SEX ADDICTS ANONYMOUS

SEX ADDICTS ANONYMOUS

LITERATURE COMMITTEE APPROVED

AUGUST 2004

First Edition
First printing, May 2005
Second printing, June 2005
Third printing, October 2005
Fourth printing, July 2006
Second Edition
First printing, August 2007
Second printing, March 2008
Third printing, September 2010
Third Edition
First printing, December 2012

SEX ADDICTS ANONYMOUS is a registered trademark*
of the International Service Organization of SAA, Inc.

ISO
P.O. Box 70949
Houston, TX 77270
800-477-8191

Website: http://www.saa-recovery.org
E-mail: info@saa-recovery.org

ISBN 0-9768313-1-7

Printed in the United States of America

CONTENTS

FOREWARD TO THE THIRD EDITION

The book you hold in your hands, the first full-length book by the fellowship of Sex Addicts Anonymous, was produced in response to the expressed need of our members for a text providing an overview of our program of recovery from sexual addiction.

It includes descriptions of our addiction as we have experienced it; the purpose and structure of our groups; the vital importance of sponsorship as a guide through the program; the process by which members define their abstinence from addictive sexual behaviors; and the Twelve Steps of SAA. Other areas of interest included are various "tools" used by members; and the Twelve Traditions of SAA, which guide our groups and their service committees in the task of carrying our message of recovery. Following the text, we have included personal stories from members sharing their experience, strength, and hope regarding their addiction and recovery.

This book was not intended to be a complete instructional workbook covering every aspect of working the steps. As we grow in experience and wisdom, we trust that more literature will be written to address the developing needs of our fellowship as they are expressed.

The ultimate tool of recovery is the recovering sex addict. Our commitment to helping other sex addicts seeking recovery, and our working together towards that common goal, carry the message of SAA more than any piece of literature could. Each member's experience of working the steps ultimately determines how recovery looks. Here we must emphasize what is often stated in the text itself: the importance of working with a sponsor in order to gain the full benefits of our program. Not alone, but together, through a Power greater than ourselves, we can and do recover from sexual addiction.

In this faith, in the spirit of selfless service, and with profound gratitude for the gift of recovery we have received, we offer this book to sex addicts who are seeking a new way of life.

INTRODUCTION

We are sex addicts. Our addiction nearly destroyed our lives, but we found freedom through the recovery program of Sex Addicts Anonymous. In the fellowship of SAA, we discovered that we are not alone and that meeting regularly together to share experience, strength, and hope gives us the choice to live a new life.

Our addictive sexual behavior was causing pain—to ourselves, our friends, and our loved ones. Our lives were out of control. We may have wanted to quit, making promises and many attempts to stop, yet we repeatedly failed to do so. For each of us, there came a moment of crisis. When we finally reached out for help, we found recovery through the program of SAA.

We have found, through long and painful experience, that we are unable to achieve recovery from sexual addiction through our own efforts. Our program is based on the belief, confirmed by our experience, that a Power greater than ourselves can accomplish for us what we could not do alone. By surrendering our addiction to a Higher Power, we receive the gift of recovery, one day at a time.

Sex Addicts Anonymous is a spiritual program based on the principles and traditions of Alcoholics Anonymous. Although we are not affiliated with AA or any other organization, we are deeply grateful to AA for making our recovery possible.

Our primary purpose is to stop our addictive sexual behavior and to help others recover from sexual addiction. We find a new way of living through the SAA program, and carry our message to others seeking recovery. Membership is open to all who have a desire to stop addictive sexual behavior. There is no other requirement. Our fellowship is open to women and men, regardless of age, race, religion, ethnic background, marital status, or occupation. We welcome members of any sexual identity or orientation, whether they are gay, lesbian, straight, bisexual, or transgender.

In our groups, there is a collective wisdom that has grown and been handed down over the years. We learn many new solutions to old problems. Central to these are the Twelve Steps, a spiritual program of recovery. Following these steps leads to freedom from addictive sexual behaviors and to the healing of our minds, bodies, spirits, relationships, and sexuality.

Desperation brought us together. We found in each other what we could find nowhere else: people who knew the depth of our pain. Together we found hope and the care of a loving Higher Power. Our commitment is to help others recover from sexual addiction, just as we have been helped. This book contains our stories and our wisdom. It is dedicated to sex addicts everywhere.

CHAPTER ONE

OUR ADDICTION

Before coming to Sex Addicts Anonymous, many of us never knew that our problem had a name. All we knew was that we couldn't control our sexual behavior. For us, sex was a consuming way of life. Although the details of our stories were different, our problem was the same. We were addicted to sexual behaviors that we returned to over and over, despite the consequences.

Sex addiction is a disease affecting the mind, body, and spirit. It is progressive, with the behavior and its consequences usually becoming more severe over time. We experience it as compulsion, which is an urge that is stronger than our will to resist, and as obsession, which is a mental preoccupation with sexual behavior and fantasies. In SAA, we have come to call our addictive sexual behavior *acting out*.

Acting out altered our feelings and consciousness, and we found this altered state very desirable. The obsession and rituals that led up to the sex act itself were part of the "high." We sought this addictive high repeatedly, preferring it to many other activities, and feeling our compulsions more strongly than our basic needs to eat, drink, sleep, or be safe. These compulsive desires were irresistible, persistent, and insatiable. They went off like alarms in our heads that made it difficult to focus on anything else. When we wanted to act out, the urge didn't go away. Nor did we feel satisfied when we got our "fix." Instead, the more we acted out sexually, the more we wanted to act out. We lost more and more of our lives to our addiction, which cost us time, money, relationships, our health, our jobs, and even our freedom. The consequences of our addiction did not make us stop or limit our acting out. The more we tried to control our behavior, the worse it got. We were unable to stop on our own, and the pleas or threats of the people in our lives didn't help us to stop, either.

We acted out in many different ways. Sometimes we had trouble with one unwanted behavior, sometimes with many. We struggled with promiscuity; anonymous sex; compulsive masturbation; destructive relationships; romantic obsession; infidelity; obsessive fantasizing; cybersex; compulsive use of pornography, including internet pornography; excessive fear or avoidance of sex; prostitution or use of prostitutes; compulsive cross-dressing; phone sex; voyeurism; exhibitionism; sex in public places; inappropriate touching; sexual assault or molestation; bestiality; or other behaviors that involve risk to ourselves—physical, legal, emotional, or spiritual—and harm to others. These are only examples of acting out; there are many more. The common thread among all these behaviors for us as sex addicts is that we engaged in them compulsively, our willpower was helpless against them, and they had negative, painful effects. It didn't matter if others appeared to do the same behaviors without ill effect. We could not engage in them without consequence.

Over time we have become aware of certain characteristics of our lives as sex addicts. While none of us fits the profile perfectly, we can all identify with some of the following traits. We chose sex and romantic obsession over those things we cherished the most—including friends, family, and career. Sexual thoughts, romantic fantasies, and seductive planning filled our minds and distorted our thinking. Sex became our way to escape our feelings and responsibilities. We repeated our sexual behaviors even though we knew they would bring harm to ourselves and others. We made attempts to stop the behavior, but they failed. Much of our time was spent either being sexual, or managing crises and problems that arose because of our sexual behavior. We violated our own values, and sex became the chief measure of what was important. Our sexual choices created fear and despair. Our lives became filled with deceit in order to hide our behaviors. We found ourselves isolated and alone. We felt spiritually empty.

In our addiction, we lost control over our behavior; the disease had a life and an agenda of its own. This is a hard fact to accept. We may think that we acted out only when we wanted to. But if we look closely at our experience, we see that we couldn't maintain control of our behaviors. For example, many of us thought that we could act out for a while, and then go back to our lives. We would engage in one of our favorite behaviors, such as cruising the internet, only to find that we didn't stop when we said we would. Sometimes we didn't stop until we absolutely had to.

OUR ADDICTION

When we were active in our addiction, it was difficult to stop our sexual preoccupations. They intruded into our thoughts, especially when we were under pressure. These included fantasizing about sex, thinking about past sexual acting out, and planning to act out again. Sexual obsession had consequences of its own. When we were preoccupied by sex we had a hard time concentrating on anything else. We would use sexual fantasy to deal with emotions and situations that we didn't want to face. The more we did this, the more our sexual obsession grew. Before long, many of us were thinking or fantasizing about sex around the clock. Our fantasies would become more compulsive and more extreme. If we acted on our fantasies, in the hope that fulfilling them would satisfy us, we found ourselves simply hungry for more. The longer we stayed in this fantasy world, the more we lost touch with reality. Our sexual obsession often led us to believe that other people were obsessed like we were. As a result of this belief, some of us would make sexually inappropriate suggestions, jokes, or remarks. It's not that sexual fantasy is necessarily unhealthy, in and of itself. Our problem was that we lost ourselves in these compulsive fantasies, becoming more and more isolated from others and from reality.

We would try to establish boundaries around our behavior, but eventually we'd violate these boundaries. Some of us decided that we would engage in certain behaviors, but that we wouldn't get involved in other things that were dangerous, caused harm to others, or were illegal. We would act out in so-called "safe" ways, and only fantasize about acting out in the forbidden ways. Then one day, we crossed those boundaries. We paid for sex when we thought we never would. We took risks meeting strangers for sex. Or we violated the sexual boundaries of others. We may have promised ourselves that we would not do these things a second time, and yet we did. Before long, we did them repeatedly, hoping we could stop, while praying that we wouldn't get caught.

We tried to stop our behaviors, to give up some or all of them. We would swear to never act out again, and then be right back in our addiction within days, hours, or even minutes. We would throw out all of our pornography or paraphernalia, only to dig it back out of the trash or buy more. We would promise ourselves, and sometimes our loved ones, that we wouldn't repeat our behavior. Sometimes we could keep our promises for weeks, months, or years. But eventually we would act out again.

We may have believed that, given time or changed circumstances, we would stop acting out. We may have thought that we would stop when we got married or into a committed relationship. And for some of us that was true—but only for a time. We believed that if we could just change our situation, the behavior would go away. We thought that as soon as we finished school, training, or a difficult period, we would be able to get a handle on our problem. Yet we often found ourselves acting out after we got through a crisis.

Many of us lived a double life. We might have felt appalled by our acting-out behavior. But when we were in our addiction, we would slip into a kind of trance. What we usually considered immoral or shameful became sexually exciting. We went to places we wouldn't normally go to, spent time with people we wouldn't normally associate with, and did things we wouldn't want to tell anyone.

To hide our acting out, we lied to our families, friends, and co-workers. We also tried to hide our addiction from ourselves—by working hard, being perfectionists, or perhaps being very religious. Still, with all the self-discipline we could muster, it wasn't very long before we felt compelled to act out again.

Sex addiction impaired our judgment. In our obsession, we acted as if we were invisible, immortal, and invincible. We may have believed, for instance, that we could spy on others or expose ourselves or drive to sex shops without being seen. We may have believed that we could have unprotected sex with strangers without risk of disease or violence. We may have believed that we could engage in cybersex without anyone finding out or any damage to our intimate relationships. We may have thought we could lie to our partners, our bosses, or our friends without any consequences. When we were caught, or when we tried to explain what we were doing, we couldn't make up plausible reasons for our behavior. Our behavior didn't make sense, even to ourselves, until we understood that we were sex addicts.

For some of us, the compulsive avoidance of sex and intimacy became a destructive pattern, dominating our thoughts and actions. We may always have felt unable or unwilling to be sexual. Or we may have experienced periods of feeling "shut down" alternating with other periods of sexual acting out. We have come to realize that both extremes represent symptoms of the same disease. Whether we were acting out or not being sexual at all, our addiction involved being emotionally unavailable.

Being a sex addict felt like being trapped in endless contradictions. We sought love and romance, but when we found it, we feared and fled from intimacy. We neglected or even avoided sex with those who loved us, preferring new conquests, the unknown, and the solitary. Some of us had periods of time when sex and relationships were unbearable and we avoided contact with others. Then we would plunge into a period when no amount of sex was sufficient. The more sex we would have, the less satisfied we felt, and the more our desire seemed to increase. The harder we tried to stop or moderate our behavior, the worse it became. Some of us remained loyal to those who would hurt us, abandoning the ones whose care was proven and true. Or we focused on behavior that we never even liked, or that violated our values. We sought comfort and security through dangerous, risky, and traumatic behaviors that left us more wounded, abused, and traumatized than when we started. Our sexuality, which should have been a source of happiness and pleasure, became joyless, and even destructive and dangerous to ourselves and others.

Some of us also had other addictive behaviors—such as addiction to alcohol and other drugs, compulsive eating habits, or addiction to gambling, work, smoking, spending, or any number of other behaviors or substances. These addictions tended to aggravate our sexual addiction, compounding the negative consequences of our disease.

These consequences were many and various. Some came as a direct result of our acting out: we were arrested, or got a sexually transmitted disease. We lost jobs due to sexually inappropriate behavior. Our marriages and relationships broke up when our behavior was revealed. Our reputations and livelihoods were damaged by publicity about our illegal behavior. We suffered an emotional hangover after coming down from the high, or contemplated suicide.

Often the consequences were an indirect result of our addiction. We may have lost friendships or relationships because our acting out interfered with the energy and commitment they required. We may have performed poorly at work because we couldn't concentrate, due to staying up late acting out, or to being distracted by sexual obsession. We were often depressed and dissatisfied with our lives; we were resentful and blamed others for our unhappiness.

We thought of acting out as the peak experience of our addiction, but often it was only a prelude to the physical and emotional crash that followed. The high usually wasn't as "good" as we hoped it would be. It rarely matched our fantasies, and didn't recapture the excitement that it may once have had. When we realized that we had been seduced by our fantasies again, we often felt despair. The strange thing was that our despair, rather than deterring us, led us right back to acting out. Our feelings of pain and shame were often more than we could take. Without having any reason to hope we could stop, we looked for ways to dull the pain. That led us to be preoccupied with sex again.

Shame is a common experience for sex addicts. It is the feeling that we are never good enough, that there is something wrong with us, that we are bad people. Shame played a part in the addictive cycle, undermining our resistance to acting out. To the extent that we felt that we were unworthy people, it didn't seem to matter if we acted out or not. Acting out helped us to escape or hide from our shame. Sometimes shame became part of the addictive high itself, so that we'd actually get a sexual thrill from being "bad." Shame also caused us to hide and isolate from others so that we did not seek the help we needed.

For many of us, even if we tried to quit, the distress of withdrawal impelled us to act out again despite ourselves. Abstaining from our addictive sexual behaviors prompted a reaction in our minds and bodies that was similar to that of a drug addict going through withdrawal. We could not tolerate the physical and emotional discomfort we felt when we stopped these behaviors, so we acted out again.

By the time we came to SAA, people could usually tell that something was wrong with us, even though we tried to hide our behavior. In many cases, our partners or family members knew about our addiction before we recognized it, and often had already sought help for us, or for themselves. We were frequently the last ones to recognize our problem.

One of the most dangerous aspects of our addiction is our inability to see it for what it is. This difficulty recognizing what we are doing, how serious and risky it is, and how much harm it causes or might cause, we call *denial*. Denial conceals the awful truth of our addiction by convincing us that what we are doing is not that bad or dangerous, or that other people or external circumstances are responsible for our behavior. Usually our denial is subtle. We may remember acting out, but we deny the pain of acting out, the consequences, the risks, or our inability to stop. Unfortunately, this often prevents us from seeking help.

For many of us, the spiral of sexual addiction led to what we call *hitting bottom*. To hit bottom is to reach such a low point—mentally, physically, emotionally, and spiritually—that we break through our denial. The depth of the bottom varies from person to person. For some, it may have taken the form of an external crisis: we lost our career, our partner left us, or we were arrested. For others, it came in a moment of despair, with the realization that if we didn't stop, we were going to live a miserable, lonely, nightmarish existence. Or we reached a point where we felt we might die if we acted out much longer.

OUR ADDICTION

Sex addiction is not just a bad habit. Nor is it the result of poor self-control, a lack of morals, or a series of mistakes. If it were something we could stop on our own, the negative consequences would be enough to make us stop. Many of us tried to cure ourselves with religious or spiritual practice, moral discipline, or self-improvement. Despite our sincerity and our best efforts, we continued to act out. Our behavior eluded all rational attempts at explanation or correction. We had to face the fact that we had a disease, and that we could not stop the addictive behavior by ourselves.

For all of us now in recovery, there came a time when we realized that we simply could not keep on living as before. Our denial cracked and we felt the full force of our unbearable situation. We saw that we were at the end of our rope, and that all that was left was the knot. To continue to act out seemed impossible, and yet not to act out seemed equally impossible. We knew we had to change, even if we didn't know how. Out of this despair, we came to Sex Addicts Anonymous.

CHAPTER TWO

OUR FELLOWSHIP

Meetings

Many of us first come to Sex Addicts Anonymous feeling deeply isolated and ashamed of our behaviors and past actions. We may believe that no one could understand us or relate to the things we had done or been through. Discovering that we are not alone is a liberating experience for us. It is a great comfort and relief to know that a fellowship of recovering sex addicts exists and that we have somewhere to turn to help us recover.

Meetings are the heart of the SAA fellowship. At meetings we emerge from our shame, secrecy, and fear, into a community of people who share the common goal of freedom from sex addiction. They give us the opportunity to talk about our lives and our addiction with other sex addicts, people who have had similar experiences and understand the problems we face. Attending our first SAA meeting is a crucial step in moving away from isolation into fellowship, and ultimately into recovery. For many of us, our first meeting was a freeing experience. We sat among others like us, and heard their stories. It did not seem to matter if we identified with everyone's behaviors. We were often amazed to find other people honestly sharing their challenges around sex addiction. As we witnessed their honesty and openness, we felt invited to speak candidly about ourselves. Revealing our sex addiction to others gives us a sense of freedom and relief, even if we initially felt some fear or resistance.

An SAA group consists of two or more individuals who, using the Twelve Steps and Twelve Traditions of SAA, meet regularly for the purpose of recovering from their addictive sexual behavior. At our meetings, we read SAA literature and share our experience, strength, and hope with each other, focusing on how the SAA program of recovery works in our lives.

SAA meetings are run by members. There are no professional or outside facilitators. We meet as equals: sex addicts helping one another to achieve sexual sobriety and to practice a new way of life. We all contribute to making our meetings places that foster our recovery and carry the SAA message to the sex addict who still suffers. Our fellow members depend upon us, as we depend on them.

Because of the sensitive nature of sexual addiction, many of our groups are "closed," meaning that only those with a desire to stop addictive sexual behavior may attend. Anyone else interested in finding out about SAA may attend "open" meetings. While we all strive for sexual sobriety, its achievement is not a requirement for attendance or participation. All participation is voluntary. We are not required to speak if we don't want to. Just by listening we can learn how other members become honest, confront their addiction, find support from fellow addicts, and practice the program. We can learn how others have faced problems that are similar to ours, and how they have used the tools of the program to deal with them. Members can have any religious belief, or no belief at all. All sex addicts seeking recovery are welcome.

Many groups suggest that newcomers attend at least six meetings before deciding if the program is right for them. If we don't feel comfortable at a particular meeting, we can try another. It is suggested that we make attending meetings a priority in our lives. We need the support, encouragement, and sense of belonging that meetings give us, in order to make the dramatic changes in our lives that recovery brings.

As sex addicts, we are especially prone to isolating. Many of us acted out alone or in secret. Meetings are an important way of breaking this isolation. At meetings we discover that we are not unique. If we listen to the experiences and feelings we have in common, we will find that we are more alike than we are different. At meetings we learn that we can trust others to know who we really are, and still be accepted by them.

If there are no SAA meetings in our area, we can still find recovery through program literature, long-distance connections with other addicts, or eventually starting our own meetings. The idea of starting a meeting may seem intimidating, but someone took the risk to establish every one of the meetings we have today. Support is available from the International Service Organization of SAA, and from other SAA groups.

Over the years, our groups have developed different formats and customs. Although no detailed description is valid for all meetings, there are some general principles and guidelines followed by most groups. We listen respectfully to what others have to say and share our experience as it seems appropriate. We use the words "I" or "we" instead of "you" when sharing about our recovery. We do not interrupt or give advice unless asked. We address our sharing to the whole group, not to one or more individuals. A meeting is not a place to meet sexual partners, nor is it group therapy. We try not to use offensive language, or descriptions that are too explicit. We avoid mentioning specific names or places associated with our acting-out behavior. Because of the nature of our addiction, we are careful about touching or giving hugs to others in the fellowship without permission. Our focus remains on the solution, rather than the problem.

We strive to practice anonymity and confidentiality, so that the meeting will be a safe place for each and every sex addict. We generally use only our first names in the group, to help ensure anonymity. Whom we meet or what is said in a meeting is treated as confidential and is not discussed with non-group members.

It takes some courage to show up at our first meetings. We may fear being recognized at a meeting by someone we know. This can be awkward, but it's helpful to remember that when we acted out, we risked consequences greater than any embarrassment we might experience at a meeting. Eventually, discomfort gives way to a sense of belonging and a feeling of relief that there are others like us.

Meetings are places where we can drop our emotional defenses and get honest in a way we are rarely able to experience outside of the fellowship. SAA is one of the very few places where we can talk candidly about our sexual behavior without fear of judgment or ridicule. Once we break our self-imposed silence, we are able to be more honest and to form stronger bonds with the members of our group. It is these bonds that enrich our recovery process. In time, we learn to trust our fellow members and to receive their trust in us.

Many things happen in our groups that are important for recovery. We share our experience with each other, which reminds us that we have a common illness and that we are not alone. By sharing our stories, we remind ourselves of our progress in recovery, and we give each other hope. We recognize ourselves as we used to be and commit even more deeply to the changes we are making. Being open to the experience, strength, and hope of others can also give us new strategies and attitudes to try in our own recovery. We can take what works for us and leave the rest. At the same time, sharing our experience with others helps to reduce our shame and pain. Not only do other members understand the pain we are feeling—they are willing to help.

We also learn specific tools to help us change our behavior and disrupt the compulsive cycle of sexual acting out and despair. We clarify what our abstinence is, what we need to avoid, and what we need to add to our lives in order to experience healthier sexuality. We also get support to do the hard things that will help us find the freedom we seek. When faced alone, these tasks can seem overwhelming. But with others of like mind, we discover a new courage and a new faith. Finally, we learn about the Twelve Steps of SAA, a program of recovery that provides freedom from addictive sexual behavior, and guides us in a new way of life.

Sponsorship

One of the most vital aspects of the program is sponsorship. A sponsor is a person in the fellowship who acts as a guide to working the program of SAA, a fellow addict that we can rely upon for support. Ideally, a sponsor is abstinent from addictive sexual behavior, has worked the steps, and can teach us what he or she has learned from working the program. We can learn from a sponsor's experience, struggles, successes, and mistakes. Our sponsor can help explain program fundamentals, such as how to define our sexual sobriety. Most importantly, sponsors guide us through the Twelve Steps.

If we feel like acting out, we can call our sponsor to talk about it. A sponsor can help hold us accountable for our behavior. If we make a commitment to attend a meeting, our sponsor can note whether we got to the meeting or not. Sponsors can tell us if they think we are at risk of relapse. They can suggest when we are not being fully honest with ourselves. Often a sponsor is the person in the fellowship who knows us best.

As new members, we are encouraged to get a sponsor as soon as we can. Many of us ask someone to be our sponsor who has shared things in meetings that helped us, or inspired us through example. We may have temporary sponsors until we get to know people better. It is recommended that we do not enter into a sponsorship relationship with anyone we are attracted to sexually, since that might compromise the trust and safety we all need. If someone declines to sponsor us, we need not take it personally. We simply ask someone else. Members are also free to change sponsors. The important thing is to have and use one, because we can't keep trying to solve problems by ourselves.

Sometimes it is hard to find a sponsor who has more experience in SAA than we have. This is often the case when the meetings in an area are fairly new. There are solutions to this problem. We can contact a member of the program with more experience who attends a different SAA meeting. We can maintain a long-distance sponsoring relationship, by phone, e-mail, or letter. We may consider entering into a co-sponsorship relationship with a program friend for mutual support. We can also ask a person who may have less experience in SAA, but has experience working recovery in another fellowship.

The sponsorship relationship is flexible: it is up to the sponsor and "sponsee" to decide exactly how they will work with each other. We stay in regular contact with our sponsor, reaching out for support, guidance, and encouragement. As we work the Twelve Steps of SAA, our sponsor acts as an ally in our recovery, sharing the experience and wisdom of the program with us.

Sponsors and sponsees often form an intense bond that is very healing. We can go to our sponsor with problems that we might feel are too personal to share with a group. Many of us come into recovery feeling unlovable and unworthy. When a sponsor takes the trouble to listen to us and help us through hard times, it helps us to develop trust in another human being. We begin to see that we are worthwhile and deserving of all the gifts that recovery can bring.

Once we have worked the SAA program ourselves, gained abstinence from the sexual behaviors that were addictive for us, and experienced some degree of spiritual growth, we are ready to consider sponsoring other members who ask us to do so. SAA has no formal requirements regarding this decision. Most of us know that we are ready to sponsor when another member asks us, or when our own sponsor encourages us to take on a sponsee. We don't need to be experts about life, or even about addiction, in order to sponsor someone. We simply share the knowledge and experience we have gained from working the Twelve Steps and using the tools of the program, and we pass on the wisdom we've learned from our own sponsor and others in the fellowship. We are not responsible for the decisions of our sponsees, or for how well they progress in recovery. All we need to do is be ourselves and share what we have, knowing that a Higher Power will take care of the outcome.

Defining Abstinence

Our goal when entering the SAA program is abstinence from one or more specific sexual behaviors. But unlike programs for recovering alcoholics or drug addicts, Sex Addicts Anonymous does not have a universal definition of abstinence.

Most of us have no desire to stop being sexual altogether. It is not sex in and of itself that causes us problems, but the addiction to certain sexual behaviors. In SAA we will be better able to determine what behavior is addictive and what is healthy. However, the fellowship does not dictate to its members what is and isn't addictive sexual behavior. Instead we have found that it is necessary for each member to define his or her own abstinence.

We are individuals, and our addictive behaviors, while similar, are unique to each of us. What may be healthy for one member could be clearly addictive for another. SAA simply cannot predict every possible way of acting out and define them all for everyone. As a fellowship, we wouldn't want to deny that any particular behavior might be acting out for a member. Nor would we want to restrict behaviors that are healthy for some of us. Since different addicts suffer from different behaviors, and since our sexuality is experienced in so many different ways, it is necessary that SAA members define for themselves, with the help of their sponsors or others in recovery, which of their sexual behaviors they consider to be "acting out."

This can be a difficult challenge. If we are too lenient with ourselves, we might not get sober. If we are too strict, we might restrict ourselves from healthy behaviors that we have no need to give up, and an inability to meet our high standards could set us up for relapse. We need the help of other recovering sex addicts, and the reliance on a Power greater than ourselves, to find the right balance between these two extremes.

We carefully consider which sexual behaviors we feel powerless to stop, and which sexual acts lead to feelings of demoralization or other negative consequences. These are the addictive behaviors from which we seek to abstain. We also consider which sexual behaviors are acceptable to us, or even experienced with a sense of gratitude and enjoyment. Our program acknowledges each individual's dignity and right to choose his or her own concept of healthy sexuality.

We have learned that our ideas of what is healthy and what is addictive evolve with experience. In time, we are able to define our individual abstinence with honesty, fairness, and gentleness. This process is a valuable exercise in our recovery. It requires us to carefully examine all of our sexual behaviors, decide which ones are healthy or addictive, and note those cases where we're not sure. It is a way of taking stock of our sexuality that teaches us a lot about ourselves and our behavior.

When we look at particular sexual behaviors, it is helpful to ask ourselves a few questions. Do we find ourselves repeating behaviors that we don't want to do? Does doing them make us want to do something that we know is harmful to ourselves or others? Do they violate the rights of others or go against their will or permission? Do we find ourselves engaging in these behaviors in times of anxiety and stress, or when dealing with unpleasant situations or emotions? Are there emotional causes or consequences of our behaviors? Do we notice unpleasant feelings such as anger, shame, or depression, before we do them? Do we feel shameful, depressed, remorseful, or lonely afterwards? Are there other negative consequences, potential or actual? Do we feel uncomfortable with the amount of time or money we spend on these behaviors? Do we risk our health, relationships, families, or jobs? The answers to these questions, and the honest sharing on this subject with our sponsor and other recovering persons, will help us to better understand what we need to abstain from in order to recover.

To help us define our sexual sobriety, many of us use a tool developed within SAA called The Three Circles. This is only a tool and not a requirement. Not every recovering sex addict uses this method. But many members have found that this tool helps establish a foundation for recovery.

We draw three concentric circles, consisting of an inner, middle, and outer circle. With the help of our sponsor or others in recovery, we write down various behaviors in each of the three circles. In the inner circle we put the sexual behaviors we want to abstain from, the ones we consider "acting out." These are the behaviors that we identify, with our sponsor's guidance, as addictive, harmful, or unacceptable for us. In the middle circle we put behaviors that may lead to acting out, or that we are not sure about. In the outer circle we put healthy behaviors that enhance our life and our recovery.

Our circles are not set in stone for all time. As our recovery progresses, and we gain new understanding about ourselves and our addiction, we are free to add or delete behaviors, or move them from one circle to another, in order to reflect new growth and insights. We have found, however, that changing our Three Circles should not be done on a whim, but only after careful consideration and prayer, and with guidance from our sponsor and our groups.

In the inner circle we write down the sexual behaviors that we want to stop. Inner-circle behaviors are the addictive sexual behaviors that brought us to SAA, the things that made us hit bottom in our disease.

Some of us put certain behaviors in the inner circle simply because they lead to an addictive pattern that can cause us trouble. For example, we may put using pornography in our inner circle, or cruising (driving around or otherwise looking for sexual possibilities), if we experience

powerlessness over these behaviors and find that they fuel a desire to act out more, or in more destructive ways. Some of us may consider the same behaviors destructive and dangerous in their own right. We may, for instance, list pornography in our inner circle if it takes up all of our time; leads to isolation, loss of employment, or damaged relationships; or causes ill health or emotional problems.

In the Sex Addicts Anonymous program, acting out can be defined as *engaging in sexual behavior that we have put in our inner circle.* Sexual sobriety, then, means abstaining from these inner-circle behaviors. By the same token, relapse (or loss of sexual sobriety) means engaging in an inner-circle behavior. When we define our inner circle, or otherwise identify what acting out is for us, we eliminate possible confusion concerning our program, and about what we mean when we use terms such as "acting out" or "abstinence." This clarity helps us to be accountable to ourselves and to those who are helping us in our recovery.

The middle circle helps us to avoid being perfectionists about our standards for sexual sobriety. In the middle circle we identify behavior that is "slippery" for us or about which we are uncertain.

Most of us come to SAA without really knowing what healthy sexuality is. We're usually uncertain about whether some behaviors are addictive or not. We place them in the middle circle until we can determine if they are compulsive or have negative consequences. If we put masturbation in the middle circle, for instance, we might look at how frequently we masturbate, what kinds of fantasies we use, whether we are masturbating in an appropriate location, and how we feel afterwards. If we become convinced that a behavior is addictive, we may then decide to move it to our inner circle.

Slippery behaviors are things we do that make us vulnerable to acting out. For some of us, examples may include driving by places where we used to act out, flirting or intriguing, wearing revealing clothing, or watching TV for sexual content. We may fool ourselves into believing that we have a legitimate reason to be in a slippery situation, when in fact this is part of an addictive pattern that can lead to inner-circle behavior. Putting slippery behaviors in our middle circle is a way of warning ourselves when we are in danger of acting out.

If we engage in middle-circle behavior, we have not lost our sobriety, but it's a signal that we need to reach out to others and use the tools we have learned in SAA to get us back on track. It's also important to remember that what is slippery behavior for some may be acting out for others. We need to decide what feels right for us in this process, rather than relying on comparisons with other members whose histories may not match our own.

We may also put non-sexual behaviors in our middle circle that we know lead us to slippery states of mind—unhealthy behaviors that don't support our recovery. Examples may include isolating from people, missing meetings, overworking, and other potentially addictive behaviors, such as drinking, gambling, or overeating.

When we're new in the program, our sponsor may suggest that we put compulsive sexual behaviors that don't have obvious serious consequences in our middle circle rather than our inner circle. This allows us to concentrate on our most destructive behaviors first. We might have been engaging, for instance, in illegal or life-threatening behaviors, such as masturbating while driving, or having anonymous sex in public places. Let us say that we were also masturbating to pornography in the privacy of our home. A sponsor might suggest that we first stop the more dangerous behaviors. Once we've had time to get some support, and we've started thinking more clearly, we may decide to put masturbation with pornography in our inner circle as well.

Some of us, on the other hand, may find this gradual approach ineffective, and our sponsor may suggest putting all compulsive sexual behaviors in the inner circle from the start. Once again, there is no single correct way—our special relationship with a sponsor helps us to work with the circles in a way that best fits our individual needs.

The middle circle can be seen as a safety net, allowing us to walk the tightrope of abstinence without having to fear that a false step would necessarily be disastrous. We may also think of it as a warning track or a guardrail. If we climb over the guardrail, we haven't fallen off the cliff. However, we should recognize that we are in a dangerous place.

Finally, we put those behaviors in the outer circle that we consider healthy, safe, and beneficial to our recovery. Practicing these behaviors is a way of being gentle with ourselves. They are acts of self-nurturing that help bring meaning, fulfillment, serenity, and joy into our lives.

Outer-circle behaviors encompass a wide range of healthy activities. They are frequently the things we didn't have time to do when we were acting out. Examples may include working our recovery program, rediscovering hobbies we once enjoyed, playing sports and exercising, spending time with friends and family, socializing and making new friends in a safe environment, volunteering our time to a cause we believe in, or engaging in any other activities which make our lives more enjoyable and meaningful.

Most of us also include healthy sexuality in our outer circle. Healthy sexual behaviors are ones we choose that enhance our life, our recovery, our connection to others, and our spiritual life. Examples might include dating, safe and loving sex within a committed relationship, non-compulsive masturbation, taking a dance class, wearing attractive clothes, or enjoying affectionate touch.

Throughout this process, it is extremely helpful to have the guidance of a sponsor or other more experienced members of the fellowship. Experience has shown that it is too difficult to sort through these issues by ourselves or to see through the denial that often obscures the truth about our behavior. With the help of other SAA members, we gain the awareness and sense of support that we need in order to move into recovery.

Establishing our definition of abstinence helps to answer the "what" questions that face us when we enter SAA: What must we abstain from? What are our goals? But the crucial "how" questions still remain: How do we get sexually sober? How can we live differently than before, so that we stay abstinent? The answers to these questions are contained in our spiritual program of recovery, the Twelve Steps of Sex Addicts Anonymous.

CHAPTER THREE

OUR PROGRAM

The Twelve Steps of SAA

Attending SAA meetings starts us on a new way of life. But while the SAA fellowship supports our recovery, the actual work of recovery is described in the Twelve Steps. Meetings are forums for learning how to integrate the steps into our lives. Working the Twelve Steps leads to a spiritual transformation that results in sustainable relief from our addiction.

When we start attending meetings of Sex Addicts Anonymous, many of us are surprised to meet people who are enjoying life and experiencing freedom from the painful, compulsive behaviors that had brought them to SAA. Listening to other members share about their recovery, we gradually realize that in order to make the same kind of progress, we need to be willing to do whatever it takes to get sexually abstinent, and to stay abstinent. We have learned from hard experience that we cannot achieve and maintain abstinence if we aren't willing to change our way of life. But if we can honestly face our problems, and are willing to change, the Twelve Steps of SAA will lead to an awakening that allows us to live a new way of life according to spiritual principles. Taking these steps allows fundamental change to occur in our lives. They are the foundation of our recovery.

The Twelve Steps of Sex Addicts Anonymous

1. *We admitted we were powerless over addictive sexual behavior—that our lives had become unmanageable.*

2. *Came to believe that a Power greater than ourselves could restore us to sanity.*

3. *Made a decision to turn our will and our lives over to the care of God as we understood God.*

4. *Made a searching and fearless moral inventory of ourselves.*

5. *Admitted to God, to ourselves, and to another human being the exact nature of our wrongs.*

6. *Were entirely ready to have God remove all these defects of character.*

7. *Humbly asked God to remove our shortcomings.*

8. *Made a list of all persons we had harmed and became willing to make amends to them all.*

9. *Made direct amends to such people wherever possible, except when to do so would injure them or others.*

10. *Continued to take personal inventory and when we were wrong promptly admitted it.*

11. *Sought through prayer and meditation to improve our conscious contact with God as we understood God, praying only for knowledge of God's will for us and the power to carry that out.*

12. *Having had a spiritual awakening as the result of these steps, we tried to carry this message to other sex addicts and to practice these principles in our lives.*

These steps are the heart of our program. They contain a depth that we could hardly have guessed when we started. Over time, we establish a relationship with a Power greater than ourselves, each of us coming to an understanding of a Higher Power that is personal for us. Although the steps use the word "God" to indicate this Power, SAA is not affiliated with any religion, creed, or dogma. The program offers a spiritual solution to our addiction, without requiring adherence to any specific set of beliefs or practices. The path is wide enough for everyone who wishes to walk it.

There is no one correct or SAA-sanctioned way to complete the Twelve Steps. Most of us learned how to work the steps from our sponsors. Many of us have also gained insight from books or adapted methods from other twelve-step programs. In this book we suggest ideas for how to work each step, based on approaches that have worked for many of us.

Each step presents a significant action, with each action linked to the other steps, in a process that establishes our new life of recovery on spiritual principles. The steps are numbered because they are meant to chart the course of our spiritual progress. We work the steps in order, as each step creates a foundation for the steps that follow. The actions of the steps often involve the completion of specific tasks, such as writing lists, that require an honest examination of ourselves and our way of life. Each action also takes place within us, as we gradually let go of old ways of thinking and establish conscious contact with our Higher Power.

No step is done well in isolation. We work the steps with someone who understands our problem and cares about our recovery, preferably a sponsor. A sponsor will help us prepare for each step, give us guidance and suggestions, and listen to us as we share the experiences and insights we gain.

But the steps are more than a series of exercises. They provide basic principles for living. Most of us find opportunities on a daily basis to apply one or more of the steps to some challenge in our life. Over time, the spiritual principles in the steps become integrated into our thoughts, feelings, and behavior. We find that we are not only working the steps— we are living them.

Step One

We admitted we were powerless over addictive sexual behavior—that our lives had become unmanageable.

In our addiction we held on to the belief that we were in control of our sexual behavior and could successfully manage our lives. This kept many of us from seeing that we even had a problem. We told ourselves that if we had tried harder, we could have stopped. But our experience has shown otherwise. No matter how many promises or resolutions we made, no matter how strong our efforts and our determination, the behaviors eventually returned, along with their painful consequences. Only when we admit our powerlessness over these behaviors, and our inability to manage our own lives, are we able to begin walking a path of recovery.

In taking the First Step, we admit that our addiction is destroying us, and that we are unable to stop it. We surrender, raise the white flag, and accept that the battle is over. The principle behind this admission is honesty. For many of us, the first crack in our denial comes with hitting bottom, and the despair of facing an unbearable situation. The next breakthrough occurs when we are honest enough to take the First Step, acknowledging that we are powerless over the behavior that brought us

Sex is not my problem—
Sex is my solution to my problems

22

to this point and that our lives are in shambles. We make this admission without excuses or rationalizations. With the First Step, we stop lying to ourselves.

As long as we can be honest, even a little bit, we can move forward in our recovery. Honesty is the foundation on which all further progress is based. We start by admitting that we are completely powerless to stop our addictive behaviors on our own. We admit that our lives are out of our control. This is enough for our recovery to begin.

Admitting that our willpower is insufficient allows us to be open to new ways of thinking and living. As long as we retain a belief in self-control as a remedy for our addiction, we will continue to fail. With this step, we recognize that we have a disease, not a mere weakness or character flaw, and that we are powerless to change this fact. We honestly admit that we don't have all the answers and that we need help. When we admit our powerlessness, we start letting go of control and become more open to receiving the help we so desperately need.

Admitting that our lives had become unmanageable allows us to honestly examine the painful consequences of our sexual behavior, consequences that affected every aspect of our existence. It is difficult to accept that we are unable to manage our lives, and even more difficult to admit this to others, but our experience has shown that we have no choice but to surrender, or else return to acting out, and all that follows from it.

Many of us have found it helpful to examine our sexual behavior in detail when working this step. Some of us write a history of our sex addiction, from as far back as we can remember up to the present, trying to leave nothing out. Looking at our own story helps us see how we were powerless over our addiction. In writing a First Step, we list examples of our powerlessness, including the progression of our acting-out behaviors, actions that violated our own values, efforts we made to stop, and occasions where we knew that these behaviors would lead to serious consequences yet did them anyway.

In a written First Step we also list the ways that sex addiction made our lives unmanageable. If we spent money on our addiction, we can try to estimate how much money we spent. If we spent time, we can consider how many hours we spent, including the time we spent in fantasy or obsession. If we took the risk of arrest, violence, or disease, we can examine each specific risk we took. We also write about the specific ways our behaviors affected our physical and mental health, our work, the lives of those we love, and any other consequences, internal or external, that we experienced.

Our disease left us with little time, energy, or money for anything else. Our fantasies and obsessions distracted us from the things we needed to do. We often neglected our responsibilities and put off doing things that we didn't want to face. Many of us had a number of simultaneous problems. We had relationships that needed mending, we had financial crises, and we sometimes faced legal problems. The consequences to our inner life were just as serious. Addictive sexual behavior increased our loneliness and insecurity, damaged our self-worth, estranged us from our spiritual nature, and often resulted in emotional trauma. All of these consequences add up to an unmanageable life.

In listing examples of powerlessness and unmanageability, we include specific details, which helps us to recall the thoughts and feelings we had at the time, and makes the reality of our sexual addiction more and more evident to us. Although we work this step the best we can, more may be revealed later in our recovery. The important thing is to work the First Step now, to the best of our ability, in the knowledge that we can always work it again when we need to.

We get help from someone in the program, usually our sponsor, to work the First Step. We need support while facing our addiction. A sponsor can also help us face those parts of our disease about which we are in denial. We may think, for example, that the risks we took were not that dangerous, or that the consequences were not that severe. Our sponsor can help us see more honestly and clearly what our situation was really like. If we choose to do a written First Step, we usually share what we have written with our sponsor. For many of us, this is the first time we've told the whole truth about our addiction to another person.

In some SAA groups, members share their First Step at a meeting. With help from our sponsor and others in the group, we select the most important parts of our story to tell. These include the most significant examples of our powerlessness, and the worst moments of unmanageability, no matter how much shame we may feel about them. We also share critical points in our addiction story, illustrating the progression of our disease. We tell how we finally sought help, and what it has been like to recognize our powerlessness and unmanageability. Our sponsor can also help us decide beforehand whether certain details of our story are too intense to be shared with the group.

The group needs to make sure that we are supported before and after a step presentation. Sharing our story in a group can bring up intense feelings. We feel very vulnerable. But it can also help break the bonds of shame and isolation, deepen the process of healing, and increase our commitment to recovery. Sharing a First Step in a group creates an opportunity to connect with other members. We allow ourselves to be known when we take this risk. And when we hear others share their First Steps with us, we are reminded of similar aspects of our own addiction. Experiencing the common bond of our powerlessness promotes the healing of every member.

Each of us chooses to work this step in the way that is most effective and meaningful for us. Not everyone works Step One in written form. What is important is that we get honest about our addiction, and let go of the idea of controlling our behavior with our willpower or managing our lives without help. We cannot change the fact that we have an illness. By practicing rigorous honesty and giving up the dream of overcoming our addiction by ourselves, we become open to the spiritual solution offered by the Twelve Steps.

We also begin to learn how to ask for and receive help from other recovering sex addicts. Asking for help releases us from the toxic isolation that drives our addiction. As we receive help, we learn to let the walls down and to accept nurturing and care from others. Learning to be vulnerable, admitting that we don't have all the answers, and asking for and receiving help are all essential to our recovery. As we fully admit our dilemma, and our inability to find a way out, we find that we are now ready to hear the solution. We are ready for Step Two.

Step Two

Came to believe that a Power greater than ourselves could restore us to sanity.

When we accept that our way doesn't work, Step Two opens the door to a new way that does. In the First Step, we admitted that our addiction was going to destroy us if we did not stop and that we could not stop on our own. We discovered that our addiction was a problem too big for us to solve by ourselves. Without some Power greater than ourselves to assist us, our situation is hopeless. In the Second Step we are presented with the possibility that this Power can restore us to a basic sanity and well-being.

Step Two offers hope that sanity is possible, and at the same time it implies that, in our addiction, we were insane. Our insanity manifested in many ways. We would often put our addiction first and everything else second. We may have placed ourselves in dangerous situations or taken terrible risks. And the more we denied our addiction and its consequences, the less we were in touch with reality. To be restored to sanity is to rediscover the spiritual nature we have always had but which was hidden by the insanity of our disease.

Belief in a Higher Power can be difficult for many of us in SAA who come to the program with a faith that was damaged in one way or another, or those of us who never had any spiritual beliefs at all. Some of us came from strict, judgmental religious backgrounds that reinforced our fear and shame. Some of us attempted to find refuge from our addiction in religion. Yet after making great commitments and efforts in our religious practice, we found little lasting relief from our disease. Others never took up a religion, or tried a few and found them unsatisfactory. Many of us didn't believe in God, or were uncertain as to what spiritual beliefs we were willing to accept, if any. Whether we are atheists, agnostics, or those with strong religious convictions, we may find ourselves having reservations about the spirituality needed to work Step Two.

We may be so used to self-reliance as the only way of functioning in the world, that we resist the notion of any Power greater than ourselves. We can start to open ourselves to this idea by considering the forces that are clearly more powerful than we are, such as nature, society, or even our addiction. When we recognize that our own power is limited, we can more readily acknowledge the possibility of a Higher Power.

For some of us, almost everything seemed more powerful than we were, but in a negative way—oppressing us, and preventing us from being happy or free. In contrast to this negative belief, working the Second Step allows us to accept the possibility of a Power that can free us from the bondage of our disease and restore us to a life of sanity and fulfillment.

To work this step, we only need to be open-minded enough to try something new. For most of us, *coming to believe* is a gradual process. We don't need to believe in any particular concept of a Higher Power in order to begin. We learn from others what works and doesn't work for them. We listen, and we try out new approaches. If we are teachable, we can discover the stirrings of hope within us and come to a belief in the possibility of recovery from our sexual addiction.

For many of us, this starts with simply coming to meetings. We experience the group as a Power greater than ourselves that cares. The example of those who are living in recovery, free of their sexually addictive behaviors, shows us the power of the program. We can rely on the love and support of our friends in the group. We develop a

H - honesty
O - openness
W - willingness

willingness to try some of the group's suggestions, even those outside of our usual comfort zone, when we observe the practical effects of these ideas in action. From this simple beginning, belief in a Higher Power can grow.

In time, most of us also come to believe in a spiritual Power that transcends our human willpower and thinking, and that this Power can return us to a condition of serenity and sanity. The Steps use the word "God" to indicate this Power. Nevertheless, the program is not aligned with any religion, nor do we adhere to any particular beliefs concerning the word "God," leaving this matter up to the understanding of each member. We are free to use a different word in our spiritual practice, if that's what works for us. What is important is that we rely on a spiritual reality, or Higher Power, rather than on words. In essence, our shared experience of this Power is one of loving and caring. We don't have to be religious to accept this idea, or to ask this loving Power to help us in our recovery.

One of the aspects of coming to believe in a Higher Power is finding out what spiritual concepts make sense to us. We need to be willing to set aside old ideas and prejudices, try new solutions to old problems, and listen to the spiritual experiences and ideas of others in the fellowship. What works for others may not be an exact fit for us. But if we are patient and open-minded, we will discover an understanding of a Higher Power that is unique to us, and that we are comfortable with. Ultimately, the specifics of our belief are not as important as faith. We can build our spirituality on the faith that our Higher Power can relieve us of our addiction.

Some of us have found it helpful to explore our past beliefs concerning God or religion, in order to gain clarity about old ideas and assumptions that may be blocking us now. Sharing these thoughts with our sponsor or others in recovery may help us to understand our past spiritual beliefs and to be open to new ones that are healthier for us.

Our concepts of a Higher Power may change and evolve over time. As we grow in recovery, our spiritual awareness grows. And in time we discover that our faith grows not so much from a set of abstract beliefs, but from daily practical experiences of recovery and healing, as observed in others and in ourselves. We can cultivate this awareness by drawing near to those members who demonstrate significant recovery from those behaviors we've struggled with the most, and whose practical faith attracts us.

The key to Step Two is not just believing in a Higher Power, but believing that this Power can and will restore us to sanity. Many of us thought that recovery might work for others, but not for us. We thought that our problems were different, that our situation was unique. We had become so used to defeat and despair that we lost touch with hope. In early recovery, many of us had our first experience of hope through the group. In the words of other members, and in their eyes, we saw that recovery was possible. All we needed to do was concede that if it was possible for others, it was possible for us too.

If we find it difficult to believe, we can act "as if" we believe. The willingness to act "as if" helps us to make a commitment to recovery, despite any doubts we may have. By committing to recovery, we give ourselves time to let the program work in our lives, with our understanding growing gradually along with us. We find that "acting as if" is more than just wishful thinking. In the process, we discover that a willingness to accept new ways of behavior leads to a clearer understanding of who we are and how spiritual principles work.

When we have come to believe that we can be restored to sanity, we have stepped out of the problem and become aware of the solution. Without needing to completely understand our Higher Power, we can accept and use this Power in order to find freedom from our addiction. Our belief that recovery is possible gives us the strength to take action. We are ready for Step Three.

Step Three

Made a decision to turn our will and our lives over to the care of God as we understood God.

The Third Step is a turning point. In taking this step, we find the willingness to allow a God of our understanding to work in our lives. Having accepted both the reality of our disease and the possibility that a Higher Power can help us where our own efforts have failed, we make a leap of faith, turning to that Power for assistance. Our understanding of this Power does not need to be perfect or complete in order for us to take this step. We need only an open mind and a willingness to try something new.

Taking the Third Step means acting on our belief that a Higher Power can relieve our addiction and restore us to sanity. We loosen the grip on our old destructive patterns, perhaps not knowing yet what will replace them, but in the faith that something better will be revealed. When we surrender our old way of living to a Power greater than ourselves, we don't always know where we're going, but we can be sure that it will be better than where we were.

When we first encounter this step, we may have many questions and doubts. What does it mean to turn over our will and our lives? We can think of "our will" as our plans and intentions—what we want to do with our lives. We can think of "our lives" as the carrying out of our intentions—the full scope of everything we actually do, think, and say. We turn our will and our lives over to the care of God because our self-directed thoughts and actions have so often led us to acting out, negative consequences, and despair. In Step Three, we let a Power greater than ourselves help guide our daily decisions, opening ourselves to the possibility that we may not know what is best for us, and letting go of the belief in our own power to manage our lives. In so doing, we find that God's care applies not only to becoming abstinent from addictive sexual behaviors, but to the entire course of our daily lives and to every aspect of our existence.

How can we accomplish this turning over? We may be afraid of taking this step. It may even seem impossible to surrender control and allow a caring Higher Power to direct our lives. But it is helpful to remember that all we are doing is *making a decision* to turn our will and lives over. At this point in our program, we are simply willing to move forward. We decide to make a commitment to recovery, and to our spiritual growth. For most of us, the actual turning over of our will and lives to the care of God will take place gradually, through working the remaining nine steps.

The Third Step invites us to turn our will and lives over to the care of God, not the control of God. We are not abandoning ourselves to the direction of some powerful taskmaster forcing us to do things that are not of our own choosing. Instead, we become open to making new choices for ourselves in the light of a Higher Power's transforming love and care. Turning our lives over to the care of the God of our understanding offers a way of gentleness and compassion. We do not have to obsess about the past or worry about the future. We can turn our attention to the present, where we really live, and become open to new solutions. We are free to make different choices, gradually learning to care for ourselves as our Higher Power cares for us.

Taking this step, we become willing to walk through all experiences and emotions, including painful and difficult ones. We discover that turning our lives over is not the end of our problems, but a way of seeing our difficulties in a new light—with a developing sense of trust that solutions are possible.

In this step, we turn our will and lives over to God *as we understand*

God. This means that we each have the opportunity to develop our own understanding of God, and the right to grow and recover in ways that match this understanding. No member or group can impose a belief about our Higher Power on us. We are free to develop our relationship with this Power in whatever ways work best for us, and at our own pace. Our concepts of God and spirituality may also change over time, as our life in recovery progresses. This freedom of understanding has opened the door to spirituality for many of us who thought we would not, or could not, be spiritual.

With small but significant actions, we can work Step Three by establishing a commitment to the program. For example, many of us decide to make going to meetings a priority, and schedule them into our lives regardless of circumstances. We commit to attending, whether or not we feel like going. We come to believe that it is God's will that we not act out. In this way, we give up debating about how to handle our addiction and simply do what is right according to our program. We work the Third Step whenever we choose recovery over addiction.

At this point, we may also begin to practice opening ourselves up to the guidance of a Higher Power. For many of us, these are our first rudimentary attempts at prayer. We may ask for our Higher Power's help in staying abstinent today and working our program of recovery. We may ask for insight into how we can be of use to others and carry out God's will. Our specific words are less important than our willingness to make contact with a Power greater than ourselves and to let God's care into our lives.

To make the Third Step decision is to surrender. We give up the belief that our intellect, our knowledge, our judgment, and our will could successfully guide our lives. We accept that the control we thought we had over our lives was an illusion. This profound surrender of old beliefs, habits, and behaviors is something we learn to renew every day. We reaffirm our decision to turn our will and lives over to the care of the God of our understanding, not seeking an unattainable perfection, but acknowledging and affirming the progress we make in recovery.

With surrender, we say goodbye to our old way of life and prepare to make a transition to the new. Letting go of our addiction can be like losing a familiar friend. For most of our lives, our addiction was there to comfort us and distract us from our problems. Facing life without acting out involves feelings of grief and loss. But it can be done, through faith in a Power greater than ourselves, and in the company of others who walk the same path.

From time to time we may find ourselves "taking back" our will—attempting to control things again by only surrendering in certain areas of our lives and not in others. We need not be discouraged by these experiences. As long as we believe in the process of recovery, and have the willingness to learn and grow, we can return to Step Three and recommit to our spiritual program.

When we make a decision to turn our will and our lives over to the care of the God of our understanding, we begin to notice signs of growth and transition, evidence that the program is working. We find ourselves being more honest, more willing to share the truth about ourselves with others. We attend meetings consistently, making room in our lives for the fellowship. We ask for and accept help, reaching out to other recovering sex addicts on a regular basis, instead of living in secrecy. We may experience abstinence from our inner-circle sexual behaviors as a gift from our Higher Power rather than as the result of our own white-knuckled efforts. We start to value and enjoy a new sense of spirituality. We feel grateful for our recovery and for the gifts we are starting to receive from our Higher Power.

Reflecting on our progress thus far, we may begin to feel both relief and a new faith that the program can work for us. A growing sense of community within the SAA fellowship, and a newfound ability to live in the moment under God's care, gives us the courage to go forward in recovery. With the help of our sponsor, we are ready to take stock of ourselves, to reflect profoundly on our past and on the defects of character that keep us from fully turning our will and our lives over to the care of God. The decision has been made, and the work of fearless self-exploration can begin. We move on to Step Four.

Step Four

Made a searching and fearless moral inventory of ourselves.

In taking the Fourth Step, we begin to know ourselves for who we really are. Building on the foundation of the first three steps, we take stock of the feelings and patterns that have shaped our lives. We come to realize that our addiction is more than just unmanageable sexual activities; it includes an entire system of underlying thoughts, feelings, and behaviors. If we neglect this inventory, we risk being stuck in our old habits and mistaken beliefs, and our unexamined defects of character will eventually lead us to relapse. By looking honestly at our moral nature—the failings that kept us trapped in our addiction, as well as our virtues and aspirations—we start to move away from being self-centered and toward being God-centered.

The Fourth Step takes courage, because we are gradually giving up our old rationalizations, dishonesty, and self-pity, in order to discover the truth about who we are. In the process, most of us find ourselves peeling away many layers of denial. Our distorted view of ourselves led us to avoid responsibility for our actions. Our denial about our addictive behaviors prevented us from seeing our faults. At the same time, our belief that we were horrible people kept us from believing we could ever change, or be deserving of a better life. In taking the Fourth Step, we become willing to challenge these old ways of thinking and examine ourselves with a new clarity.

A searching and fearless moral inventory is one of the means by which we open ourselves to the care and healing of our Higher Power. It is one of the first and most profound ways we put our Third Step decision into action. As we work Step Four, we practice honesty, courage, and faith, keeping in mind that others have walked this path before us and have found their recovery strengthened through this work.

A moral inventory can be described as a systematic examination of all the beliefs, feelings, attitudes, and actions that have shaped our lives from our earliest years. It is a careful survey of how we have responded to people, circumstances, and the world around us. An inventory allows us to go over our lives methodically and objectively, reevaluating assumptions, beliefs, and feelings that we have held onto for years but perhaps never examined or questioned. In making this inventory, we take special care to identify those aspects of our character that have caused harm to ourselves and others, so as to bring them forward for healing and change in later steps.

The Fourth Step inventory is a written inventory. If we merely say it aloud or think about it, it is too easy to miss or ignore important things. All inventories have to be recorded in some way in order to be accurate. Imagine trying to take inventory of all the merchandise in a store without writing anything down. In the same way, our inventory needs to be documented in order to be useful. The written inventory serves as a snapshot of the current state of our moral being and allows us to get an accurate, realistic perspective on ourselves, perhaps for the very first time. We may also draw on this inventory for reference when working Steps Five through Nine.

Experience has shown that it is helpful to work this step one small amount at a time, without trying to rush the process. Most of us cannot write a thorough Fourth Step in one sitting. There is too much work to do, and we need time to reflect on our work as we do it. If we break the step down into manageable pieces, all we need to do is focus on the piece in front of us.

The support of others in doing this work is essential. While making our inventory, we stay in close contact with our sponsor and our friends in the fellowship. A sponsor can help us pace our work and keep us on track, encourage us to explore new areas, or give us permission to move on when we are stuck. Some of us have found it helpful to set a date for our Fifth Step as part of the Fourth Step process. We may also share parts of our inventory with our sponsor as we go along.

There is no single format that is used by all members in their inventories. We work closely with our sponsor to discover what kind of writing we need to do and what form of inventory is most effective for us. The common element is that we write about a number of aspects of our lives that, when put together, give us an honest picture of ourselves, including our shortcomings. Our inventory is searching, because we try to examine ourselves as thoroughly and painstakingly as possible. It is fearless, because we don't let our fear stop us from digging deeper. It is moral, because it concerns our values and the consequences of our actions for ourselves and others.

Examining our sexual conduct is an important aspect of our inventory. While in our First Step we examined the patterns of our sexual behavior and disclosed specific instances, here we explore more deeply our sexual history and look at every instance in which our sexual behavior directly or indirectly harmed others or ourselves. We look at whom we hurt, what we did specifically to hurt them, and why we did it. In the process, we may uncover the secret agendas, fantasies, beliefs, and rationalizations contributing to our behavior. While violating others sexually is an obvious example of a harm done, we also acknowledge that using people for our sexual exploits, violating trust, committing infidelity, lying and covering up our behaviors, manipulating others covertly or overtly, and taking advantage of others by using power or authority are other ways we may have caused harm. We may also examine our traumatic sexual experiences or sexually abusive relationships and their effects on ourselves and others. Clarity, honesty, and self-disclosure are essential as we explore each instance. We take full and unequivocal responsibility for what we've done. Even if we were co-partners in sexual misdeeds, in working Step Four we focus only on our part. We look honestly at the defects that drove our behavior, such as selfishness, desire for control, an attitude of entitlement, or feelings of inferiority or superiority.

We also inventory our resentments. For sex addicts, resentment is one of the most stubborn obstacles to our spiritual growth. Resentment means holding on to old hurts, anger, and grudges. When we cling to hurts or anger, we get a negative attitude. We feel victimized. And each time we play the event over in our minds, we feel victimized again. From this victim attitude, we often slip into an attitude of entitlement. If life is unfair, we are entitled to get what we need and want by any means necessary. So feeling entitled, we play by a different set of rules. We lower our moral standards to allow ourselves to get our fair share. We use dishonesty, blaming others, manipulation, or theft to even the score.

In our inventory we list the people and situations that have hurt us, citing specific instances. We list what resentments we hold against people, and why—trying to identify exactly what they did, instead of writing in generalities. Many of us write about how we felt when we were hurt, and how we feel now. We may list what we think was lost, taken, or threatened by another person's actions. Some of us have also listed resentments against society or certain institutions. We also write about our blame of others—how we believe their actions have harmed us and affected our lives for the worse. We may find ourselves feeling uncomfortable about this, but it is important to write honestly about our feelings, even if they seem unreasonable.

We then go back over the list of resentments, looking at each incident, and ask ourselves what role we played in the situation. We must take responsibility for our part, however small. Sometimes, especially for resentments from childhood, we determine we had no role in the problem at all. When we review the resentments from our adult lives, however, we discover, often to our surprise, that we've almost always contributed in some way to the troubles that have beset us. When looking at the actions of others, for instance, we need to ask ourselves, "What is it about their actions that may have been a response to something I said or did?" A sponsor can help us sort this out and see where we need to take responsibility, and where we need to let go of carrying responsibility for the actions of others.

When we review our responsibility in conflicts, we see the pattern of our character defects emerge. Character defects are flaws in our moral nature that prevent us from aligning ourselves with God's will; they are expressions of our willfulness. These defects include dishonesty, selfishness, self-centeredness, lack of humility, grandiosity, pessimism, the desire to control everything around us, or any other shortcoming that we see coming up again and again in our relationships with others. For example, if we repeatedly got into conflict with people because of jealousy, we list jealousy as one of our character defects. In our inventory we do our best to list whatever such defects we can identify. We will refer to our list of character defects later in Steps Six and Seven.

In the same way that we write about our sexual conduct and resentments, we may inventory other emotions and behavior patterns in our lives. Examples of troubling emotions that bring out our character defects may include fear, envy, loneliness, shame, embarrassment, or self-hatred. This list may not fit for everyone, and we may inventory other patterns instead. Our sponsor can help us narrow or broaden our focus as needed.

Our emotions have often been a source of pain and confusion in our lives, and they frequently triggered our addictive sexual behavior. We may have acted out whenever we experienced anger, fear, anxiety, or even joy, rather than responding to these emotions in a healthy way. We also may notice that our feelings increase in intensity when we stop acting out. In taking inventory, we may write about the many ways that these feelings have ruled our lives, using specific examples from our experience. We strive to isolate and recognize each feeling, to the best of our ability, and we practice acceptance of all our emotions, rather than denying or fearing them. In each case we search for the defects of character revealed by our emotional unmanageability, as well as giving ourselves credit for the times we were responsible, caring, and appropriate with our emotional responses. If we find ourselves hesitating, we turn to our Higher Power for help, trusting that with God's care we cannot fail.

In the case of fear, we may write about times in which we risked our lives, health, careers, or relationships, while denying that we were in danger. We can list the ways in which we have been handicapped by our fears: how fear motivated actions that we later regretted, how it prevented us from achieving the things we desired, or how the fear of intimacy and commitment contributed to our loneliness. Many of us have found that fear was a pervasive influence throughout our lives, profoundly affecting our beliefs, our relationships, and our self-worth. Yet we also need to credit ourselves for the times when we have been courageous—the times we felt fear but still did what was worthwhile or healthy for us.

In writing about envy, we may look at all of the ways we compare our insides with the outsides of others. We might list the things others have that we think we're lacking, write about our responsibility for not pursuing these goals, and then list the things in our lives for which we are grateful.

When examining loneliness, we may write about the ways in which we have isolated ourselves. If we keep ourselves too busy to have friends, or otherwise avoid intimate contact, we note that. We list the ways we have avoided emotional intimacy with those closest to us. And we list the ways we still avoid it. If we have kept secrets or kept parts of our lives hidden, we record that as well.

We may want to write down the things we've done that brought us shame or embarrassment. Although embarrassing events might seem trivial, we sometimes feel as much embarrassment as if the events happened yesterday. We can also list the things we feel guilty about. We look at things we did that we knew were wrong and about which we feel remorse. And we write down any secrets that we feel ashamed about, or other events that bring up shame when we recall them. These painful events and feelings must come to light if we are to continue on our path of recovery. As long as they remain secret, they have the power to lead us back to our addiction.

We may inventory self-hatred by listing the things we've done that we feel we cannot accept or forgive ourselves for. These are the things time does not seem to heal. We look at the ways we let ourselves down. We list the resentments we hold against ourselves. We record the things about ourselves that we don't like, or that we wish were different. We write about how we have acted in self-hating ways, listing the ways that we've abused our bodies, our emotions, and our spirits. We look at how we have neglected our physical, emotional, mental, and spiritual needs. We examine the ways in which we allowed others to abuse us and treat us poorly. We list the negative things we believe about ourselves, and the abusive messages we tell ourselves. We look for the patterns in our self-hating behaviors, trying to identify the character defects underlying them.

A moral inventory wouldn't be complete without some acknowledgment of our positive aspects. We list the ways we have acted in a self-loving manner. We may write about the friendships we have nurtured and the people we have helped. We list the things we are genuinely proud of, such as healthy accomplishments that we worked hard to achieve. We write about our love, faith, and gratitude. We give ourselves credit for the success we have had at turning our addiction over to our Higher Power.

We need to remember that our Fourth Step is *an* inventory, not *the* inventory. We may always return to our inventory when we need to. We may have only been ready to face certain truths about ourselves when we first worked the step. We may work a Fourth Step again when we have new challenges to face or when we need to examine ourselves more closely. There is no one right inventory, and there are no perfect inventories.

Completing Step Four is a major milestone in our recovery. To complete it we need patience, persistence, honesty, and courage. It takes support, for we do our Fourth Step with the help of our Higher Power, our sponsor, and our group. And it takes gentleness in the form of self-care. By completing this step we show a commitment to our recovery and to living in reality. Now, after gaining such hard-won insight into ourselves, it is time to open up and share our truth, and in this sharing help make our recovery secure. It is time for Step Five.

Step Five

*Admitted to God, to ourselves, and to another
human being the exact nature of our wrongs.*

Each step of the program is a leap of faith that moves us forward in our recovery. After completing our moral inventory, we are challenged in Step Five to take another leap. We now need to admit the whole truth we have discovered to God, to ourselves, and to another person. Working the Fifth Step helps relieve us of the burden of our secrets, break through our isolation, and face ourselves honestly in a way we cannot do alone. With the Fifth Step, we come out into the open.

As active sex addicts, we hid who we were and what we were doing—from others, but also from ourselves. We take the Fifth Step when we come out of hiding, let go of self-deception, and acknowledge our reliance on a Higher Power. Our belief that we were isolated, estranged from the care of a loving God, had kept us in fear. Now, breaking free of secrecy, we admit our wrongs in the light of our relationship with the God of our understanding. If we trust, we will be given the power to acknowledge our shortcomings. Admitting our wrongs to God opens the door to change within ourselves. We have found that God will help us find the courage and honesty we need in order to work this step.

Although we have recorded a detailed inventory in the Fourth Step, it is a different thing altogether to admit the truth to ourselves. We need to be careful to acknowledge the exact nature of our wrongs inwardly, so that denial can give way to acceptance. Sharing our inventory with another human being helps in this process. When we hear ourselves admitting our wrongs to someone, explaining all of the details out loud, our past begins to make more sense, and we can start to view our lives with more clarity. As the reality of our shortcomings sinks in, we can bring them, in humility, to our Higher Power. Our deepest acceptance comes when we know that the God of our understanding loves us no matter what we have done.

In the Fifth Step we reveal all our secrets to another person, many of us for the very first time. Despite our commitment to the program, we often find ourselves feeling afraid at this point. We expect to be judged harshly and rejected if we tell someone our secrets, especially those acting-out behaviors of which we are most ashamed. These fears are only natural, but we cannot allow them to prevent us from taking this step. We call on our Higher Power for strength and for the willingness to share our story. We discover that the person hearing our Fifth Step will not reject us, but will often respect us for our honesty and courage, and love us all the more.

We pick someone we trust to hear our inventory. Most of us share our Fifth Step with our sponsor. Some of us choose a friend in the program, a therapist, a spiritual advisor, or another wise confidant with whom we feel safe. It is best to take this step with the help of a person who has worked this step in his or her own recovery and who already knows and accepts us unconditionally.

We do not take the Fifth Step with our partners, parents, or families. This is not the time for selfish confessions. We need time in the program, and the help of experienced members, before we can judge what to reveal to our families or those closest to us.

Admitting our wrongs means admitting all the ways in which we were dishonest, unfair, abusive, inconsiderate, unjust, or unethical. Our wrongs include all of the ways we broke the rules to get ahead or to avoid consequences we didn't want to face. They may also include actions we neglected to take, as well as ones we took.

We admit our wrongs in a detailed and thorough way. We describe what we did, when we did it, and what we were thinking or feeling when we did it. We describe what the consequences were for ourselves and for others. Many of us tell the story of each wrong rather than simply listing them. In the process, we reexamine situations in which we may have seen ourselves as the victim or minimized our wrongful actions. Striving for thoroughness, we admit all the wrongs we can remember, not just those related to our acting out.

Most importantly, we admit the character defects that motivated our actions, such as pride, envy, selfishness, or greed. These defects or failings are *the exact nature of our wrongs*. They are those aspects of temperament that hold back our spiritual growth and keep us locked in self-defeating avoid sex for fear of being victimized again or becoming perpetrators ourselves. In taking this step, we acknowledge that many of our feelings, thoughts, and patterns around sex are beyond our ability to manage and won't disappear overnight. Our part is to become willing and ready for our Higher Power to move us toward healthier ways of being with our sexuality.

We may feel as powerless over our defects as we did over our addictive sexual behaviors. Yet if we are unwilling to let go of our defects, we risk being led back into our addiction. Our Step Four inventory revealed to us how defects such as resentment, self-centeredness, and self-pity led us time and again into our addictive behaviors. By becoming ready to relinquish our defects, we show our willingness to do what it takes to stay abstinent.

Becoming entirely ready involves a deeper commitment to recovery, a willingness to let the God of our understanding effect important changes within us—changes in our ways of thinking and feeling, changes in our behavior. The readiness in the Sixth Step is one of the practical results of our Third Step decision to turn our will and life over to God's care. For our Higher Power's will to work in our lives, we must be willing to let it work. If we feel that we are not yet willing, we can pray to become ready to have these defects removed. Although there is no perfect, infallible way of knowing that we are "entirely" ready, we will know when our doubts and reservations are no longer blocking our way.

Many of us had tried to purge ourselves of our worst traits, and our efforts failed, just as our attempts to be free of our addiction failed. We may have tried vows and resolutions, or adopted beliefs or practices designed for self-improvement, only to see our defects manifesting again, despite good intentions. We wondered how God could remove our character defects. But we need not concern ourselves with this in order to work Step Six. All we have to do is become willing, and leave the rest to our Higher Power.

On the other side of every character defect is a character asset. Part of the process of becoming entirely ready is to practice these character assets in our actions and choices, instead of our defects. If we suffer from emotional rigidity, we can look for ways to become more flexible. If we are perfectionists, overly self-critical, or impatient, we can practice acceptance. Practicing new ways of behavior can help open our hearts to the spiritual changes God wants for us.

The prospect of having life-long habits removed may seem overwhelming. We have learned that the Sixth Step is not a single

habits, attitudes, and beliefs. We have found that admitting these defects is essential to experiencing a positive breakthrough in our relations with others, and with ourselves.

This may seem like a very difficult task. We should not lose heart. During the Fifth Step, our sponsor will often share his or her own experiences with us, letting us know about similar actions, feelings, and shortcomings. Knowing that others feel the way we do, and have done some of the same kinds of things, helps to relieve us of our shame and isolation. Our sponsor supports us emotionally as we face the most painful parts of ourselves, allowing us to look at our wrongs without flinching.

Although the Fifth Step focuses on admitting the exact nature of our wrongs, it is also very helpful to acknowledge the good things about ourselves. Admitting the ways we have been caring, resourceful, and talented helps us get a balanced picture of the whole of our moral nature. By acknowledging our character assets, and with our sponsor's encouragement, we establish a foundation on which our further recovery can be built.

While we might wish to share our entire Fifth Step in one sitting, some of us may in fact need several meetings to complete the entire step. Once we start, we make a commitment to finish it. We are often emotionally vulnerable while working this step, so we want to be sure to complete it in a timely fashion and to get some extra support. With the help of our Higher Power, and support from our sponsor and others, we can face our pain without becoming consumed by it. Once we finish Step Five, the rewards will prove to have been worth the effort.

When we finish Step Five, it may feel as though a great burden has been lifted from our shoulders. Many of us feel a sense of wholeness and integrity for the very first time. We have acknowledged and taken responsibility for the whole of our being, to ourselves, our fellow addict, and our Higher Power. The acceptance we receive is a profound spiritual experience. Having gained a greater faith in the love and care of the God of our understanding, it is now time to take a good look at our character defects in the light of our relationship with God. Our new awareness leads to a desire for change. We go on to Step Six.

Awareness
Acceptance
Action

Step Six

*Were entirely ready to have God remove
all these defects of character.*

Wanting our lives to change is not the same as being actually ready for change. The negative patterns uncovered in our inventory represent a lifetime of ingrained beliefs, attitudes, and habits of behavior. Just becoming aware of them can be painful; imagining life without them may seem almost impossible.

Much of our resistance to change is based in fear. We may find it easier to continue in an unhappy, yet familiar way of life, than to face an unknown and uncertain future. For many of us, our problems and shortcomings seemed to define us as people: what would we be without them? Often we find that our character defects started as ways to deal with difficult circumstances, in childhood or later. It is hard to let go of beliefs and behaviors that once helped us cope, or even kept us alive. If we are fearful, we can gently and courageously allow ourselves to consider the possibility of surrendering our familiar defects, trusting that our Higher Power will not give us more than we can handle.

Character defects are undesirable traits, attitudes, and beliefs that make our lives unmanageable, cause pain to others, and block our spiritual growth. Our problems did not begin with our sex addiction, nor do they end when we get into recovery. Step Six builds on the recognition that our malady has roots that run deeper than just our acting-out behavior. It requires the willingness to change fundamentally, to be free of the failings that continue to create serious problems in our lives.

Most of us are well aware of our worst character defects long before we get to this step. If we rage, are uncontrollably jealous, are full of resentments, or feel like a doormat, we probably have had some sense of how these patterns have poisoned our lives and relationships. But rather than solving these problems or accepting our lives, we had hunkered down with our addiction. In the Sixth Step, we become open to the possibility that God can remove the defects we had felt helpless to control and had masked with our acting out.

In working this step, we have found it helpful to refer to the list of character defects we made in our Step Four inventory and perhaps expanded with the help of our sponsor when we took Step Five. Our list includes all of the self-defeating attitudes and behavior patterns that have been revealed to us. Examples of unhealthy attitudes may include resentment, grandiosity, self-pity, perfectionism, blaming others, feeling

like a victim, and entitlement. Our list of behaviors mig habitual actions such as raging, isolating from others, lying, ma or avoiding conflict. We may also have noted our negativ approaches to life, such as greed, envy, selfishness, and self-h important to realize that the words "these defects of charact the "exact nature of our wrongs" admitted in the Fifth Step. we focus on those defects that have come to our attention t inventory work.

We may see, for example, that our expectations of others disappointment and resentment. We may notice that our pe caused us to procrastinate rather than complete a task impe may remember instances when our stubbornness, judgment or self-righteousness produced conflict with other people. areas of unmanageability in our lives can help us recognize when we identify our responsibility for events that felt painf control. We can also look at where we've been "stuck": areas that repeatedly gave us trouble. If, for instance, we are the kin who won't commit to things, we can recognize this defect in of problems we have had, such as not staying long in any jumping from one relationship to another. We look for thos our personality that hold us back in life, whatever they migh

We can ask our sponsor and friends in recovery for help in our character defects. We can ask them to tell us when making choices that are not in our best interest. They can t we seem to be repeating the same mistakes. Often they wi the situations that cause us trouble, rather than tell us di they think our problems are. It is also helpful to ask our H to reveal our character defects to us. When we pray or medi step, new insights about ourselves and our shortcomings will to us.

As sex addicts, we may find that our character defects ta of unhealthy beliefs and attitudes about sex. These defects believing that sex is inherently bad or wrong, or that sex is i with being religious, spiritual, or "good"; having difficulty difference between sex and love, or understanding how to each other; having feelings of sexual inadequacy or sh avoiding healthy sexual risks; and having feelings of sexual or associating sex with power and control. If we have bee sexual trauma or abuse, we may feel stuck in the role of e or perpetrator, repeatedly reenacting abusive patterns,

event, but an ongoing process. We do not need to be willing to have all of our defects removed at once. We can concentrate on being ready to have one or two debilitating character traits removed first. And just as we stop acting out one day at a time, we can allow ourselves to be ready for changes in our character one day at a time. When we see ourselves reacting to a situation in an old way, we can try handling it differently for one day. We will never know perfection, but we can experience progress.

As we let go of old ways of approaching life, and trust that God will reveal new ways, many of us begin to have a greater vision of what our life in recovery could be. We are ready for real change, and our attention now turns directly to our Higher Power, so that we may ask in all humility for the help we need. It is time for Step Seven.

Step Seven

Humbly asked God to remove our shortcomings.

The preceding steps bring us to a realization that our character defects, the flaws or shortcomings in our personality, have caused us a great deal of suffering throughout our lives and prevented us from completely aligning ourselves with our Higher Power's will for us. When we become entirely ready to have these self-destructive aspects of our character removed, we then ask God to do so in Step Seven. Whenever we ask for this help, we invite God into our lives in a new way.

We may wonder why it is necessary to ask *humbly*. Many of us have confused humility with humiliation. We were more familiar with pleading for, or demanding what we wanted, than with asking. In fact, it takes humility to truly ask for help. It means admitting that we are not wholly strong and self-sufficient. It means that we are not too proud or ashamed to believe that we can be helped.

Humility is a result of the self-honesty we have gained through working the preceding steps. It comes from a realistic view of ourselves, a knowledge of both our strengths and limitations. We recognize that our shortcomings are not unique, and that we are not better or worse than anyone else. When we live with this knowledge, we do not expect perfection from ourselves or others. We know that we are bound to make mistakes, and we choose to learn from them rather than punish ourselves for them. Humility means being teachable, vulnerable, and open.

Ready for fundamental change in our lives, and knowing that we can-not change without help from our Higher Power, we humbly ask God to remove our shortcomings. The power of this step is in the asking, not in the result. Asking is a very powerful act—it expresses a deepening surrender on our part. The Seventh Step does not guarantee, or even predict, an outcome. We have found that God's will for us is usually different, and ultimately greater, than our expectations. Simply putting ourselves in God's hands is all that's needed.

Many of us work this step through prayer. Often we include our request in our regular prayers. We may also ask for a particular shortcoming to be removed when a situation demands it. We often find relief as soon as we pray, because our attitude toward the situation has changed through the act of asking.

Change occurs in God's time, not ours. As addicts, we are accustomed to seeking instant gratification. But in recovery, most of us experience gradual improvement rather than sudden transformations. We need patience to work the Seventh Step, and trust that our Higher Power can help us. Some of our defects may indeed be quickly removed. Others may arise again and again, challenging us to a greater reliance on God. We may even find that certain shortcomings have gone into hibernation, allowing us to move forward in our recovery, only to reappear later when we are better able to recognize and surrender them. However we experience this step, the result is a steady increase in our serenity, freedom, and spiritual growth.

One of the main ways God works in our lives is through other people. Asking to have our shortcomings removed is also expressed through opening ourselves to other recovering sex addicts. Our fellow addicts help us in many ways. They can give us encouragement when we lack confidence. They can help us see shortcomings that we have been unable to recognize on our own. And they can support us by sharing their own experiences with taking this step. Simply telling others about our defects can reduce their power over us. And just having someone listen to us in our struggles is often the very help we need.

In working Step Seven, we may also see our conception of a Higher Power becoming more personal. Up to this point, many of us still felt a certain distance and remoteness in our relationship to God. By experiencing how reliance on God has a practical effect on our day-to-day lives, and influences our attitudes and behaviors in tangible ways, we begin to see our Higher Power as a much closer and more intimate presence than we had been aware of before. We can ask for God's help at any time, and in any situation. Humility and openness become a part of everyday life.

As we grow in humility, we gradually come to view our lives, and even our problems, with gratitude. When we are free from self-importance, we can recognize that we have much to be grateful for. In our addiction, we felt that no matter what we had, we were missing something. We often risked the wonderful things we had in order to act out. In recovery, with the humility we receive through working the steps, we become thankful for the things we used to take for granted. And we can look at our shortcomings as opportunities to learn and grow.

We also discover that our character defects can become useful in God's hands. Our struggles with our own shortcomings help us to understand and empathize with the struggles of others and to reach out to the still suffering addict by sharing our own experience, strength, and hope. Aspects of ourselves that we were ashamed of and tried to keep hidden can sometimes blossom unexpectedly into gifts that enrich our recovery, when brought into the light of a loving Higher Power. Anger may contain the seeds of courage; envy can turn to empathy; self-centered pride may grow into a healthy self-love. Each character defect we turn over to God becomes one more way of opening ourselves to God's care.

In the process of asking our Higher Power to remove the flaws in our character, we exercise and deepen our humility. Only when we have come this far in our program, and have begun the change from a self-centered approach to life to a new approach based on spiritual principles, are we ready to constructively face the damage that we have inflicted on other people. With the willingness to let go of resentment, fear, and the other defects that have isolated us from God and our fellows, we are spiritually prepared to consider repairing the harm we've done in the past. We move on to Step Eight.

Step Eight

Made a list of all persons we had harmed and became willing to make amends to them all.

With the Eighth Step, we begin to take responsibility for the harm we inflicted on others when we acted on our character defects. Most of us know that we caused harm in one way or another, but in the past we chose to feel guilty without doing anything about it. It was frightening to consider the consequences of our wrongs, and we felt helpless to take action. Or we were too self-absorbed to notice the wreckage in our wake—so wrapped up in our own resentments and hurts that we were unwilling to recognize our part of the problem. However, as we progress in recovery, we seek to reclaim the truth about our actions. Working

Steps Four through Seven helps our responsibilities become clearer. In Step Eight we claim both our integrity and our compassion, and become willing to free ourselves from the guilt we have carried.

We start by writing a list of all the persons we have harmed. Our Fourth Step inventory can be very helpful in making this list. Going back over our inventory, we will see the names of many people we resented, feared, neglected, or harmed with our sexual acting out. Most of these names will go on our Eighth Step list. Paying attention to the shortcomings outlined in our Fourth Step may also trigger memories of the harm we have caused to other people over the years because of these defects. The point is to make the list as complete as possible, trying not to leave anyone out. Whereas in Step Four we looked at our painful relationships to help us uncover our character defects, in Step Eight we focus on the individuals affected by these defects, in order to see how we have harmed each one.

The harm we have done to others can take many forms. We may have harmed people sexually or physically, or hurt them verbally or emotionally. Harm may have resulted from our actions or from what we failed to do. The degree of harm could vary, from our being inconsiderate or neglectful to outright abuse. We list anyone we have harmed in any of these ways. Many of us include details in our lists, such as when we hurt the person, what we did to cause harm, and what harm resulted. Listing these specific details helps us to take responsibility for our actions in a concrete way.

We have found it helpful to start by considering the people who were directly harmed by our acting-out behavior. We may have exploited and manipulated others, taken advantage of their vulnerability, convinced them to violate their values, or pressured them into having sex. Some of us engaged in sexual abuse and other harmful or illegal sexual activities. We may have forced people to have sex or to participate in our sexual activity. We may have exploited children or used violence or threats to keep others from exposing our behavior. The important thing is to be thorough, including all the people we can remember who were harmed by our behavior, whether we know their names or not. If we start to feel overwhelmed, we pray to our Higher Power and turn to our sponsor and friends in recovery for support and guidance.

We also list those who have been harmed by our dishonesty, self-centered attitudes, or other behaviors that arose from our character defects. We may have lied or made false promises to people, even to those we felt closest to. We may have been critical, impatient, argumentative, judgmental, financially irresponsible, vengeful, or mean. We also list people we harmed by our neglect, by not "showing up" for our lives. Perhaps we were too busy for family or friends, missed important events, were preoccupied, withdrawn, isolated, or uninvolved in our work, or completely abandoned our families or loved ones.

We work this step most effectively when we keep our attention squarely on the Eighth Step, concentrating only on our willingness to make amends to those we have harmed, rather than worrying about how to actually make our amends in Step Nine. The amends process is broken into two steps for a reason, allowing us to take the time we need to become truly willing before moving forward. At this point, we only need to be honest with ourselves about the harm we have done. We stay focused on this work, letting go of any worries we may have about the future. Our Higher Power is with us throughout this process.

Many of us were surprised when it was suggested that we put our own name on our amends list. We forgot to take into account the harm we did to ourselves. In our addiction, we often took poor care of ourselves and acted in self-destructive ways. We may have betrayed our own values or damaged our sense of self-worth. Putting our own name on the list helps to develop a sense of compassion for ourselves and encourages us to begin treating ourselves with care and respect.

When we have completed our list, most of us ask our sponsor to go over it with us and provide feedback. Our sponsor may make suggestions about people or incidents that we've overlooked, or suggest that we take certain names off the list. Some of us feel guilty for things we are not responsible for. Our sponsor can help us sort these things out, encouraging us to be thorough without being too hard on ourselves.

After we have completed our list, we often experience difficulty in becoming willing to make amends, especially if we feel that the people we hurt caused us harm as well. Justifications and rationalizations for our behaviors may reassert themselves. If we are angry with someone, it is hard to think about making amends to that person. We may wish that he or she would make amends to us first. But in order to become willing, it is essential that we focus only on our own behavior, not on someone else's. Our part may be small, but we concentrate on that part.

We have found that when we hold on to old grievances, we are prevented from growing spiritually. In many cases, our list contains names of people with whom we have unfinished business. If our life is full of these unfinished conversations, our mind is filled with regrets and "what-ifs." Working this step means finding the willingness to bring resolution to these relationships, regardless of whether or not those involved behaved rightly towards us. This process of becoming willing to make amends involves a deeper surrender to our Higher Power's will than we have known before.

Some of us have felt trapped in our feelings about the past. We have felt great sorrow and grief over our actions and the losses that resulted from them. Sometimes we felt so ashamed that to talk of it further seemed almost unbearable. If we feel overwhelmed in this way, we turn to the God of our understanding and to our program friends for support in facing the pain of our actions and finding the willingness to make amends. Our lives are in God's care, no matter what harm we may have caused. We muster our courage, in the faith that our willingness to continue with this step will both dramatically reduce our suffering and allow us to acknowledge the suffering we have caused to others.

Empathy with those we have harmed is a sign of our willingness to make amends. This process cannot be rushed. We may never be able to fully understand what those we have harmed have gone through, but we can ask for the willingness to have this understanding given to us, in God's time.

Eventually we find the willingness to proceed with our amends. However, we don't expect to work Step Eight perfectly. If we're not feeling totally ready in every case, or if we're still unsure about some names on our list, we can still move forward and not get stuck here. We can always return to Step Eight at another time and go deeper. Now that we have been honest about the harm we have caused, and have become willing to do what we can to make amends, it is time to take action. We are ready for Step Nine.

Step Nine

Made direct amends to such people wherever possible,
except when to do so would injure them or others.

In taking the Ninth Step, we act on the knowledge that what we do really matters—that our actions have consequences in the world, for good or ill. The damage we did in our addiction is cleared away not only by honestly admitting what we have done, but by committing to setting things right. Reaching out to others to acknowledge and heal the wrongs of the past brings us freedom and serenity in the present. We call this process *making direct amends*. In Step Nine we make our best effort to contact the people we have harmed, admit the wrongs we have done them, express our remorse, and offer some kind of reparation. Most importantly, we change how we behave today. We do our utmost not to repeat the behavior that caused harm in the past, and we communicate this resolve to those we've hurt.

Many of us find ourselves worrying about the reactions of those to whom we make amends, hesitating to proceed with this step because of our fear. We can rely on our Higher Power to be with us throughout this process and to grant us the courage we need to move forward. Our part is to make the amends, without taking responsibility for the reactions of others. Some of the people we approach may accept our amends with understanding and forgiveness, and others may not. The response of any particular person, positive or negative, is not a measure of how well we make our amends. The success of our amends depends only on how honestly and thoroughly we make them.

The Ninth Step can be a project of some magnitude. We work this step only when we have a strong foundation built on the preceding steps. Rather than be overwhelmed by the number of people on our Eighth Step list, or all of the harm we've done over the years, we simply make amends to one person at a time. Each person and situation has much to teach us. We can take our time, patiently dealing with the challenges we are ready for, and trusting that we will become ready for others in the future.

Throughout this process, we are mindful of our motives in making amends. Effective amends are as selfless and sincere as we can make them, with no hidden agendas. We want to be sure we are not using the amends process as an excuse to re-engage with people who prefer not to have contact with us. We also guard against using Step Nine as an opportunity to defend our past behaviors or to burden others with detailed confessions in order to relieve ourselves of our own guilt. In all cases, we check to see whether we are acting out of selfishness, simply in order to feel better, or from a desire to be liked and admired for having changed our ways.

We need to exercise good judgment here. We seek the counsel of our sponsor and other members who have experience working this step. Rather than rushing into premature amends, we take the time to get clear about exactly what we are making amends for and what harm we think we caused in each situation. We also take time to clarify our emotions before we proceed. An attitude of humility and sincere regret for the harms we have done will carry us far. For each amends, we also decide whether it is appropriate to make contact with that person, how much we reveal to the person, and whether we put ourselves at risk when we make amends.

If we have good reason to believe that we will do someone harm by making contact, then we refrain. Sometimes we might ask through a third party if contact for an amends would be appropriate. If the answer is no, we need to show our respect and stay away. If we contact a person we have abused, it may need to be through someone that person knows or under the supervision of a professional who can make the interaction safe. When it comes to those we have harmed through sexual abuse or illegal behavior, we should be very cautious about harming them again, not even offering to make amends unless we're certain they would welcome it.

We are careful about how much we reveal in our amends. To those we have harmed in the past that are not close to us today, we need not explain that we are sex addicts. Revealing our disease is less important than taking responsibility for the harm we did, and may actually distract us from focusing on our amends. We also use judgment about how specific we are when making the amends. Going into great detail about our sexual behavior, for instance, might do more harm than good. Instead, we can share the general pattern of our hurtful behavior, taking our cue from the person to whom we are making amends if more detail would be helpful. We are fearless, however, in revealing those consequences of our behavior that directly affect the other person, such as if we have exposed him or her to a sexually transmitted disease. Throughout this process, we carefully examine our motives, always balancing the willingness to take full responsibility for our wrongs with care and concern for the well-being of those we have harmed.

We usually don't need to put ourselves at grave personal risk when making amends. Some of us committed serious offenses in our sex addiction. Admitting to them can have dire consequences for us, as well as for our loved ones. Before we take action, we look at those we may harm in the process, including ourselves. On the other hand, we don't want to leave room for rationalizations. We consult with our sponsor, and perhaps an outside professional, before attempting to make amends that could have legal consequences. Ultimately, after praying to our Higher Power for strength and guidance, we come to our own decision regarding such amends.

When setting things right, we consider what would be appropriate in each case. If we took money or property, we do our best to replace it. If our behavior has caused psychological harm, to our children or others, we can offer to pay for therapy. If we were distant and neglectful, we can make ourselves available and emotionally present. Many situations are more complex than this, requiring prayer, careful thought, and consultation with our sponsor. It is often helpful to ask the people we harmed what they think we should do to help make things right. We bear in mind that we can't always fully repair the harm we've done; nothing can change the past. This does not keep us from doing our best to set things right in the present. Many of us have seen great healing occur in ourselves and our relationships from even seemingly inadequate acts of reparation.

If we cannot make our amends directly, we can still take meaningful actions. We may, for instance, donate time or money to an appropriate charity or institution. It may be best to make our donations anonymously, in the spirit of our newfound humility. In the case of those people who are deceased, we can still write letters to them, containing everything we would have said to them if they were alive, and then read these letters to our sponsor. We can remember such people in our prayers and allow their memory to motivate us in our new way of life. In all cases where we cannot, for whatever reason, make direct amends, we grieve our losses and then use our experience to make better choices in the future.

Despite our best efforts and intentions in working this step, regaining the trust of those we have harmed is usually not a quick or easy matter. In our addiction, many of us apologized over and over to our loved ones, only to repeatedly harm them again. Our apologies will be seen as sincere only when it becomes evident that we now live differently. Often it takes longer for the people hurt by our behavior to trust us again than it takes for us to make significant progress in our recovery. In some cases, trust may never be restored. We can only make amends to the best of our ability, and leave the rest in God's hands.

In the long run, the most effective amends we can make to others and to ourselves is in our commitment to recovery. Some call this making "living amends." We find we can redress the wrongs of the past by not hurting those we have harmed, or anyone else, in the same way again. As we complete our Ninth Step, we know we have done everything in our power to clean up the wreckage of our past and move forward with our slates clean. By continuing to stay abstinent and work the SAA program, we commit to maintaining this new freedom from the consequences of our acting out. We become accountable for our behavior. Our relationships improve, both with those we have harmed in the past and with new people in our lives. We see that we are becoming better people, and we begin to experience a new sense of self-worth. We feel free to live in the present and enjoy our lives, no longer having to carry a load of despair, resentment, and fear.

Working Step Nine brings us many gifts: true empathy for those we have harmed, compassion, self-respect, and respect for the humanity of others. God willing, we may experience the forgiveness of those we have harmed. If we have been diligent in our amends, we will certainly grow in self-forgiveness too. As a result of accepting responsibility for the harm we have done, even to those who may have hurt us, we glimpse new possibilities for loving and forgiving others. Our faith in our Higher Power increases when we realize that we've squarely faced the wrongs in our past, made amends for them, and received the gift of a better future. The process that began in the Fourth Step, and culminated in the Ninth, now becomes a part of our lives, a daily stance, a practice that will keep us sexually sober and spiritually connected. We will now take Step Ten.

Step Ten

Continued to take personal inventory and when we were wrong promptly admitted it.

In the Tenth Step we embrace the discipline of regular spiritual housecleaning. Just as we took action to repair the damage we caused in the past, so we continue taking inventory of our behavior, and making amends when needed, in our lives today. Working Step Ten helps us deal with our shortcomings on a daily basis. Even with our best efforts we make mistakes. We are human, and we fall short of the mark regularly, even when we are abstinent from our addictive sexual behavior. In taking the Tenth Step, we commit to keeping our house in order, whether old failings reappear or new ones arise, as they inevitably will.

Regular inventory is the cornerstone of the Tenth Step. We set aside time to review our behavior, our dealings with others, our emotions, and our spiritual condition. Quiet time for self-reflection, without distraction, is essential. We may each find different ways to set aside this time, and different methods for taking stock. However we work this step, we act on our commitment to making continued self-examination part of our new way of life.

Honest self-examination can take many forms. We may mentally review the events of our day or write our inventories in a journal. We may check in with our sponsor or others in recovery, or we may pause for a "spot check" inventory in the moment. Many of us work the Tenth Step daily, though we can also work it as needed when we feel upset, angry, or off balance. Some of us set aside a block of time weekly, monthly, or annually for a more thorough inventory. The important thing is that we repeat the process we began in Steps Four through Nine, in order to keep the gains we have made in recovery and to strengthen our connections with ourselves, with others, and with our Higher Power.

Many of us take inventory at the end of each day. As we look back, we note what emotions we have felt throughout that day, checking whether particular emotions, such as anger or fear, took center stage. We take stock of our attitudes, the things we say to others, and whether we're taking care of our own needs. We look at any character defects or old habits that may have revealed themselves. We consider whether we have harmed anyone and need to make amends. We also find it helpful to remember the things for which we are grateful or things we have done well. Gratitude provides a needed perspective on our problems and helps us feel connected with our Higher Power. We ask God's help with the challenges that face us, while thanking God for the blessings of life and recovery.

Some of us choose to put our Tenth Step inventories in writing. We needn't try to solve all of our problems in these written inventories—we just record our current challenges and difficulties, as well as the positive things we notice about ourselves. If we write regularly in a journal, we can use some of our journal time to work this step as well. The act of writing can give us a sense of clarity that we don't always experience in other ways. It can also help us break through the rationalizations that spring from our character defects. Many of us find it useful to later share with our sponsor what we have written.

We can also work the Tenth Step by checking in regularly with our sponsor or other members, or by giving a thorough and rigorous accounting of ourselves at meetings. In addition to honestly admitting our shortcomings and mistakes, many of us use these check-ins to assess how well we are working our program in general. We report honestly any slippery thoughts or behaviors we have been engaging in. We examine the pressures that may tempt us to act out. We review how well we have been using tools of recovery, such as attending meetings, reading recovery literature, making phone calls, or praying. We report how we are taking care of ourselves and what positive risks we are taking to challenge ourselves and grow.

When we feel our serenity disturbed, we can use a spot-check inventory to restore our emotional balance. These quick inventories are often helpful when we find ourselves in conflict with someone or otherwise bothered by uncomfortable emotions. We take a moment to look inside and to gain perspective. We often discover unexamined resentments or other character defects at play. We can pause and ask ourselves what our part is in the situation. We can then admit our part and prepare to do whatever is needed to set things right, whether it is making direct amends, adjusting our attitude, or simply letting go.

It isn't always easy to know when we've been wrong. We may not discover the truth about our behavior until later. When we review our day as part of our Tenth Step, we find ourselves recognizing actions and emotions that we weren't completely aware of at the time. With practice, we learn how to recognize how we are feeling in the moment. We gradually learn to listen to the quiet, gentle voice of our conscience and to notice from within when something feels wrong. As we continue to take personal inventory, we begin to notice our mistakes and hurtful behaviors more quickly.

Sometimes our wrongs may carry significant harm to others, as when we lie, cheat, or act out of anger. We don't need to seriously harm someone, though, in order to be wrong. In fact, our less severe wrongs are often far more pervasive and difficult to recognize. We may forget or be late for appointments, make thoughtless comments, break promises or twist the truth, not follow through on commitments, or test other people's boundaries. Over time, we become better at seeing and admitting the influence of our character defects on all aspects of our behavior.

When we recognize our error, we promptly admit it. First we admit it to ourselves, which means letting go of defensiveness and the desire to be "right" at all costs. Next we may admit it to our sponsor or other support people, especially if we need help in sorting out our amends, and to our Higher Power in prayer. Finally we admit it to those affected by our behavior, and make any amends that are necessary. In some cases, we may need to approach our amends as carefully as we did in Step Nine, and offer reparation if appropriate. Often, however, we don't need to do more than simply acknowledge our wrongdoing to the person affected.

Whatever our wrongs, our promptness in admitting them is essential to the success of this step. The longer we wait to make amends for even minor wrongs, the greater the chance that the situation will worsen. Even more importantly, the longer we wait, the greater the risk to our serenity. Admitting our wrongs as soon as possible helps keep shame and regrets from building up inside us, and allows us to more quickly regain our peace of mind.

Taking regular personal inventory doesn't mean that we beat up on ourselves. Neither self-punishment nor excessive vigilance is the purpose of this step. Instead, we come to accept that making mistakes is a fact of life and an essential part of recovery. Step Ten says "when we were wrong," not "if we were wrong." Our experience shows that we will be wrong on a regular basis. Some of our mistakes stem from the influence of our familiar defects. Other mistakes will result whenever we grow and take new risks in our recovery. In either case our imperfection is certain, and mistakes are inevitable. We adopt the attitude of learning from, rather than denying, our mistakes. Working this step allows us to let go of both perfectionism and grandiosity. We gradually discover the relief and humility of not having to be perfect.

At this point in our recovery, we may have already experienced surprising growth in the quality of our relationships and the quality of our faith. Practicing the Tenth Step helps us continue to grow in self-acceptance, self-awareness, and rigorous honesty. We discover a greater willingness to take risks and learn from our mistakes. We are living in such a way as to keep our accounts balanced and our serenity intact. In gratitude for all we have received from our Higher Power, we move forward to Step Eleven.

Step Eleven

Sought through prayer and meditation to improve our conscious contact with God as we understood God, praying only for knowledge of God's will for us and the power to carry that out.

In taking the Eleventh Step, we dedicate ourselves to an increasing spiritual awareness and a greater connection with our Higher Power. As we progress in recovery, we come to realize that our Higher Power has always been with us, even in the depths of our addiction. It is our conscious contact with this Power that has increased for us as we work through each step. By making contact with God a conscious practice, we have allowed God into our lives, healing us, directing us, and changing us in ways that were never possible before. In Step Eleven we seek to improve this conscious contact, so that our spiritual connection will become not only the means by which we recover from our sex addiction, but our daily source of guidance and strength.

The Higher Power we seek is loving and supportive. This step works best when we have faith in the goodness of our Higher Power's will for us, even if we can't see the outcome yet. We may still go through hard times or periods of confusion. Yet we hold on to the belief that God's will is for our good and that the knowledge and power we need will be given to us in God's time.

The two practices through which we seek to improve our spiritual connection in this step are prayer and meditation. The quality of our contact with God, the depth and richness of our spiritual life, is the goal; prayer and meditation are the means. The forms that our prayer and meditation take will depend, in large part, on our personal beliefs about our Higher Power. We find help and guidance by asking our sponsor and other friends in recovery about their experiences working this step. We are free to discover what works best for us; the important thing is the goal of maintaining and improving our connection to the God of our understanding.

For many of us, prayer simply means talking with God. Rather than struggling with our life's challenges as if we are alone and need to "figure it out" ourselves, we share our thoughts and feelings with our Higher Power. When we pray, in effect we're saying, "Here I am, God, and these are my concerns." By sharing ourselves in this way, we bring ourselves regularly into the open, into the awareness of God's care.

At first, some of us were not very comfortable with praying. Often, we held assumptions about what prayer was, or what it looked like, that held us back. We learned that prayer need not be formal or associated with a religious tradition or text. We can pray in our car or in the shower. We can just say what's on our mind. With practice we become more comfortable. In time, our prayers become regular conversations with our Higher Power.

We have found it very helpful to pray at regular times during the day, as well as other times when we need to feel close to our Higher Power. In the morning we might pray for God's help in facing the challenges of the day. In the evening we may express gratitude for our lives and for the gifts we have received in our recovery. These prayers frame our day, reminding us that nothing is more important than our relationship with our Higher Power. We also pray at unscheduled times when we want or need to. We pray for guidance and courage when we are tempted to act out, or when we're in a difficult situation of some kind. With time, we find ourselves praying spontaneously, as an expression of trust in our Higher Power.

If prayer can be thought of as talking to God, then meditation can be compared to listening. It starts when we take the time to slow down and focus without distraction. We set aside time without work, other people, TV, or other media demanding our attention. For the space of time devoted to meditation, seeking God's will becomes our conscious priority. When we are quiet, we become receptive to wisdom that isn't available otherwise.

Some of us felt resistance when we tried to meditate. Learning to be quiet and pay attention can often be quite difficult for us. In addition, we may be disturbed by unpleasant thoughts and feelings rising to the surface. We can be gentle with ourselves, gradually getting used to the experience of being still and attentive. If we are patient and stay with our meditation, we also find that the disagreeable emotions eventually pass. Any small effort we make to slow down and listen is a step towards connecting with our Higher Power, and will bear fruit in time.

There are many ways to meditate. Once again, we are free to discover whatever works best for us. For example, we may meditate by reading spiritual literature, by practicing one of many techniques to still the mind, or by simply sitting in nature. Whatever method we use, we make ourselves available to our Higher Power, opening ourselves to whatever insight we may receive.

Many of us practice reading meditation, in which we read and contemplate literature that inspires us. This may include spiritual texts of our choice. It may also include daily meditation books that feature a short passage to read for each day of the year. Some of us read meditations written specifically for people working twelve-step recovery. We may then take time to think about what we have read and how it applies to our lives today.

Some of us have found that being out in nature is also a form of meditation. We recognize the natural world as part of a Power greater than ourselves. We find serenity looking at the stars or listening to the ocean. Connecting with God through nature gives us perspective and a special sense of God's presence.

Some of us practice one of the many forms of meditation intended to calm the mind. These practices can be done in a sitting position or while walking. Often the key to this kind of meditation is concentrating on something simple, such as one's breathing. Or we may just sit quietly, turning our attention to our Higher Power, allowing ourselves to be open to God's grace and wisdom. There are meditation practices associated with particular traditions, and there are practices that are wholly personal and unique. No matter which method we choose, we seek to clear our minds so as to become aware of God's presence and available to God's influence.

By the time we get to Step Eleven, we already enjoy some level of conscious contact with our Higher Power. We have also grown used to asking God for help and for such spiritual gifts as wisdom, serenity, and courage. We have no need to give up these kinds of prayers when we come to this step. Yet in taking Step Eleven, we go further. We surrender our desire for particular results and ask only for knowledge of God's will for us and the power to carry that out. We go beyond asking for things from God, into a practice of seeking to join our will with God's will for us.

Working this step means being aware of the higher purpose of our spirituality, rather than focusing on personal desire. We learn to accept that reality is not tailored to the limitations of self, and that hardship and loss are as valid a part of life as joy and pleasure. This doesn't mean that we will stop asking God for spiritual gifts or for help in life's challenges. But working Step Eleven lends greater meaning to these other kinds of asking. We come to recognize God's will as our highest good, and in so doing, our asking becomes founded in gratitude rather than self-seeking, faith rather than fear.

When we sense what God would have us do, we also ask for the power to carry that out. We need faith and strength to carry out God's will, for we cannot always foresee the results of the actions we are being led to take, or take into account all possible effects. Our belief that our Higher Power knows what is best for us, and that more will be revealed, grows as we work this step. We also gradually accept that God's will for us extends over all aspects of our lives, not just over our recovery from sex addiction. We find our serenity growing as we align our will with God's in each new area that is revealed to us.

We have been given a new chance at life, awakening to a spiritual dimension we never knew was available to us. We become open to sharing with others what we have gained and to helping others on the path of recovery. In gratitude, we seek opportunities for service to God and our fellow sex addicts. Our path leads to Step Twelve.

Step Twelve

Having had a spiritual awakening as the result of these steps, we tried to carry this message to other sex addicts and to practice these principles in our lives.

Working this program leads to a spiritual awakening. Our relationship to the God of our understanding becomes an essential part of our lives. Through the process of the Twelve Steps, we let go of ways of thinking and acting that are based on fear, shame, and isolation, and we learn to rely on the guidance and care of a Higher Power. When we first came to the fellowship of Sex Addicts Anonymous, we may have sought only to stop acting out. But every step of the program contributes to a fundamental change in our outlook, from self-obsession and control to surrender and acceptance. Our sexual sobriety goes hand in hand with our spiritual growth.

For some of us, this awakening may be a sudden and dramatic gain in awareness. For others, it may be slow and gradual, and we may not even realize we've had one until we reflect upon the changes that have occurred. Although our experiences are different, certain aspects are common to many of us. We notice in ourselves a deepening humility that allows us to ask for and receive help when we need it. We find ourselves being less judgmental, more ready to let go of resentments and admit when we are wrong. We make the effort to repair relationships that we have damaged. We choose to keep the company of people who respect us, care for us, and treat us well. We start to see life in terms of growth, change, and transformation. We have a greater sense of belonging, intimacy, and true friendship. We endeavor to live according to our true purpose, which is God's will for us.

In Step Twelve we put our awakening into practice by serving others. With spiritual awareness comes the responsibility, the desire, and the need to help other suffering sex addicts, just as help was freely given to us. This impulse springs from selfless love and gratitude, but it is also essential to our own sexual sobriety and spiritual growth. Carrying the message to our fellow addict is as important in maintaining our own recovery as it is in helping others find theirs.

Our message is simple and profound: that recovery from sex addiction is possible through working the Twelve Steps of SAA, and that following this program results in a spiritual awakening. Each of us carries this message by means of the wisdom gained through working the program ourselves, rather than through ideas or theories borrowed from someone else's experience. We are not experts, only sex addicts sharing honestly with one another. Our authority comes from our experience. We share what we know: how we got here, and how the SAA program has worked for us.

When we carry the message directly to other sex addicts, we connect with them in a way that non-addicts cannot. We speak from experience. We have found that telling our stories is one of the most effective ways of carrying the message. We tell about our sex addiction:

the pain, sorrow, suffering, and despair it brought; how we tried to stop or control it and how our efforts failed; the way our lives became unmanageable; the loss and suffering our addiction brought upon ourselves and others; and how we finally found recovery. By telling our stories, we demonstrate that we truly understand where others have been. And by sharing our recovery, we offer hope and show that there is a way out of our common addiction.

There are many other ways to carry the message. Any service we do that helps bring our message to other sex addicts is in the spirit of Step Twelve. We can start by regularly attending meetings. When we show up, we help create a place where others can pass on the message of recovery, even if we don't say anything ourselves. This is more significant than we may think, for many meetings have died out through lack of attendance. If we are new to the program, we can contribute by helping set up the meeting and cleaning up afterward. There are always ways we can help, regardless of how much experience in recovery we have.

We carry the message to our fellow sex addicts with every act of encouragement, support, and service. We can help start a meeting and reach out to others in an area where there are no SAA groups. We can carry the message one-on-one, talking with another addict after a meeting. Or we may serve as part of larger groups or committees, contributing our time and talents to provide various services to the fellowship, to publicize our meetings, or to organize fellowship activities.

One of the most direct and profound ways we can serve other members is by sponsoring them. We walk through the Twelve Steps with those we sponsor, passing on what we have learned from those who sponsored us. Ultimately, we carry the message through example. When we practice new ways of acting and thinking, we show that the program works, and we offer hope to others who are seeking a new life. We continue to ask our Higher Power's help in carrying the message of recovery, so that we may be a channel for God's love and wisdom.

However we do service, we receive much more than we give. First and foremost, our experience has shown that working with others safeguards our own abstinence. We keep the priceless gift of our sexual sobriety by being of service to other sex addicts. We receive many other gifts as well. We break out of the isolation and self-centeredness of our addiction. We grow as we practice generosity, empathy, and humility. We forge new bonds with others that nourish and sustain us. And we experience the joy and satisfaction of giving something of ourselves to a larger cause.

The Steps are an expression of spiritual principles that can be practiced in all aspects of life. Honesty, willingness, courage, humility, forgiveness, responsibility, gratitude, and faith are just some of the names we give to the spiritual principles that gradually come to guide us in our lives. As we progress through the program, establishing conscious contact with the God of our understanding, we become aware of these principles within us—like gifts that were always there, unopened until we were ready to receive them. Opening these gifts brings about our spiritual awakening. Continuing to apply them on a daily basis keeps us spiritually fit and growing in recovery. With the Twelfth Step we seek to consciously practice these principles in our lives, not only as ways to keep us sexually sober, although that will always remain important, but as lights to guide us in everything we do.

Practicing these principles in our lives means applying program principles at home, at work, and wherever else we gather with others for a common purpose. As we grow spiritually, we find opportunities for service in virtually any situation. Our closest relationships may offer the most challenges to our honesty, compassion, and integrity, but we are often rewarded beyond our expectations. We find that spiritual principles can guide us in the everyday challenges of life, and they can help us face even loss, grief, and death with fortitude and grace. What we gain in this program is a blueprint for full and successful living, whatever may come.

We maintain our recovery by working a daily program, in the knowledge that although we can never be perfect, we can be happy today. We can live life on life's terms, without having to change or suppress our feelings. Our serenity and sobriety grow as we continue to live according to spiritual principles. We enjoy the gifts that come from being honest and living a life of integrity. We ask for help when we need it, and we express our love and gratitude every day. We realize that everything we have been through helps us to be of service to others. We learn that the world is a much safer place than we had ever known before, because we are always in the care of a loving God.

CHAPTER FOUR

OUR LIFE IN RECOVERY

Tools of Recovery

Sex Addicts Anonymous offers a spiritual solution to the disease of sexual addiction. Every aspect of our program is founded on the experience of a Power greater than ourselves helping us live healthy and productive lives, free of addictive sexual behavior. With time, and continued abstinence from our inner-circle behaviors, we have found that the desire to act out becomes less intense and less frequent. The sense of compulsion is lifted from us—we now have a choice. We also experience relief from the obsession with sex, and we are grateful to be free of a craving that we thought would never leave us.

Sexual sobriety is a gift that makes possible many other spiritual gifts. But it is not a cure. We need to remain humble, continuing to practice our program on a daily basis, in order to stay sexually sober and grow spiritually. We cannot afford to be complacent or to live unconsciously. Maintaining the freedom we have found requires daily conscious contact with the God of our understanding, expressed by practicing the spiritual principles we have learned in recovery. We came to the fellowship of SAA out of a desire to stop acting out. Through the steps, we have been given the abstinence we sought, but in the process we have been given much more: an entirely new way of life based on spiritual principles. Our journey of recovery lasts a lifetime.

In taking this journey, we commit fully to the process of recovery. We make the program our top priority, in the knowledge that anything less puts us at risk. We learn to listen with an open mind at meetings. Gradually, we stop picking and choosing what we are willing to change, and begin to open ourselves to the changes our Higher Power wills for us. We learn to go to any lengths for our recovery—because we are worth it.

Rigorous honesty is one of the essential principles on which our program is based. Without honesty, we do not stay sober. We share honestly with our sponsor, and at meetings. We learn to be honest about who we are, what we have done, what brought us here, and what we are doing now. Honesty helps us gain self-respect, eventually becoming our normal stance in the world at large and in all our relationships. We don't lie or cheat, even when we can get away with it. We learn not to use half-truths to manipulate others. We accept responsibility for our actions and our lives. We live in the faith that God's care is enough for us and that we don't need to be dishonest to survive.

In addition to the Twelve Steps, there are many suggested tools that we have found to be beneficial in our recovery from sex addiction. A tool is an action that supports recovery and that has been used successfully by other sex addicts. We practice honesty, openness, and willingness when we adopt a new tool, and we trust in the experience, strength, and hope of the fellowship that we will benefit as others have before us. We offer here some common tools that we have found to be helpful, but there are many others.

Our experience has shown that we move forward in our recovery when we take action. Understanding our addiction benefits us in many ways, but ultimately, we can't think our way out of the problem. Our best thinking got us into trouble in the first place. Instead, we move into action. We go to a meeting. We call someone in the fellowship when we feel like acting out, or when we feel shaky. We avoid places and situations that are associated with our addictive behavior. We get a sponsor. We carry the SAA message, contribute to the fellowship, and help others recover, while helping ourselves in the process.

As we work the program, we become more aware of how the addictive process operates. One of the most important skills we gain is connecting our behavior with its eventual consequences. When we feel like acting out, we tend to slip into fantasy and focus on our addictive desires, losing touch with our knowledge of the consequences that inevitably follow. In recovery, we practice reminding ourselves about the possible results of our acting-out behavior. We consider how we will feel afterward, what it will cost, what we are putting at risk, and what harm we may be bringing to others. Often we may need the help of other members to do this successfully, so we have learned to call our sponsor, or someone else in the fellowship, when we are feeling the desire to act out. Another sex addict can bring us back to earth, supporting us in our recovery and reminding us of the consequences of relapse.

Most of us use the telephone on a regular basis, just to let someone else in the program know how we are doing or to reach out when we are struggling with our addiction. Some of us have made a commitment to call a friend in recovery whenever we're in a slippery situation or when obsessive thinking and desires begin to arise. Sometimes all we need is for someone to ask us what is going on and to listen to the answer. Before long, we know what is bothering us, and once we know, the urge to act out usually passes.

Reading recovery literature is another important tool of the program. It helps to educate, motivate, and inspire us. Reading SAA literature helps us learn how to stay sober and work a recovery program specifically tailored for us. This unique identification with our disease and our fellowship is invaluable in fostering a sense of belonging and a commitment to recovery from sex addiction. Some of us also consult outside literature on sex addiction or read literature published by other twelve-step fellowships. Such literature may help us understand our disease in depth and give us additional insight on how to work a program of recovery.

Many of us use the tool of setting boundaries. Boundaries are the limits we put on our behaviors. When we decide that we need to stay clear of a behavior that is a problem for us, we can set a boundary around that behavior. For example, we may set a boundary around driving through neighborhoods where we used to act out. If we have a problem with inappropriate sexual talk or intrigue, we may set a boundary around making sexual jokes or flirting with people. If we are sexually attracted to children or have molested children, we may set a boundary around being alone with children or driving past schools or playgrounds. We set boundaries in order to keep ourselves safe and away from situations that can lead us into our acting-out behaviors.

Boundaries may also be limits we set and maintain with others in our lives. We learn how to let other people know how we wish to be treated and what kinds of behavior we will and will not accept. Unless we accept personal responsibility for establishing and sticking to healthy boundaries in our relationships, we run the risk of harboring resentments or casting ourselves in the role of the victim. The danger in playing the victim is that we might develop a sense of entitlement to act out. Our sponsor can help us set appropriate boundaries and keep us accountable.

Some of us use journaling as a tool to help us discover and express how we feel, relieve our obsession, record our progress, and give us a creative outlet. Sometimes we write about a particular topic or a problem that we are trying to deal with. It can help us sort out what we think and feel. When we are confused, we can write in order to gain clarity. Writing can also help us to stop obsessing about things. Just the act of writing can help calm the mind. As a daily routine, writing helps us stay in touch with our feelings, issues that may be bothering us, and challenges we are facing in our lives.

Over time our journals become records of our progress. We can look back at old entries and see what we used to struggle with. We can see how the things we used to fear often didn't come to pass. We can discover the progress we've made in our recovery, noticing changes in our behavior and outlook that we might otherwise have overlooked, since they are often subtle and happen over a long period of time.

Developing our creativity helps us play and heal. We express ourselves in different ways. We might play a musical instrument, write poems, paint, dance, or draw. Or perhaps we cook, garden, or decorate. Some of us had given up on being creative when we concluded that we weren't good enough or that we didn't have time. In recovery, we rediscover our creative side. Many of us choose to put our artistic and creative activities in our outer circle.

Many of us need to recover physically as well as spiritually and emotionally. One of the amends that we owe to ourselves is to take better care of our bodies. This may include eating better, seeing the doctor or the dentist, or getting some exercise. Exercise is also a way to reduce anxiety, establish a new relationship with our bodies, and enjoy pleasure from our bodies that is not sexual.

There are many other tools and suggestions that have been passed along from one addict to another through the years. Some of these informal traditions are expressed through various recovery sayings and slogans. Examples include: *HALT* (get help when you are Hungry, Angry, Lonely, or Tired), *Let Go and Let God* (the principle of surrender), and *Progress, not Perfection*. It can be very helpful for us to recall these sayings when we find ourselves in difficult situations.

A slogan that expresses one of the fundamental truths of the program is *One Day at a Time*. Rather than thinking in terms of forever or always, we simply focus on staying sexually sober today, letting go of worry about tomorrow or the rest of our lives. Keeping our attention in today helps us to show up and be present for our own lives, while resting in the faith that God's care is sufficient for the future.

Through our experience of God's care and the love and care we find in the SAA fellowship, we learn the importance of being gentle with ourselves. We know all too well the brutality of our addiction. Gentleness is a different way. We are gentle by taking good care of ourselves, making sure we get what we need, and not pushing ourselves too hard. We forgive ourselves for our past and present mistakes. We acknowledge the positive changes in our lives. We learn to love and affirm rather than punish ourselves. We allow ourselves to experience the full range of human feelings.

We may have setbacks and difficult times. We may suffer the painful consequences of past behavior, or experience the pain of new growth. It is important that we not give up. Using the tools, and practicing the spiritual principles we have learned, we can move through the pain without acting out, and find serenity. The miracle of recovery from sex addiction becomes a reality we experience every day.

Withdrawal and Relapse

Long-term abstinence is possible through the SAA program. Through the grace of God, we can find freedom from addictive sexual behavior. We don't just act out less frequently or stop the worst behaviors while continuing others. We are abstinent from all of our inner-circle behaviors, one day at a time, over months, years, and decades. Many of us live this miracle every day, and it is possible for us all.

Many of us experience a period of intense emotional upheaval and physical discomfort when we stop our addictive sexual behaviors. We call this *withdrawal*. We may be assailed with powerful memories, feelings, and physical sensations. Other withdrawal symptoms can include intense mood swings, physical pain, anger, anxiety, depression, exhaustion, insomnia, nightmares, or acting-out dreams.

In withdrawal we often feel a powerful urge to resume acting out in order to stop the discomfort. We may find ourselves repeatedly confronted with temptations to sabotage our recovery, or mysteriously drawn to new sexual behaviors that we never thought would interest us. Yet we know that if we act out again we will only postpone or prolong the inevitable withdrawal.

No one can go through withdrawal for us, or take away all the pain. But we have the support of our sponsor and others in the program to help us get through this. During withdrawal, we are advised to keep in regular contact with others through phone calls, meetings, and fellowship. We also need to be gentle with ourselves, honoring our needs for self-care, comfort, safety, nourishment, rest, exercise, and affirmation.

If we experience withdrawal, we can be confident that it will not last forever. Many of us with long-term abstinence have gone through some form of withdrawal and have come out on the other side, often far healthier and happier than before going through it. We may continue to experience some form of withdrawal with each new level of surrender in our recovery. We have faith that our Higher Power is guiding us through this process and that we are cared for along the way.

As sex addicts, many of us face great challenges in maintaining abstinence from our addictive behaviors. Those of us who have experienced recovery in other twelve-step programs that deal with addiction to substances often feel that it is harder to stay abstinent from addictive sexual behavior than from alcohol or other drugs. Our sexual obsessions are inside of us and seemingly available on demand, not just when we ingest a mood-altering chemical. In addition, we may experience a wide variety of addictive sexual behaviors, which may switch and change over time. Our disease is powerful, baffling, many-sided, and deeply ingrained. It is no surprise that many of us have experienced relapse.

Relapse means engaging in something that we have defined in our personal program as addictive sexual behavior, or "acting out." In terms of the Three Circles, relapse means engaging in sexual behavior that we've put in our inner circle. It is vital, therefore, that we use the Three Circles, or some other tool that exactly defines our abstinence, so that there is no ambiguity about when we have relapsed and when we have not. Clear definitions allow us to recognize our progress. Lack of clear definitions leaves room for denial and rationalization, and prevents progress.

There are no failures in this program. We do not judge members who relapse, because we know that we are all powerless over this disease. If we relapse, it is important that we get right back into recovery immediately. We need not turn a mistake into a self-destructive binge. Often we feel ashamed when we relapse. Our addiction becomes charged, and the thought arises that we might as well try to get the urge out of our system. But we have learned that this is only the shame and the addiction talking. Our addictive desires cannot be satisfied. Instead, we can go to an SAA meeting, and we will be welcomed there. Whatever situation we face, no matter how badly or how recently we acted out, no matter how defeated we may feel, we can stay abstinent today. All we need to do is make it a priority to use the tools of the program and seek help from our Higher Power and our friends in recovery.

A relapse is an opportunity to take inventory of how well we are working our program. Here are some questions to consider: Do we find ourselves returning to slippery situations or places? Are we attending meetings regularly, or are we finding excuses to do something else instead? Are we listening at meetings? Do we judge what others are saying rather than trying to relate to it? Are we being honest when we share? Do we have a sponsor, and have we been keeping in touch with our sponsor? Have we been fully honest with our sponsor? Are we using all of the tools of the program? Are we making phone calls? Are we praying and meditating? Are we working the Twelve Steps? Are we stuck on a particular step? Are we avoiding a step? We need to work all of the steps if we want to continue our progress.

When evaluating our program, we are ultimately asking if recovery is our highest priority. We all have responsibilities and obligations. But if we allow ourselves to fall into our addiction again and not return to recovery, we jeopardize everything we have.

We also need to examine the circumstances surrounding a relapse. These give us clues about how we can be better prepared in the future. What was going on in our life before the relapse? Perhaps we are vulnerable during holidays. Or we may need to get extra support when we are around our family of origin. How were our relationships at the time? We may have acted out when we were having difficulty in our relationships. Some of us discovered that we've actually started fights as part of our acting-out pattern. How was our self-care? Were we isolating? Did we allow ourselves to get too hungry, angry, lonely, or tired? Illness can weaken our boundaries and make us more vulnerable to our addiction. By recognizing the circumstances surrounding a relapse, we can get more support when we are in similar circumstances in the future.

Gradually we learn to identify our "triggers." Triggers are any situation or behavior that causes us to feel a powerful desire to act out. One of the most difficult challenges for many of us is learning how to turn back from acting out once we have been triggered. It is one thing to get back on track after a relapse, and another to pull away from our addiction once the familiar pattern has been set in motion. We learn that we don't need to wait until after a relapse to recommit to our recovery. If we feel on the verge of engaging in an inner-circle behavior, we can use program resources to break the pattern before we act out. We remind ourselves that acting out is not a healthy option and that we are powerless to stop the addiction on our own. We may say a prayer to call upon our Higher Power for help, or we may reach out to another addict. Calling someone on the phone, even if no one is there to answer the call, is a powerful act of surrender. Sometimes that is enough to break the spell. Many of us have found that automatic interventions are better than trying to evaluate whether we are at risk for relapse. We can make a phone call whenever we are exposed to a trigger, regardless of whether we feel like acting out. This gets us in the habit of turning away from a relapse even before the addictive craving kicks in. We also find it helpful to identify our part in the slippery situation and take responsibility for using the program's tools to address it.

Some of us have found ourselves relapsing on a regular or periodic basis. In these cases, we need to make some fundamental improvements in our program. If we haven't found a sponsor and worked the Twelve Steps, it is time that we do so. If we are continuing to act out as a pattern, it is possible that we aren't fully willing to admit powerlessness over our addiction. Sometimes we put ourselves in difficult situations over and over without sufficient support to stay abstinent. In this case we need to ask ourselves if we have accepted powerlessness over our addiction in every aspect of our lives. It might also be necessary to make adjustments in our Three Circles. We may need to add new items to our inner or middle circle, or move certain behaviors from one circle to another. If we find that we are relapsing around a certain situation, we need to change the situation or find new ways to respond to it. Regular contact with our sponsor and other friends in recovery helps us gain the insights and discover the resources we need, so that we can be open to changes in our ways of thinking and acting.

When we have been abstinent for a length of time, complacency can become a stumbling block for us. We can't take recovery for granted. Many of us have found that our disease continues to progress, even as we work our program. If we relapse, we often don't just return to our old behavior, we go on to new, more destructive behaviors. And our disease may tend to escalate faster than it used to. To avoid complacency in our program, we need to cultivate and maintain a sense of gratitude and a commitment to sexual sobriety.

We didn't choose to be sex addicts. But we are each responsible for our own recovery. As a fellowship we believe that long-term abstinence is possible for all of us. If we "keep coming back," and work the program to the best of our ability, our Higher Power will help us stay sexually sober today.

Healthier Sexuality

Sexuality is a fundamental part of being human. It can bring great pleasure and deep satisfaction to our lives. And yet, non-addictive sexuality has seemed elusive for us. One of the tragedies of our addiction is that we may never have learned to enjoy our sexuality in a healthy way.

In our addiction we experienced sex as compulsive. We felt driven, as if by an irresistible force, to engage in sexual behaviors, rather than freely choosing to be sexual. For many of us, it often seemed that we weren't being sexual to satisfy our sexual needs, but were using sex as a way to escape from reality, cope with anxiety, or deal with emotions we didn't want to face. In our disease we used control and isolation in order to feel safe. We would spend increasing amounts of time in fantasy, which tended to alienate us from others and from a real sense of ourselves. For some of us, our addictive sexuality was centered on power and ego. Our fantasies were about having the power to be sexual whenever, however, and with whomever we wanted. Or we constantly looked to relationships to "fix" us, fill our emptiness, and make us feel worthwhile. Some of us were abusive to others and treated them as objects. We were unaware of, or failed to respect, others' sexual rights and boundaries. No matter how much sex we had, we still felt unsatisfied. We were afraid of vulnerability and intimacy.

These symptoms of our disease, and many others like them, made deep impressions on us, becoming habitual patterns of thought and action. When we gain abstinence from addictive sexual behavior through the program of Sex Addicts Anonymous, we find ourselves still challenged by these patterns, which become more evident to us once we've stopped acting out. For most of us, these symptoms only begin to fade away gradually, through working the Twelve Steps. And as our old way of life and thinking unravels, we are encouraged to explore what healthier sexuality might mean for us. This, too, is a slow and gradual process for most of us. The distortions in our sexuality caused by this disease can be quite persistent, sometimes making it difficult to discover new behaviors that feel healthy.

Some of us have found it useful to choose a period of refraining from all sexual activity as part of our recovery. We decide on a length of time in which we will not be sexual with anyone, including ourselves. This allows for a withdrawal period, when we can begin to discover who we are without the familiar distraction of sex. We need the guidance of our sponsor to decide if and when this is the right choice for us. Our sponsor can help us judge if our motives are healthy and if we have enough support to be successful. For most of us, this is a temporary tool we use for our recovery, but some of us choose celibacy as a fulfilling way of life in its own right.

The Twelve Steps of SAA lead to a spiritual awakening. If we remain abstinent and practice the principles of the program in our lives, we may find our attitudes towards our sexuality and our ways of experiencing sex changing as well. For some, this happens quickly; for others, slowly or not at all. In SAA, we do not measure the success of our program by the frequency of our positive and healthy sexual experiences. While exploring healthy sexuality is a part of life in recovery for many of us, it is not the primary purpose or goal of SAA. Our program offers freedom from addictive sexual behavior. Where we focus our energy in our new way of life is a choice that is left up to each member.

As SAA members, we face diverse challenges in recovery, and our needs, situations, and experiences are diverse as well. Just as we do not define in advance what behaviors constitute addictive sexual behavior for individual members, SAA does not endorse any specific definition of healthy sexuality. There is no formula, no single answer to our questions. We can explore this realm whether we are single, dating, or in partnerships. It takes patience and honesty to gain insight into what our needs and desires really are. Our sponsors and other members can support us and share what has worked for them and what has not. For more specific or complex guidance and advice, we may choose to consult a qualified outside professional.

Many of us had extremely intense sexual experiences in our addiction. We know that we can't continue to act out, but we may fear that healthy sexuality will be boring by comparison. The truth is that most of us didn't really experience sex when we were acting out. In our most intense experiences, we tended to be disconnected, lost in a bubble of repetition, fantasy, and obsession. Our disease kept us from being fully present when we were sexual. In recovery, we learn not to let exaggerated notions of sexual excitement prevent us from learning and practicing healthier sexual behaviors.

Many of us recognize healthier sexuality when we experience something very different from what we knew in our addiction. We notice this by the difference in our feelings. We don't feel compulsive, driven, or off in another world. Instead, we are emotionally present during sexual activity. This may seem uncomfortable or frightening, especially at first. By practicing honesty, open-mindedness, and willingness, we are able to discover healthier experiences of sexuality. There are numerous ideas and suggestions about healthier sexuality that have been offered by SAA members, based on our experience. Many of us describe our sexual behavior as healthy when we are present, intimate, flexible, nurturing, and appropriate during sex. We are free to consider these suggestions and decide what feels true for us.

We may discover that healthier sexuality begins long before any actual sexual acts, with a change in our emotional presence and connection with others. When we allow ourselves to be intimate with our own emotions, we become aware of how we are really feeling, without judging or censoring ourselves for it. We gradually learn to be honest about our feelings with others, while being open to their feelings as well. In the process, we learn to express our affection rather than seek power and control. To be intimate is to let go of control and begin to have trust—trust in another person, trust in ourselves, and faith in a Higher Power.

When we are safe and emotionally present, we can be flexible. We learn that sex doesn't have to be the same way every time, and that it doesn't need to have a goal. If we are aware of how we're feeling, we can decide what we want and need. We learn to have sexual boundaries—limits around the kind of behavior we may or may not want to engage in. We also learn to respect the boundaries of others. We find that we experience being sexual as a way to satisfy appropriate sexual needs and desires, rather than as a way to manage anxiety, self-medicate, or escape.

Some of us have experienced the avoidance of sex as addictive, in some cases choosing to identify as "sexual anorexics." In the same way that compulsive starving of oneself, or anorexia, is considered an eating disorder, avoidance of sex can be seen as an addictive sexual behavior. Some of us have found ourselves "shut down" sexually in recovery, afraid of sex because of its association in our minds with our addiction or with past sexual trauma, or because of a fear of intimacy and vulnerability. Trying to control our sexuality in this way is just another symptom of our disease. The solution lies in turning our will and lives over to the care of our Higher Power, knowing that however unfamiliar we are with the challenges of healthier sexuality, we can put our trust in the God of our understanding.

These are all hints, suggestions, and descriptions from the varied experiences of SAA members. They are not rules, and they don't all fit for everyone. Part of recovery is acknowledging that we have more questions than answers and allowing room for mistakes. The freedom we gain through sexual sobriety helps us to accept differences and to be open to new possibilities.

The promise of recovery is a restoration of self. Sexuality is part of who we are, a part that became lost and distorted through our addiction. When we reclaim the possibility of healthier sexuality, we regain a vital aspect of our being. In our addiction, sex was something we did outside of our "normal" lives. In recovery we try to find ways to make our sexuality an appropriate part of life. We also acknowledge what we have lost, grieve the harm we suffered, and eventually come to acceptance about our past, which opens the way for being present today, sexually and spiritually. And as we grow in recovery, many of us choose to integrate our sexuality with our spirituality. When we are sexual with love, gratitude, and generosity, sex can be an expression of our highest spiritual ideals. We can use our sexuality to express our love, appreciation, and faith.

Outside Help

SAA offers a program of recovery from sex addiction. Although our experience has shown that the Twelve Steps lead to a spiritual awakening, and provide invaluable guidance for a new way of life, we do not claim that our program provides answers to every problem or situation that we might face. Many of us have felt the need to seek help from outside the fellowship, in addition to the support we receive in our SAA groups. We are encouraged by our friends in recovery to take whatever action necessary to further our well-being and personal growth.

For some of us, sex is not our only addiction. We may have come to SAA from another recovery program. Or we may discover, in the course of working our program in SAA, that our lives are unmanageable in other areas as well. We might find that we need more support for our other issues and behaviors than SAA alone can provide. Although we are not affiliated with and do not endorse any other twelve-step fellowship, we acknowledge our common roots in the Steps and Traditions of Alcoholics Anonymous as they are practiced in AA and other twelve-step programs. Open meetings of other twelve-step fellowships, and the literature they offer, are always available as resources.

Some of us have also found support for our recovery through our involvement with some form of religious organization. We may seek more structure in our spiritual practices, or to establish a sense of community with others who share our religious or spiritual beliefs. Some of us find that participating in a religious community or attending religious services can strengthen our own spirituality and help our program. At the same time, some of us choose to practice our spirituality without being involved in any religious tradition. Once again, we are encouraged to do whatever feels right for us. All of us are free to go wherever our faith may lead us.

Many of us have sought therapy in order to help ourselves heal from deep-seated emotional and psychological wounds, including sexual abuse and trauma. We may have suffered grave losses associated with our addictive behaviors or past abuse, and our grief over these losses may seem overwhelming. Or we may find that we need professional support in coping with the effects of sexual trauma. We are free to seek whatever professional help we need in order to aid our grieving and healing process.

We may also seek therapy as part of a commitment to self-improvement or awareness. For example, some of us have turned to couples therapy for help with issues that come up in our relationships. We may simply consider therapy part of an ongoing program of psychological self-care.

In addition, some of us have sought professional medical treatment for depression, anxiety, or other mental health issues. We may take prescription medications under the care of a doctor. Many of us have found medication to be helpful, particularly with conditions that aggravate our addiction, such as clinical depression.

Those of us who are sex offenders may find ourselves court-ordered into group therapy or outpatient treatment. SAA does not have an opinion on these programs. For some of us, both the SAA program and treatment may be necessary for full recovery. However, the process of recovery through working the Twelve Steps is a completely different process from therapy, although the two may complement each other.

For us, it was important to recognize that none of the resources mentioned above are substitutes for working the SAA program. SAA neither endorses nor opposes any other fellowship or religious organization, or the use of any particular medication or form of therapy. As SAA members, we view all of these as outside help that is available if we need it.

As we grow in recovery, we discover what we need in order to take care of ourselves, and give ourselves permission to meet those needs. Outside resources are available as part of our self-care. We also grow in our willingness and ability to reach out beyond the SAA program, enjoy a greater connection with people, and engage with life. We gain not only freedom from our disease, but the freedom to be at home in the world.

CHAPTER FIVE

OUR PURPOSE

Service

We depend on each other to stay sexually sober, and SAA depends on our service to keep functioning. Service in SAA ranges from one-on-one outreach over a cup of coffee to the worldwide outreach performed by the International Service Organization (ISO). Helping keep SAA running is an extension of carrying our message of recovery. Our voluntary efforts are essential to the success of the fellowship and the recovery of every sex addict who is a part of it.

Personal service, one addict helping another, is the most essential way we carry our recovery message. We perform this type of service whenever we greet newcomers or listen to someone in the fellowship who needs to talk. We may sponsor others in the program, visit or write to addicts in jail or prison, or be available to take phone calls from members who are reaching out. In all cases, we share our experience and offer support. The paradox is that service helps us to stay sexually sober ourselves, regardless of the benefit that others may receive from us. We have learned that the best insurance against relapse is helping another sex addict.

In addition to personal service, we provide general services that help to keep our groups functioning. These services include finding places to meet, providing public information and outreach, and producing and distributing literature. We need trusted servants and committee members at every level: from the officers of our local groups, to the delegates we send to the International Convention, to the representatives and staff serving us at ISO. All of these efforts require the voluntary financial contributions of SAA members and groups.

Our local meeting is the foundation of our personal recovery. Without a healthy and well-run meeting, the recovery of every member is threatened. Each group needs trusted servants to perform the tasks necessary to keep the meeting available to all. Some of the tasks trusted servants perform include: chairing the meeting, ordering literature, answering letters to the P.O. Box or calls to the phone line, collecting donations, and paying rent. A group may hold business meetings on a regular basis or as needed, in order to elect trusted servants and make the decisions necessary for running the meeting smoothly.

Our local meeting is also the foundation of the SAA service structure. Through our local meetings, we have a voice in SAA as a whole. Our groups send delegates to the annual International Convention. The delegates bring the decisions and concerns of their local groups to bear on matters affecting SAA as a whole. In this way we each contribute to the decision-making process of the entire fellowship. We rely on our Higher Power for guidance in all our deliberations.

In some areas, local meetings band together and form intergroups to provide services that a single meeting could not provide on its own. Intergroups may publish meeting directories and newsletters, organize area events, serve as a clearinghouse for literature orders, sponsor a phone line or a website, provide outreach to the community, or perform any number of other services as determined by the needs of the member groups.

At the international level, the ISO provides services that member groups and intergroups cannot provide on their own. ISO helps to ensure that our SAA message remains uniform and available to new groups worldwide as they arise. In addition, ISO answers letters, phone calls and emails asking for information, maintains the world meeting directory, operates a website, publishes and provides translations of SAA literature, organizes international events and conferences, and provides many other services determined by the needs and funded by the contributions of the member groups.

At every level of our service structure we are guided by the Twelve Traditions of SAA, as adapted from the Twelve Traditions of Alcoholics Anonymous. Just as the Steps teach us the spiritual principles necessary for healthy individual recovery, the Traditions embody the spiritual principles necessary for the healthy functioning of our groups. Adhering to these principles safeguards our fellowship, thus protecting the recovery of each individual member. We have found that they also help us to act with integrity in our personal relationships and as responsible members of society.

OUR PURPOSE

The Twelve Traditions of Sex Addicts Anonymous

1. *Our common welfare should come first; personal recovery depends upon SAA unity.*

2. *For our group purpose there is but one ultimate authority—a loving God as expressed in our group conscience. Our leaders are but trusted servants; they do not govern.*

3. *The only requirement for SAA membership is a desire to stop addictive sexual behavior.*

4. *Each group should be autonomous except in matters affecting other groups or SAA as a whole.*

5. *Each group has but one primary purpose—to carry its message to the sex addict who still suffers.*

6. *An SAA group ought never endorse, finance, or lend the SAA name to any related facility or outside enterprise, lest problems of money, property, and prestige divert us from our primary purpose.*

7. *Every SAA group ought to be fully self-supporting, declining outside contributions.*

8. *Sex Addicts Anonymous should remain forever nonprofessional, but our service centers may employ special workers.*

9. *SAA, as such, ought never be organized, but we may create service boards or committees directly responsible to those they serve.*

10. *Sex Addicts Anonymous has no opinion on outside issues; hence the SAA name ought never be drawn into public controversy.*

11. *Our public relations policy is based on attraction rather than promotion; we need always maintain personal anonymity at the level of press, radio, TV, and films.*

12. *Anonymity is the spiritual foundation of all our traditions, ever reminding us to place principles before personalities.*

Tradition One

*Our common welfare should come first;
personal recovery depends upon SAA unity.*

As recovering sex addicts, we all need the love and support of our fellow SAA members. We need to hear each other's experience, strength, and hope. We need sponsors and other recovering addicts to guide us through the steps of the program. If we're having a hard time and want to act out, we need to be able to pick up the telephone and call someone in the fellowship who understands. We can't recover alone. Instead, we find the freedom we seek as interrelated parts of a greater whole. In the same way, our groups are strengthened when we forge supportive connections with other SAA groups and with the fellowship as a whole. Unity means that, as a group, we set our sights on the common needs of all recovering sex addicts, and this links us together across all languages and borders. Each member's recovery depends on the well-being of all.

Just as we all share the same disease, so we share an all-important need for recovery. Our common welfare consists in whatever supports this basic need. As individuals, we have different ideas about how to meet that need, and this is healthy. Diversity of thought and opinion helps make our service work vital and creative. The First Tradition channels this creative energy towards a single goal: the welfare of recovering sex addicts. When we put this common need ahead of our individual desires, we can enjoy our differences while maintaining our unity of purpose.

Our groups work together to make SAA a place where sex addicts can recover and grow spiritually. Each group receives support from other groups and from SAA as a whole, by cooperating in providing services, and by presenting a consistent message of recovery. The entire fellowship, in turn, is supported by the efforts of each group. We keep in mind not only the welfare of those who are members of SAA today, but of all the sex addicts in the future who will come to our meetings hoping to find freedom. A stable and united fellowship provides a safe haven for those seeking help.

Disagreements are a natural part of any healthy community. The spirit of unity prevents disagreements from turning into quarrels, factions, or destructive personal conflicts. We cultivate tolerance and good will towards other members, holding the welfare of the group above our own personal preferences, desires, or opinions. A group that splinters or divides over conflicts puts all of us at risk. Our groups are strongest when we can solve or accept disagreements as they arise, continuing to carry the message of recovery with equal compassion for all.

As a fellowship, our commitment is to the common welfare of recovering sex addicts everywhere. The First Tradition makes it clear that each member's recovery depends on the strength of that commitment. We all play an important part, and as long as we work together, united by faith in a loving Higher Power, sex addicts will continue to find recovery in SAA.

Tradition Two

For our group purpose there is but one ultimate authority—a loving God as expressed in our group conscience. Our leaders are but trusted servants; they do not govern.

The Second Tradition builds on the principle of SAA unity: in all aspects of the program, our wisdom derives from the group, not from any single individual. This tradition also builds on the principle of humility: our best group decisions are guided by our reliance on a loving Higher Power, rather than on natural intelligence, special expertise, personal power, or skill at debate. This ideal of basing our group decisions on spiritual principles rather than personal opinion or power is different from what we may be used to. We discover that in SAA, no single member has authority over any other SAA member, but that God has ultimate authority over us all.

We all have opinions on group issues, but keeping a spiritual focus raises us above the personal level and shows our commitment to finding solutions that fulfill the group's needs rather than our personal desires. We find ourselves asking, "What is right?" instead of "Who is right?" As we listen to one another while drawing on our relationship to a loving God for guidance, an understanding of how to solve issues according to spiritual principles begins to arise within the group. We call this *group conscience*. Sometimes the conscience is so clear that a group will come to a quick, unanimous decision. In other instances, we may call for a vote to decide the issue. Whatever mechanism is used to make decisions, we strive to keep our minds open. Our experience has shown many cases where a so-called minority view came, over time, to be recognized as the group conscience after all. In the spirit of SAA unity, we strike a balance between supporting the group's decisions as our own, while continuing, as a group, to seek the will of our Higher Power.

Group conscience is not the same as unanimity, consensus, majority vote, or compromise. Rather than expressing the will of the group, it is the will of our Higher Power as expressed through the group. There is no one method used by groups to determine group conscience, but it is always wise to test our decisions against the Steps and the Traditions as we proceed. In some cases, the group conscience may be expressed by one individual. More typically, the group conscience is discovered only after sifting through many different perspectives, and often represents a view no individual member could have come up with on his or her own. Regardless of our personal views or opinions, we each have a responsibility to play our part in discerning and supporting the group conscience.

Learning to seek the will of our Higher Power through group conscience takes time, patience, and good will. Love is the force that guides our service activities, rather than the familiar methods of human power and control. It can be difficult for us to relinquish old ideas about authority, especially if we believe that our motives are good. We may, out of a genuine concern for the fellowship, want to take control of what happens in our groups and service committees. But with time and experience, we learn to trust the group conscience and to value the guidance we receive as a group more than our own power or wisdom. We also learn that the group conscience grows and changes just as we do in our personal recovery. New challenges call for new solutions. Sometimes growth can be painful, and the changes we experience may not look anything like what we'd expected. By practicing the principle of surrender, we can trust that God's guidance, as expressed in our group conscience, will take us right where we need to be.

Those of us who are chosen by our groups to carry out the decisions called for by group conscience are known as *trusted servants*. Asking members to serve does not put them in a different rank or class than other members. Instead, it establishes a relationship of trust. We trust that those we elect to positions of service will act according to the spiritual principles of our Steps and Traditions, be guided by group conscience, communicate accurate information to and from the group, and help carry the message of recovery to the best of their ability. Leadership in SAA means a commitment to serving the fellowship of SAA and promoting our common welfare.

This concept of service is distinct from the idea of government. To hold a governing authority over others means to exercise our individual power and control over them. As trusted servants, however, we do the will of our Higher Power as discerned by the group conscience, with full responsibility for carrying out the tasks entrusted to us, but with no power to compel or sanction any of our fellow members. Doing service work together, we learn to relate to each other on a basis of trust, caring, and selflessness, rather than the desire for control. When we acknowledge a loving God as our one ultimate authority, we are guarded from the pride and self-will that could divide us from each other and obscure our message. The mutual trust that we experience in service springs from this reliance on a loving God working through our groups.

Tradition Three

The only requirement for SAA membership is
a desire to stop addictive sexual behavior.

The disease of sex addiction does not discriminate according to race, gender, age, sexual orientation, class, religion, or any other social category. There are sex addicts all over the world and in every walk of life. All of us have a right to seek recovery in Sex Addicts Anonymous. The Third Tradition protects us from the human tendency to set up applications, tests, qualification procedures, or other demands that are meant to control the membership of groups.

No one can judge whether or not another person is a sex addict, or make decisions about someone's fitness for membership in SAA. In order to belong, all we need is a desire to stop addictive sexual behavior. Since desire is subjective, it can't be determined by anyone but ourselves. Neither can the honesty, clarity, or strength of our desire. Our motives for attending meetings may seem unclear at first, and many of us experience varying levels of desire and willingness over time. But if we are having trouble with sexual behaviors that we can't seem to stop, we can reach out to SAA for help, and be guaranteed a place in the fellowship with no strings attached.

We can rest assured that as long as we seek to stop our addictive sexual behaviors, we belong in SAA, even if our acting-out patterns differ from everyone else's in our meeting. Since membership in SAA has only this single requirement, we are reminded not to focus on how we are different from others, or to imagine that only those who have acted out in certain ways are truly sex addicts. If we can look inside and honestly say that we have a problem with any addictive sexual behavior, then the help SAA has to offer is meant for us, too.

This tradition opens the door to all sex addicts seeking help, so that we will be welcomed in our meetings and encouraged to keep coming back. The SAA program is offered in the form of suggestions based on our collective experience, rather than as a requirement. There are no fees for membership, and addicts may always attend meetings, regardless of what stage of recovery we are in, or what progress or setbacks we've experienced in the program. Although it has become customary for members to identify as sex addicts in meetings, it is not required that we do so. This freedom from judgment, restriction, and control helps us feel safe to open up and share about our addiction, many of us for the first time in our lives. Although meetings do have structures and rules concerning appropriate behavior, these apply only to our words and actions in a meeting, and never to our status as members or our right to attend.

As a fellowship, Sex Addicts Anonymous is open to anyone with the desire to stop addictive sexual behavior. Some groups, however, have made the autonomous decision to gear their meetings toward a specific group within the fellowship. For example, there are meetings for men, women, gays and lesbians, sexual anorexics, professionals, and those who have committed felonious behaviors. Such meetings are meant to allow those of us who attend them to speak more freely, to give us the opportunity to meet with others who may understand us better, or to better protect our anonymity. These kinds of meetings have proven to be valuable. Our experience suggests, however, that we gain much by also attending meetings that are as open and diverse as possible.

The Third Tradition is based on trust rather than fear. When we live in the spirit of this tradition, we acknowledge that we cannot stand in judgment over any of our fellows, or believe any sex addict unworthy of recovery or unfit for our program. We are challenged to open our hearts and our meetings to those different from us and to seek ways to show the compassion and hope that have been given to us. The Third Tradition's clarity and simplicity reflects the compassion of a loving Higher Power, who grants us freedom from addiction regardless of who we are or where we have been. Everyone with a desire to stop addictive sexual behavior is welcome here. The welcome we receive in SAA inspires us to extend the same welcome, and the same message of hope, to those who come after us.

Tradition Four

Each group should be autonomous except in matters affecting other groups or SAA as a whole.

Our basic and most important vehicle for recovery is the SAA group. Whenever two or more sex addicts gather together to share their experience, strength, and hope, we have a meeting. Meetings are not created or maintained by some outside authority. Sex addicts start their own meetings, and the groups are self-governing. This level of self-determination may seem extreme. How can an organization function without any outward control in establishing its groups? We have found that one of the reasons this process works so well is precisely because we do it ourselves. Our autonomy stands in sharp contrast to the dependence and compulsion we felt in our addiction. Autonomy goes hand in hand with self-respect and a new sense of freedom, as we take responsibility for our groups and the carrying of our message.

We have the freedom to develop our meetings in different ways, in order to meet the varying needs of our diverse fellowship. Some groups choose to devote their meetings to studying the Steps. Others have speaker meetings, with members telling their stories and sharing solutions, or topic meetings in which the group discusses one or more subjects relating to our addiction and recovery. Groups may create any number of such formats, or include several different options in the same format. No single type of meeting can meet the needs of every sex addict. Some addicts will be more receptive to certain kinds of meetings than others. By maintaining group autonomy, we ensure that our message is carried to as many sex addicts as possible.

Autonomy also means that each group has the freedom to make mistakes and learn from them at its own pace. As addicts, most of us react negatively to control. As long as we keep to the Steps and Traditions and do not affiliate with any other organization, we are free to experiment. Some of our ideas will prove effective, and others will not. We have found that this freedom contributes to the overall health of our fellowship, as the best innovations take root and thrive.

While Tradition Four safeguards the self-governing nature of our groups, it also balances this autonomy with the awareness that we are all part of a greater whole, the fellowship of Sex Addicts Anonymous. Each group has its individual character, but there are matters that can affect other groups, or even SAA itself. Our meetings need to be identifiable as SAA meetings—clearly following and presenting the Steps and Traditions of SAA as written, bearing our name and no other, and offering hope to all who seek recovery from sexual addiction. We are careful not to create uncertainty concerning our identity as SAA in the minds of those attending our meetings. Without this clarity, our primary purpose can easily become confused and entangled with other ideas, goals, or causes.

In the spirit of unity, we also strive for constructive relations with other SAA groups, even if we have a very different format or approach. We do not try to control other groups, dictate to them, or blacklist them. If a group stresses its differences from other SAA groups rather than affirming its similarities, or doesn't provide information about other SAA groups or our International Service Organization, sex addicts will be denied access to the full range of help available in our fellowship. Isolation and mistrust, with all their attendant problems, may also result. We have found it best to focus on our similarities and shared purpose, allowing each member the freedom to discover the meetings that suit him or her best.

We are also conscious of the impressions that our groups make on the outside community. When we rent spaces in which to have our meetings, we are responsible for treating those places and their owners respectfully, by paying rent on time, maintaining order and cleanliness, and being considerate to neighbors, as well as by a proper demeanor in our communications with others. The same concerns apply when SAA groups hold social events, retreats, conventions, or other activities. If a group makes a bad impression on non-SAA members, it reflects on the fellowship as a whole and may prevent sex addicts from finding us through referrals or word of mouth.

The Twelve Traditions of SAA provide a framework in which a wide range of recovery experience can find expression. Each group has an obligation to adhere to the spiritual principles of our traditions when carrying its message. By following the Fourth Tradition, we stay united in purpose while remaining free to serve our fellow sex addicts in vital and diverse ways.

Tradition Five

Each group has but one primary purpose—to carry its message to the sex addict who still suffers.

Our groups are dedicated to serving sex addicts who seek recovery, and the purpose or goal of our service is to carry the SAA message: that freedom from addictive sexual behavior is possible through the Twelve Steps of SAA. Every activity of our groups, and indeed of the fellowship as a whole, is motivated by that one purpose. Tradition Five states that no other purpose can be greater than, or equal to, that of carrying the message of recovery. Having only one primary purpose in our service activities keeps everything simple and focused. As long as we keep this purpose foremost in our minds and hearts, we can be confident that our SAA groups are on the right track.

This principle of service applies at every level of our experience in SAA. We find that we attend meetings not just to receive support and wisdom from others. Nor do we only talk about our problems. Instead, we learn to be mindful of carrying the message of recovery at our meetings. By sharing the solutions we have learned through working the SAA program, we keep both our recovery and our groups healthy. Although we enjoy the company of the friends we've made in the fellowship, we do not make socializing our main purpose in coming together. We remember to welcome newcomers, encourage them to stay, and answer their questions and concerns.

Adhering to our primary purpose involves many responsibilities. We make sure that SAA literature and meeting schedules are available. We strive for an atmosphere of recovery in our groups, by using consistent formats and meeting etiquette, starting and ending on time, and being respectful in our sharing and listening. When we have business meetings, or otherwise gather to discuss service, we explore new ways to make our message accessible and our meetings safe and welcoming.

Keeping to our primary purpose also means avoiding carrying any message other than our own. As individuals, we may find support and inspiration from all manner of outside literature, self-help programs, therapies, philosophies, religions, or spiritual ideas. As a group, however, we focus on the SAA message.

We take care not to give newcomers the wrong impression of what we have to offer by mixing our message with other disciplines or approaches. We guard against implying that any member needs to subscribe to a particular religion, political viewpoint, or therapeutic program as part of joining an SAA group.

Tradition Five does not tell us exactly how to carry the message to the addict who still suffers. Each group needs to work out for itself how to use its time and resources to reach out to others. There are bound to be disagreements among individuals about the best way to fulfill our primary purpose, some perhaps arising from personality conflicts or a desire for control. This is why we rely on our Higher Power and the process of group conscience to come to decisions. Throughout this process, the Fifth Tradition serves as a constant reminder to keep our priorities in order. Our groups exist to help make recovery available to any sex addict seeking help. This purpose is central to everything we do as a fellowship.

Tradition Six

*An SAA group ought never endorse, finance, or lend the
SAA name to any related facility or outside enterprise,
lest problems of money, property, and prestige divert us
from our primary purpose.*

In carrying our message of recovery, we often come in contact with other organizations. Part of our outreach efforts may involve cooperation with health care facilities, public agencies, treatment centers for addiction, or other groups and institutions. Such cooperation can play a vital role in making the SAA program available to sex addicts seeking help, but if we become too closely identified with other organizations, our ability to carry the SAA message can be seriously damaged.

There are many other groups, including other twelve-step fellowships, that present ideas about, or offer solutions to, sexual addiction or related issues. As individuals, we may or may not find these ideas and solutions helpful, but for SAA to make a public statement of support for any of these groups or organizations would constitute an *endorsement*. Our program would inevitably be confused with these other programs and opinions in the minds of the public, making it more difficult for those seeking help to hear and understand SAA's message. If we were to *financially support* another organization, such as a clubhouse or treatment center, we might become entangled in the practical business considerations of that group, taking us away from our primary purpose. And if we were to *lend our name* to some other project or institution, we would be implying an endorsement of the group or event with which the name of SAA was being associated, and thus mingling our message with concerns that are not relevant to SAA or its program. In addition, by affiliating our fellowship with non-SAA organizations, we would also be associated with their public reputations. If an outside group got into trouble or received bad publicity, this could negatively affect perceptions of SAA, and thus prevent sex addicts from being open to our message.

The Sixth Tradition wisely identifies *money, property, and prestige* as potential obstacles to effectively carrying our message of recovery. Our efforts as a fellowship are based on the spiritual principle of service, rather than on self-interest or desire for gain. Money and property are powerful forces in the world, and when we are tempted to affiliate ourselves with an outside enterprise, these forces almost always play a part, diverting energy and attention from our focus on helping the suffering sex addict, or even damaging the integrity of our service structure. We need to remember that our purpose is not to make money, nor even to grow as an organization. SAA's growth and financial stability are only instruments helping us carry our message—they must always be secondary to that purpose, never ends in themselves.

Prestige is perhaps the greatest challenge to the principle of service. It may seem that affiliation with an outside group or enterprise would increase our influence or credibility as a fellowship. But experience has shown that we need only rely on our Higher Power and our steps and traditions to sustain us, and that compromising that reliance through outside interests clouds our vision. When we apply notions of status, authority, and control to ourselves, either as individuals or groups, we risk being motivated to extend or increase this perceived power and prestige, at the expense of the humility and reliance on a Higher Power that is central to our program. Prestige also fosters differences among us, fracturing the unity on which our recovery depends.

From the group to the international level, we maintain our identity as a fellowship of sex addicts, offering a program of recovery to all who seek freedom from addictive sexual behavior. To ensure that our message will not take second place to any outside interest, Tradition Six puts healthy boundaries around our relationships with other groups and causes. In this way we are able to cooperate with those outside of SAA who can help us, without being entangled in many of the problems that groups experience when working together. Of course we cannot avoid all problems, but by always keeping in mind that we are separate and distinct from other organizations and enterprises, and communicating only SAA's unique message, we stay on the simple path of service to our fellow sex addict.

Tradition Seven

Every SAA group ought to be fully self-supporting, declining outside contributions.

The Seventh Tradition ensures that every SAA group takes full responsibility for its own needs and expenses. As addicts, we were often all too ready to shirk responsibility and allow others to take care of us, clean up our messes, and attend to the necessities of life. In the program we learn instead to be accountable for ourselves and our recovery. On the group level, this means accepting complete responsibility for the maintenance of our meetings and not looking to anyone outside us to help pay our bills or facilitate our groups. The Seventh Tradition also ensures that other influences or organizations, however well-meaning, never interfere with our primary purpose. By declining outside contributions, we are free to focus on carrying the SAA message, and that message only.

Each group must meet certain basic requirements in order to sustain itself. We need members who are willing to meet together and share experience, strength, and hope on a regular basis. We need a meeting place that is reasonably accessible to sex addicts who wish to attend. We need to have SAA literature and meeting schedules available. Once a group has established itself, it can usually pay the rent and other expenses by passing a basket and taking voluntary contributions during the meeting. Experience has shown that if we are unable to fully support ourselves this way, it is better to lower our expenses than to rely on fundraising or other special events to sustain us. Once we have met our own basic needs, most groups pass any extra funds on to the local intergroup or the ISO, in support of coordinated services and outreach efforts.

Being self-supporting involves more than just paying our bills. Each group needs not only money in the basket to pay the rent and buy literature, but members willing to fulfill service commitments. To be self-supporting, each group needs volunteers to perform basic functions, such as chairing the meeting, sponsoring newcomers, and answering the mail. We may think of the Seventh Tradition as "the money tradition," but non-monetary contributions are just as necessary and valuable. When we each accept responsibility for contributing to the meeting, financially or otherwise, we help our group to be self-supporting, which in turn helps carry our message.

Our experience has shown that not soliciting or accepting outside contributions encourages us to become better stewards of the group's resources. Although we have expenses and a treasury, we are not a business, and we need not be concerned about making a profit or carrying out an elaborate business plan. Many SAA groups choose not to accumulate extra money beyond what is necessary for ongoing expenses, annual projects, and a prudent reserve. Our needs are simple, and we should not lose sight of SAA's primary purpose as our foremost concern.

Being fully self-supporting means being aware of the responsibility of every member for supporting the group. Some of us have a natural tendency to sit back and let others do all the work; others are only too willing to take on service positions and hold them indefinitely. Although this might seem to create a perfect balance between those who take over and those who sit back, in actuality such a situation works against becoming self-supporting. A group works well when all members are encouraged to serve in line with their abilities and when service positions are regularly rotated among the group's members. We are fully self-supporting when we all take ownership of our common welfare, secure in the knowledge that even if certain members leave, the group will be strong enough to continue to carry its message.

Tradition Eight

Sex Addicts Anonymous should remain forever nonprofessional, but our service centers may employ special workers.

As members of SAA, we share a common problem and a common solution. We are all sex addicts who desire to stop addictive sexual behavior. We all know from experience what it was like to suffer from sex addiction, and what challenges we face in recovery. With other sex addicts like ourselves, we experience a level of honesty and understanding that we are rarely able to reach with those who are not sex addicts. However concerned and well-intentioned those outside SAA may be, the kind of help they can offer is different from the help we receive from one another in SAA. In carrying the message of recovery, we gratefully give what was so freely given to us.

There can be no price tag on such a gift. SAA rests on the solid foundation of sex addicts helping other sex addicts, with no fees or professional qualifications. If SAA were to offer professional help, the essential nature of our meetings and our program would be altered beyond recognition. We would be divided into two groups: those who offer professional help, and those who receive the help, with the first group having an inevitably higher status than the other. If we charged a fee, only sex addicts who could afford the fee would be able to attend meetings. Our primary purpose could be compromised by budgetary and political considerations. To avoid these pitfalls, and continue to carry our message with no strings attached, SAA should remain forever nonprofessional.

The Eighth Tradition also reminds us that carrying the message as called for in Step Twelve ought not to be confused with the actions we may perform for pay in the course of carrying out our occupations. Those of us who are counselors, therapists, educators, clergy, or health care workers may deal with sex addicts and sex addiction as part of our work. The Eighth Tradition draws a healthy distinction between the paid services we provide as part of our jobs, and the twelfth-step work we engage in as members of SAA. Whenever we carry the message of SAA, we carry it only as sex addicts helping one another, never in our capacity as professionals.

As our groups expand and coordinate their services, however, it may become necessary to hire professionals, in order to fulfill our service responsibilities. We establish centers or offices, separate from the meetings, which are in charge of providing services for the fellowship, such as literature, public information, outreach, and SAA conventions and other events. We may need to pay people to help us do this kind of service work, which often involves too much labor and time to be handled by volunteers alone. These "special workers" may or may not be SAA members. If they are members, the fact that they get paid for helping with service tasks does not affect their status as equal members of the fellowship.

We may also need to seek professional advice on certain matters affecting SAA, from lawyers, insurance agents, accountants, or other experts in their fields. We practice humility when we recognize that we don't know everything and that there are cases in which we will need to ask for help from professionals. We also use good judgment by carefully deciding which situations call for such help, and which ones don't. Tradition Eight preserves our nonprofessional approach to recovery, while allowing us to take the actions we need in order to provide needed services that help carry the SAA message.

Tradition Nine

SAA, as such, ought never be organized,
but we may create service boards or committees directly
responsible to those they serve.

The Ninth Tradition is based on the insight that our groups function best when we rely on spiritual principles, rather than on conventional ideas of organized authority or control. Our fellowship is founded instead on the simple idea of sex addicts meeting together to help each other recover from sexual addiction. Within this framework, there are no dues, fees, or membership requirements. Whatever structure we may choose to give to our meetings is guided solely by our need to facilitate recovery through the SAA program, and we are all equal members within the group. This informal approach is part of the reason our meetings are so effective. We keep everything as simple as possible, and this helps us focus on recovery.

Not being organized also means that there is no membership committee determining who is in or out, and no disciplinary committee punishing members for breaking the rules. In practical terms, no sex addict can stand in authority over any other sex addict. This gives each of us an unparalleled degree of freedom and responsibility, which is one of our most precious gifts. In most other organizations, a manager, boss, or board has the ultimate power to enforce rules or sanction members. If we were to practice this type of organization within SAA, we can easily imagine the conflicts, rebellions, and resentments that would ensue. We have learned that not being organized helps ensure the very survival of our fellowship, because we rely on the spiritual authority of our Higher Power rather than on any human authority to direct us.

Of course, there are practical matters that need to be addressed if SAA is to function effectively. Usually we need to pay rent for the spaces in which we meet. We need literature that explains our program, and we need to find ways to make that literature available to members. We need to produce SAA meeting schedules, so that we will know the places and times of meetings in our area. Eventually, as the groups in our area become more numerous, we feel the need to create outreach services, such as a phone line or a program for carrying our message into institutions. Practical questions and concerns of various kinds also come up in our meetings, and we need to find ways to address them that are in line with our principles.

If we were to organize our groups to handle these services, the simplicity of the meetings would be compromised. The group's attention would have to be diverted to these practical necessities, taking precious time away from the real reason for meeting together—sharing our experience, strength, and hope with each other. For that reason, the groups create service boards or committees, which meet at a different time than the regular SAA meeting, to address these concerns and provide the needed services. At the individual group level, this might be as simple as a short business meeting that takes place after the regular meeting. When several meetings coordinate their activities, they create an intergroup, which is a board or committee through which these groups provide services. The same principle applies at the international level. The SAA groups have created the International Service Organization in order to provide services to the entire fellowship of SAA. Our service structure, therefore, is founded on the Ninth Tradition. Every service board or committee owes its existence to the SAA groups, and its sole purpose is to serve the needs of those groups.

For our boards and committees to remain accountable to those they serve, all their actions need to be directed by the groups. The service committees, therefore, consist of members who have been elected by their groups to represent them. In most matters that concern our principles as a fellowship, the trusted servant is expected to seek the group's conscience before participating in a decision. Throughout our service structure, it is vital that communication remains open between the members and their trusted servants. The groups are responsible for keeping the service committees up to date on their activities, and for clearly communicating their needs and concerns. The service committees are responsible for providing thorough and accurate information on their discussions, decisions, projects, and finances. Our committees work best when all decisions are open to the scrutiny of the SAA groups and their members.

The Ninth Tradition protects us from a danger that has threatened human societies throughout history—the abuse of power. The fact that our service boards and committees are directly responsible to those they serve ensures that our service structure will not become a separate entity with its own interests, but will remain dependent on the groups, accountable to the members, and faithful to the message of SAA.

Tradition Ten

Sex Addicts Anonymous has no opinion on outside issues; hence the SAA name ought never be drawn into public controversy.

Our fellowship, in all its activities, has really only one issue or concern: recovery from sexual addiction through the program of Sex Addicts Anonymous. When we carry our message, or present SAA to the public, that is the one subject on which we are qualified to provide information. Anything else is considered an "outside issue." SAA does not have any opinions at all on the social, political, economic, religious, or philosophical issues of our time. Because we are so diverse, any such opinion expressed publicly by SAA would fail to represent the views of many of the members, thus prompting dissension within the fellowship. In addition, if SAA took sides on an issue, it would obscure our basic message by associating our fellowship with that issue in the public mind. Public controversy could prevent sex addicts from seeking help, if we were perceived as a partisan group rather than as a fellowship that welcomes anyone with a desire to stop acting out. Negative public perception could also keep sex addicts away from our fellowship, out of the fear of being involved with a controversial organization.

We do employ certain ideas in SAA that could be construed as opinions on various issues. Not everyone who hears about our program will agree with the idea of sex addiction, or that this addiction is a disease. Others may argue with our spiritual orientation or the concept of powerlessness. When representing the SAA program to the public, we are careful not to engage in debate around these issues. Rather, we state that this is how our program works for us. At the same time, we don't claim that our program is the only way to recover, or oppose those who believe differently. Our only interest is to inform people about the SAA program, to the best of our ability, and not to try to argue or convince.

When carrying the message of SAA, we are inevitably asked our views on certain topics that are related to sex addiction, or seem to be. It is perhaps tempting to try to expound on such topics, using the principles of our program as a guide. But as a fellowship, we cannot afford to take a position on these questions, however relevant they may seem to the lives and concerns of sex addicts. SAA has no opinion on other twelve-step programs (for sexual addiction or in general), treatment centers, therapy and its various schools and methods, sexual abuse and its causes, the medical definitions of disease and recovery, sex crimes legislation or policy, or the sex scandals of public figures. We neither endorse nor oppose any point of view or organization. As a fellowship, it's simply none of our business. By confining our public statements to matters pertaining to the SAA program of recovery, we keep our fellowship free from unnecessary and possibly dangerous distractions.

The Tenth Tradition does not mean that as individuals we can't have or express opinions on outside issues. Our right to think and believe as we choose is absolute. However, we take care when making any pronouncements on outside issues within the SAA meeting itself, even if we have well-informed professional opinions or strongly held personal beliefs. In the same way that opinions on outside issues could damage our reputation when given publicly, such opinions expressed within meetings could drive away other members or cause dissension within the group. Our experience has shown that it is best to keep these opinions to a minimum when sharing, and to always identify them as personal opinions rather than the opinion of the group. In this way we keep our focus on the experience, strength, and hope that the program offers to us all.

Tradition Eleven

Our public relations policy is based on attraction rather than promotion; we need always maintain personal anonymity at the level of press, radio, TV, and films.

The Eleventh Tradition serves as a guide to our groups, and to the fellowship as a whole, in our public relations. It also guides us as members when we are representing SAA in a public capacity or carrying the message to the sex addict who still suffers. In our public relations, we strive to make our existence and our message known, so that sex addicts seeking help will know how to find us. At the same time, we strive to protect the anonymity of our members. Our purpose is not to increase our membership, make broad claims about our effectiveness as a program, capitalize on celebrity endorsements, or otherwise promote our fellowship. Instead, we simply offer our program as an option for anyone who is suffering negative consequences from addictive sexual behavior and is looking for help.

In SAA meetings, we try to share from our own experience, rather than giving advice. In a similar way, when we represent SAA to the public, we just describe how our program works as clearly as we can, based directly on what we know. The principle of attraction means that we are letting people know that there is a way to recover from sex addiction that has worked for us, and that anyone who wants to stop addictive sexual behavior is welcome to try it. We can't say whether or not someone is a sex addict, and we don't tell people that they need recovery or should attend our meetings. We act on the belief, confirmed by our experience, that a simple declaration of who we are, and what we do, will serve as an invitation to those seeking help, giving them the opportunity to try our program and find out if it feels right for them.

Attraction also means that we maintain our anonymity in order to keep the focus on SAA as a whole, rather than on any particular person who is representing us. If in our dealings with the press and media we put a lot of emphasis on the details of our personal stories, this tends to distract attention from our basic message of recovery and may involve us in outside issues or sensationalism. It is our policy to not use our last names, or in many cases to use an assumed name, when we are representing SAA in the media. In the case of visual media, such as TV or films, we have found it best to keep our faces hidden when speaking as members of SAA. This policy prevents our identity as SAA members from being publicly revealed. More importantly, it protects the fellowship from public controversy. If SAA becomes identified in the public mind with a particular individual, the credibility of our message would suffer if that person relapsed, or if some other negative behavior or event became associated with that person. Therefore, we do not attempt to promote ourselves through the use of celebrities or other well-known figures, relying instead on the straightforward presentation of our message.

Although we adhere strictly to a policy of attraction, it is our responsibility as a fellowship to make SAA's presence known, in order to carry our message to the still-suffering sex addict. Every aspect of outreach, whether it is establishing a phone line, mailing information to treatment centers and other facilities, or airing public service announcements on local stations, is a potential lifeline for the sex addict who may not know that recovery is available. And even if we are not directly involved in bringing SAA to public awareness, living in recovery from sex addiction sets an example that demonstrates, particularly to those who knew us before we got into recovery, that the program works.

Tradition Twelve

Anonymity is the spiritual foundation of all our traditions, ever reminding us to place principles before personalities.

On one level, anonymity simply means that the names of SAA members, and the details of what we share in meetings, are kept confidential and not repeated outside of the meetings. This helps foster an atmosphere of freedom and safety in our groups, without the fear that our identities as sex addicts, or our personal stories, will be revealed to others without our permission. It also helps prevent gossip or other inappropriate talk within the fellowship.

On another level, to be anonymous is to have no name. When we are anonymous in this sense, we put aside our outside identities and act only as members of the fellowship, regardless of social position, gender, occupation, race, religion, economic status, appearance, or any other quality that makes us different from one another. In a very real sense, when we join together for the purpose of recovery, we need to leave all such distinctions behind. Although we all have different personal histories, as well as unique talents and gifts, no member is more important than any other.

But anonymity also has a deeper meaning for us, a significance that underlies our entire existence as a fellowship. Just as we learn to turn our will and our lives over to the care of a loving God in our recovery program, so as a fellowship we learn to carry the message of recovery through selfless service, always keeping in mind the suffering sex addicts who are desperately seeking help, rather than our individual desires or ambitions. In our groups and service committees, therefore, we strive to emphasize "we" and "our," rather than "I" and "mine."

Being in recovery doesn't erase our personalities. On the contrary, most of us experience our personal qualities as becoming more special, colorful, and vibrant as we gain abstinence and grow spiritually, and our individual strengths help us to carry a message of hope. But personalities are also prone to the influence of character defects, such as resentment, fear, envy, or the desire for control. Our groups and service committees are founded on a stronger foundation than the will of individuals. The principles of our program, springing from our faith in a Higher Power and expressed in our Steps and Traditions, must guide us in our decisions if we are to carry our message effectively.

It is anonymity, the spirit of selfless service, that reminds us as a fellowship to always base our actions and deliberations on spiritual principles, putting aside any personal considerations in favor of a higher good—carrying the message of recovery to sex addicts. With anonymity as our foundation, we dedicate our efforts to something much greater than any one of us. Protected from the inevitable divisions and conflicts of our personalities, SAA is able to continue helping sex addicts find freedom and serenity.

CONCLUSION

KEEP COMING BACK

SAA was founded when a sex addict, weary from his addiction and feeling defeated by its consequences, called a colleague and asked for help. They took a walk around a lake near their homes, and as they talked, the colleague revealed that he suffered from similar addictive behaviors. They may not have known to call it sex addiction at first, but they decided to try adapting the Twelve Steps of Alcoholics Anonymous to deal with their problem. They began meeting together regularly, sharing about their addiction and exploring how the Steps might help them find recovery. Soon, a third member joined them, and then others.

Gradually the fellowship grew. Brave and desperate people formed their own meetings, and others joined them. Before long, regular meetings of Sex Addicts Anonymous were being held in cities around the country. As the years went by, the message of recovery was carried around the world.

Some knew that they needed help for their sex addiction, but didn't know where to get it. Some found relief by attending other twelve-step groups. And some started their own meeting of SAA. It may have started when two or three people discovered by chance that they had similar problems and began meeting informally in a private home or coffee shop. Others may have begun with just one addict who found a space for a meeting, advertised the time and location in the local paper, then waited at the scheduled time, praying for someone else to show up. All of these pioneers knew they needed help, and they were willing to go to any length to get it. Soon they were blessed with a meeting that would take hold and grow.

Some members found that the drives to their meetings were too long. Rather than drop out, they started new meetings in their own cities or towns. Others found that they couldn't always attend the one meeting in their town, or they decided that they needed more support than what a single meeting could provide. So they started a second or third meeting in their community.

What they all had in common was a desire to recover from their addiction—a desire that overcame any fear, adversity, or inconvenience. They were courageous. Perhaps they were brave simply because they were able to comprehend the seriousness of their condition.

And so it has been for all of us since then. Each of us has had to face our problem after years of denying it. Each of us has had to make the decision: "Do I want to go on destroying what I value the most and hurting those I care about, or am I willing to change?"

It took courage for us to reach out. Each of us faced our addiction and admitted our defeat. Courageously, but not fearlessly, we each took a first step toward recovery. We made contact with the SAA fellowship. We went to our first meeting. We read SAA literature. At the meetings we found people like us, and when they told their stories, we could hear our own story. The details were often very different, but the feelings were the same. When we finally talked, we often let out secrets that we once thought we could tell no one.

Once we decided that we wanted recovery, the hard work began. Few of us began working the program without some hesitation. At each step of the way of surrender that was offered to us, we could choose to do things our own way. We have had to wrestle with that choice again and again.

We have had to work at staying sexually sober, as well as rebuilding our lives and relationships. Sometimes the steps seemed overwhelming. But we found that we had several things working in our favor. We had time and energy available that we used to waste on our addiction. We had our new friends in recovery. And most importantly, we had the God of our understanding to sustain us. Through the program, we were able to face problems that we never had the courage to face before, and to do things we never imagined possible.

This is how recovery has been for us. Each of us has taken steps of courage and leaps of faith. Each of us has contributed, not only to our own recovery, but to the recovery of other suffering sex addicts as well. We have contributed by showing up at meetings and by sharing our experience, strength, and hope. We have listened to our fellow addicts and supported them in their recovery journey. Like the first members of our fellowship, we continue to remain sexually sober by helping our fellow addict stay sober. Our prayer is that every sex addict who seeks recovery will have the opportunity to find it. And keep coming back.

THE STEPS ARE THE SPIRITUAL SOLUTION*

Some of us started out as a "tourist" at SAA meetings—the member who shows up every week or every other week, who shares at meetings, who may even buy and read the literature, but who doesn't get a sponsor, doesn't work the steps, certainly never stays for a business meeting—and who doesn't stop acting out on his or her inner-circle behaviors for more than a few weeks at a time before the next relapse. This resistance to surrendering to the SAA program is rooted in pride and a stubborn unwillingness to admit defeat, despite the pain and consequences already experienced. As an SAA "tourist," we cling to the belief that we are not really powerless and that just going to meetings (maybe combined with just going to church, or just seeing a therapist, or just getting a slip signed, or just reading a book) will be enough to turn things around without too much inconvenience. Many tourists drop in and out for months or even years before one final crisis brings us to our bottom and makes us willing, at last, to get serious.

This experience brings into focus the difficult truth that no addict is compelled to work the suggested steps in this program. A member can't be kicked out because he relapsed or because she hasn't moved past Step One. Tradition Three assures us that anyone with a desire to stop addictive sexual behavior, however slight the desire, is welcome in SAA, for as long as it takes for recovery to take hold. That said, our hearts go out in compassion to those suffering sex addicts who still hang back, when the solution to our common addiction is so close and when their brothers and sisters in SAA stand ready to help and guide the way.

In our experience, though meetings are important, they are not sufficient for recovery from sex addiction. We need the spiritual solution offered by the Twelve Steps. To be sure, meetings are where most of us first encounter the steps, learn about the program, find our sponsors, and share with others our desire for recovery. But if we want to actually *experience* recovery in our lives, there are no shortcuts. We have to work the steps to experience the fruits of working the steps.

The steps are the spiritual solution to our addiction—leading not only to a life of abstinence from our addictive sexual behaviors, but to a fulfilling life of service to our brothers and sisters in recovery and beyond. The spiritual awakening described in Step Twelve puts us on the path of service and connects us with our Higher Power, our fellow addicts, and our world in ways we had never dreamed possible. This awakening is the foundation of a responsible and joyful existence as we seek and find our Higher Power's will for us—both in our individual lives and in the life of our fellowship. And for this priceless gift of recovery, so astonishingly simple, so freely available, we are humbly grateful. We invite all suffering sex addicts, inside and outside the rooms of SAA, to join with us in accepting this gift.

Written for the Third Edition

PERSONAL STORIES

The following personal stories contain the experiences and opinions of individual SAA members, and are not intended to represent the views of the SAA fellowship as a whole.

1.

HE DID NOT WANT TO BE ALONE

My earliest memory is a sexual one. I was part of a group of children aged roughly four to seven. We were in a storage building we called "the shed." We were with a young neighbor woman and playing sex games. Each of us took a turn pulling down our pants and showing our genitals to the others. I was the only boy. I found this a very powerful experience. As time went on I would try to recreate this scene. Sometimes the other kids would play. Other times I would be very alone with desire and somehow embarrassed that I wanted to continue doing this behavior and they wanted to do other things.

From that point on, sex always seemed to be intruding in my life. When I was about seven I discovered that when I climbed up my mother's clothes pole or the swing set on the playground, it was extremely pleasurable. I did not know what ejaculation was, nor would I for years. But I had discovered masturbation. And it was a comfort. I lived in a dangerous house. When my dad drank, he got angry. He was always getting into fights. First it was Golden Gloves. Then it was guys in the army. Then guys in bars. And then it was mom. I did watch my father batter my mother. We lived in the country, so in addition to being scared I was also lonely. It helped to shinny up a pole. I was not sure that what I was doing was okay. I tried to explain it to mom but she did not seem to understand what I was telling her. So I gave up.

Dad got sober when I was about eight. He went to twelve-step meetings for two years. Things got better, but I always knew that the rage was just below the surface. We all did. When I was in the eighth grade, my dad became Catholic. My mother was raised Catholic, so this meant a great deal to her. And things got better. However, each Saturday I would have to go to confession because we believed that we could not receive communion with a sin on our soul. Since I was expected to go to communion, I had to go to confession first. My father would conclude that I had committed the sin of "self abuse"—or masturbation. On the way to and from confession he would talk to me about self-control—that I would never be a man unless I could control my "urges." I would be filled with feelings of shame and failure. I would do everything I could to stop masturbating but failed continually. I felt that God would punish me for twenty-four hours if I masturbated. Since I was doing it daily, I felt cursed. Years later during a Fifth Step, a chaplain gave me the key I needed. He pointed out that I was trying to control God with my sexual behavior. If I were good, God would have to be good.

My parents sent me to a Catholic school because they thought I needed discipline. I had a hard time with classes and finishing homework. As I look back, I think that I was probably trying to cope with depression. Fortunately I had success at the school and life got better. I could go to confession without my family knowing. And dating seemed to help, although I was very fearful of actually touching a girl. Remember, these were the days for Catholics when to "French kiss" a girl was a sin.

Then some events occurred that changed my perspective. In my junior year, three different priests sexually abused me. The first occasion was in the confessional. The second was an English teacher who had been "overly friendly" for years. He would grab my belt buckle with his fingers inside my trousers. He would bring me back from school events and hold me in his car. I did not fully understand what he wanted because I was so naive, and I think I was desperate for attention from a man. When he took me on a trip to look at colleges it became very clear what he wanted, and I was traumatized. He continued to pressure me. He was a man I deeply respected, and it left me very conflicted. I realized that he had been targeting me for some time, and I felt betrayed. The third occasion was a missionary who approached me in a bathroom. I never told anybody about any of it until the English teacher was caught and fired when I was a senior. Many of the other boys had not said anything either. As a friend of mine was later to say, it was as if we were asked to disbelieve the obvious and accept the improbable. I did not share the whole story until years later when the legacy of those experiences was painfully unearthed in therapy.

One good thing happened. The tyranny of sin had been broken. I had seen the humanness of God's servants. It was not that I disbelieved. In fact, I was not sure what to believe. But I knew that I was not alone.

I went away to a Catholic liberal arts college. Going away was a good thing for me. I had success in classes and felt like I belonged. I enjoyed dating. I finally had intercourse and it was with a woman I really cared for. The next day she was voted the girl most like the Virgin Mary in her graduating class. We both felt intense shame. Our relationship grew until I met another woman who I immediately fell in love with. I had discovered the holy grail of romance. I left the woman I had been with as if all we had done did not matter. I have regretted that all my life. And I hurt a really good person—a pattern I was to repeat.

I was accepted into graduate school at an Ivy League university. My plan was to be a professor of history. I married the woman that I was so romantic with and we left for graduate school. It was there that I snapped. The competition was intense. Students had to manage two books a day, many of which were in foreign languages. Plus the other students were from big eastern colleges and I was from a small school in the Midwest. I was constantly having to prove myself. The stress was high.

It started one night sitting in my car after a late-night class. Young coeds were walking by my car on the way back to the dorms. I found myself masturbating as these young women passed my car. Being that it was nighttime, I knew they could not see me. Yet I had never done anything like that in my life. I was astounded and scared. A few nights later I did the same thing, only I added a new element by driving my car as I masturbated. Then the next threshold was actually exposing myself to women as I would drive by. It was still at night, so the risk of being seen was low. But again I was astounded at what I was doing. I was the good, hard-working Catholic who tried to be honorable in everything I did. I never dreamed I would be doing something like that.

The pleasure I experienced was extraordinary. Unlike intercourse or solitary masturbation in which I experienced pleasure, this was what drug addicts call a "rush." The excitement was different, the orgasm was different, and my whole body was different for hours. In fact, time would go by so fast that hours seemed like seconds. And there was great fatigue and feeling physically out of sorts afterwards. Emotionally I felt tremendous shame and fear. What if someone were to see me like that? For sure I knew that it was the most exciting, exhilarating, and pleasurable thing I had ever done.

Within a few weeks I was doing it in the daytime because the nighttime was not enough. My behavior was still furtive and I would use a jacket or blanket to cover up. Still, it was daytime. I knew I should not be doing this, but I was off in a fog. Every chance I had I would cruise for opportunities to masturbate while passing someone. Within a couple of months I discarded the furtiveness and was showing myself to women I did not know. From there my addiction escalated rapidly.

I began to have other problems. My time was being used to act out, so I was not getting things done. Worse, if I got in my car I could never be sure I would actually make it to where I was going. If the right circumstances presented themselves, I would be off into the trance and would come out of it in a panic because I was supposed to have been somewhere hours ago. I would try to go to school in the morning but not make it there. I would spend the whole day cruising—eight to ten hours at a stretch of masturbating and exhibiting myself when I could. I had to invent stories to explain where I had been. I remember my wife asking me to go to the store to get some milk, as we were to eat supper in a few minutes. I came back three and a half hours later. I don't think I even had the milk. I was now lying to cover up, and I had always been an honest person. I was almost chronically in despair—and the only relief came when I hit the streets again.

I went to see a priest in a nearby town. We talked and prayed. He did everything he possibly could to help me. I am forever indebted to him. But I could not stop. It was from that experience that I first got a glimmering of how much trouble I was in. He kept trying to warn me that I could get arrested for what I was doing. I never thought of myself as a criminal. I meant no harm. His concern was almost shocking to me as I realized the implications of my behavior. That concern was well placed, for in the spring of 1968 a police officer showed up at my door.

The officer informed me that I was to report to a certain police station the next morning. I politely asked what this was about. He turned and looked at me with an expression of disgust. Without a word he got back in his police cruiser. I walked back into the house and the fear was almost unbearable. I was now in trouble with the law, and everything the good father warned me about was coming to pass. I called him up and told him what happened. We sat in silence on the phone together. He said, "You better shave your beard off." In the days of the Vietnam War, bearded students were not well regarded by law enforcement people. So that night I looked at myself in the mirror and decided that was the best thing to do. I also told my wife that I had to go to the police station. She asked me if I had been exposing myself and I admitted that I had. Over the years, even though we divorced eventually, we have remained good friends. I never learned from her how she knew.

After a very restless night, I went to the police station. I sat in the waiting area and a big man approached me and said that he was a detective. He took me into his office. He started by saying that I had been seen exhibiting myself in my car. He wanted to know if that were true. I do not know where the grace came to do this, but I responded by telling him that not only was it true, but I had a problem that was driving me to despair. I told him the whole story. He listened carefully and thought for a few minutes. He told me that I was not to be charged if I went for help, and that he would make sure I got the help I needed. But if I ever got caught again I would be in deep trouble. As we walked out of the office and outside, he put his arm around my shoulders and said, "I'm just glad you're not one of those bearded university weirdos."

The detective was true to his word. He recommended a psychiatrist, and I went to a few sessions in which I told him basically what happened. One day he asked me to list three paintings from the Renaissance that I liked. I wrote the titles of three paintings on a card and handed it to him. He handed me a sheet of paper. On it were the three paintings he guessed I would pick. He had guessed all three. I was amazed. I thought anybody capable of doing that could surely fix me. So I started psychoanalysis. In retrospect, I am not sure that it helped much, even though I found it interesting. It was good to have someone to talk to about all this.

I stopped my street activities primarily out of fear. Those first weeks were unbearably painful. I could not sleep, was irritable and anxious. More than that, there was this pain of longing. I longed to be back out but knew I could not go. Even if I just did a little bit I would not be able to stop. To help myself I bought a different car. I traded my big American car with its large windows and automatic transmission for a small foreign station wagon with a stick shift. The windows were small, the seats were small and hidden, and you had to shift. In short, it made my former activities very difficult. I also had new motivation. We had a new baby son. I wanted to do the best possible thing for my family.

I threw myself into my studies and started to do very well. I received A's in almost all my courses and was awarded a teaching fellowship. I discovered that I loved teaching and motivating students to learn history. My methods got me into some trouble, however. Students were transferring from the classes of my professors into my sections. I remember having my students come dressed as the socialist of their choice and we had a great series of classes. Eventually I was called on the carpet for "cracker-barrel informality" with my students. I toned things down but still loved doing it.

I spent nine months doing nothing but preparing for my doctoral exams that were to be in the spring of 1970. I completed my written exams and went for my oral exam one afternoon in late May. My friends and family were to celebrate with me later. I went into the office to sit with these men, whom I had studied with for almost four years, to hear their verdict. They explained that they were not going to pass me. They thought I was not "conceptual enough" to be an historian. They urged me to consider teaching at a high school level because we needed those too and I apparently had some teaching talent. What I did not know then was that I was the first doctoral student in over forty years who was not allowed to repeat the exams. All I knew was that I had studied for eight years, learned three languages besides English, and had failed. Worse, I had to walk out of that room and face my friends and family. But I also believed that I knew a terrible secret. The reason they failed me, I thought, was because God was doing a final reckoning. He was finally getting me for my sexual behavior. He went two and a half years before letting me know how displeased he was. I went into deep despair. I could not bring myself to tell everyone what I truly believed my failing was about.

Remember now the tension in the spring of 1970. Nixon had invaded Cambodia. There were riots on almost every university campus. The week before my exams there was the incident at Kent State in which four students were killed by the National Guard. Almost every campus became volatile. In those days one of the common themes was how resistant the "establishment" was to creative options. The students that I taught heard what happened in my exams and it fit the model of the repressive state. Here was a creative teacher whom "establishment" professors could not handle. So there was a sit-in, and suddenly I became a cause. And once that started there was no appeal. Nor would any other university have me, because I was a campus radical. The irony was almost too great for a guy who had been absorbed with the seventeenth century, had very little knowledge of Vietnam, and was convinced that he'd been punished for being a sexual freak. I was later to find out that neither the students nor I had it right.

The immediate impact was on my sex addiction. In my distorted thinking, I told myself that all my good behavior did not matter. So why try? I started toying with cruising again, except now I had a car that made it difficult. And I was still scared of being arrested. My wife and I moved back to Minneapolis and I started looking for a new career. I did not know what I wanted to do. It was one of the most stressful times of my life. My parents, my wife, and her parents were all pressuring me to find something, and I was struggling with despair. Then I found a "cure."

I noticed a sign for a massage parlor. I checked it out in the hope that I could expose myself, but got introduced to prostitution. The masseuse did not care that I had no clothes on. In fact, she took that as a sign that I wanted to be sexual. I found that I could attain some of what I got in the street, plus be sexual. It was not as exciting, but I was not going to be arrested. I became a prostitute junkie.

We had sold our home out east, and I was going through the equity we had saved at an unbelievable rate. I could not find a job that I wanted. I finally went to see an industrial psychologist. And again I chose to tell the whole story. The psychologist I saw was very kind. He was another one of those people who helped me change my direction in life. He did a series of tests, which indicated that I actually was not that well suited to be a history professor. The professions that were recommended were counseling psychology, writing, and public speaking. All of which meant I had to go back to school. It was an agonizing moment. To spend all that time doing it all over again seemed simply overwhelming. Furthermore, no university wanted a "campus radical." So I went back to school as an adult special student—meaning I was not accepted into any program. I told a few of my professors my story, and those men, who stood by me over the next decade, helped me get into school again.

Meanwhile the industrial psychologist I was seeing told me he had found a cure for my sexual problem. It was called behavior modification. The doctor he consulted with told him that if I followed through with the treatment the problem would be over. I went to see the doctor, who explained that he did not believe in "talk" therapies, so he would not talk to me much. But if I submitted to treatment I would be free of my compulsive behavior. I remember chasing the doctor down the street in an effort to try to talk to him. True to his word, he refused to engage in conversation. I remember standing there as he drove away, feeling profoundly alone and afraid.

Treatment meant that I was put in a darkened room and technicians attached electrodes to various parts of my body. I was to fantasize exhibiting myself and then I was to raise my hand when I was fully into the fantasy. Then the doctor would administer a strong electric shock. I would do this eight to twelve times a session. The sessions were twice a week for ten weeks. It is without question the most painful thing I have done in my life. I forced myself to go. I forced myself to keep fantasizing and raising my hand. By the end it was extremely difficult to do. Yet I would do anything to get rid of my problem.

The doctor and his staff were thrilled with my efforts. I completed treatment at the end of November. They assured me that I would never be out in the street again. By January I was cruising in my car at night and the old process started again. In retrospect the whole experience had an odd comfort to it. I was very used to the idea of being punished for my behavior. And physical pain simply confirmed what I knew to be true about myself. In short, it replicated the internal system and the family rules I grew up with. I was used to being in pain around my behavior. In fact, I deserved it. And as before, excruciating pain would not stop the call of the streets.

Something did help, though. I found a job that was in keeping with my new career direction. I started working for a church as a youth worker. I found myself immersed in the drug culture of the seventies. Reaching out to runaways and to drug addicts somehow came easy. I knew the streets and how to find the kids. They would say to me, "How do you know about this? You know what we are going to do before we do. And yet you don't use drugs." I do not remember what I said to them, but I do remember that I often said to myself, "I'm just a junkie of a different kind." I knew for sure that helping others was helping me.

My marriage disintegrated, and I became a single parent with two children. I also involved myself in a number of convoluted relationships. I had a tremendously difficult time saying no to women, even when I knew better. At one point I had agreed to spend New Year's Eve with two different women. I could not say no to either. I was in such pain over it that the morning before New Year's Day I pulled out my revolver and laid it on the table. I had just taken a deep breath and said to myself that this was the way out, when the phone rang. It was a minister friend who was sending holiday wishes. He heard my voice and said, "Stay there, do not do anything, I will be there in five minutes." He helped me sort out what I needed to do. Again, someone was there to help me.

By the middle of the 1970s I had gotten a lot better. I had finished my coursework for my doctorate in counseling, I was engaged to be married, and I had a new job as director of a new chemical dependency outpatient program. Yet I felt sexually unsettled. I had done all this therapy but still was unhappy. One night as I was leaving the treatment center I watched the patients come out of their twelve-step meetings. They came out laughing and hugging. The love and care of those people was wonderful to behold. I was one of their therapists and they seemed to be doing better than I was. I sat in my car filled with envy and longing. I made up my mind that night to start a group like that for sex addicts.

Two days later a classmate of mine from college called. He was a therapist who had gotten into trouble because of his sexual behavior. He asked to see me professionally. I said I could not do that since we had a relationship already but that I had an idea I wished to discuss with him. We met at Lake Harriet, a beautiful jewel of a lake in south Minneapolis. As we walked around the lake I told him of this group I wanted to start, based on the Twelve Steps of Alcoholics Anonymous. I asked if he would join me and he said he would. I was so relieved to hear that he was willing. Two days later, a third friend called. He also was a therapist and was having trouble with affairs. I talked with him and he said he would join us as well. None of us had ever been to a twelve-step meeting. We started by meeting in a boathouse—the most secluded place we could find. Each of us took a turn telling our history. We had just finished that when a fourth member joined us. He was also a therapist.

Since more people were coming, we rapidly outgrew the little boathouse. I knew a priest who was a recovering alcoholic. I went to him and asked if we could have a meeting space and if he would show us how to do a twelve-step meeting. He agreed to both. There was a moment when I could see that he was wrestling with the whole concept. He was a big support to us and to this day I am grateful. He coached me how to do it and allowed us to meet in one of the choir rooms. We started early that summer of 1977 and by fall we had a regular meeting in the church on Thursday nights. It felt so good to be with people who had the same problem. There was a joy in the midst of our sad stories. We also felt the need to be with each other more. So we instituted a Monday morning breakfast. That way we would have two times a week to be with each other.

The first major issue that we had to confront as a group was about our professional roles. Of the first ten members, nine were involved in some way with mental health services. The other was a judge. The big problem was that people wanted to refer clients into a group like this, but it would be difficult to have one's own clients in the group. So we decided to start a Wednesday night group to which everyone could refer their clients. That group met in the same choir room. We often wondered what the people of the parish would have done had they known.

Both groups grew dramatically. In the original group we were trying to squeeze over thirty people into a choir room that would comfortably seat twenty. We knew we had to split but could not bear leaving one another. Finally we split and then split again. The Wednesday night group started the splitting process as well. An "intergroup" service committee was formed. Sex Addicts Anonymous was born.

The splitting process actually created problems later. It started with a retreat we did that second year on the weekend before Thanksgiving. We did it as a weekend-long extended meeting. We all cooked and took different responsibilities. Some of us did the sauna and jumping in the water through the ice. We all swam in the pool. There was almost a magic to the weekend. It deepened our bonding and enriched our program. Every year we repeated the retreat with the same result. As the groups split, the competition for the same retreat center became very intense. Every group wanted it on the weekend before Thanksgiving at the same place. And there were some hard feelings. So different groups started looking for other facilities. My learning over the years is that groups that spent weekends together did very well. I have heard this from members in other parts of the country as well. The group has to have a life outside of its regular meeting time.

Our intergroup hired a man named Marv to help us coordinate our services. He had good organizational skills. He also had great recovery and was a compassionate human being. He nurtured the groups until we had fifty of them in the Minneapolis-St. Paul area. Many groups in other parts of the country also depended on his warm, wise advice. He clearly is one of the most loving men I have known. At that time I started doing training workshops on sex addiction. During these workshops people would take me aside to tell me they needed a meeting and that there were no meetings in their area. I would ask them to meet me after the workshop was over. I would show them how to have a meeting and give them the coordinator's number. He would take it from there. If they wanted to do it, he would help them make it happen. We worked like that for a long time.

Then I had a crisis. My second marriage broke up and I was devastated. I found myself a single parent again, only now with four children. The woman I married had been a student of mine. Our relationship started as a tremendous breach of boundaries on my part, and as hard as we both worked, we were not able to overcome those original dynamics. I called Marv, because at that point I did not have a sponsor. I remember sitting on my back steps on a Saturday morning and telling my whole life story. He took me on as his sponsee. Because I was so early in the program, I had never had a sponsor with any real experience. There was no one to show us how it was done then. Here I was, eight years into the program and I was finally getting the benefit of a sponsor who was experienced. It was in the nick of time. Not only was there a divorce and single parenting to face, but my father started to drink after thirty years of sobriety. The stress of that was almost unbearable, and my depression, which I would fight with periodically, became a constant companion. My sponsor saw me through it.

One of the hardest parts was that I felt I should not be having these kinds of problems. After all, I was a trained therapist and one of the early members of the program. I felt deeply ashamed, and my sponsor took the time to be there for me. I remember a speech I was giving over which I was very anxious. My sponsor showed up. As I was about to walk on stage he handed me a small wooden cross, made from the timber of a church in Coventry that had been bombed out in World War II. He had carried that cross to help him with courage. He now gave that to me. He would always pay attention to how I was doing, and expected me to call him regularly. If I did not, when I did talk to him he would go into this routine about how he thought that I had "taken the cure." We would always laugh and I knew that I was gently being reminded of the importance of staying connected. For this program to work, there have to be people who know the whole story—and walk with you all the way.

The best thing I did for myself during that time was not to date or be involved with anyone. I focused on raising children, program work, and doing therapy. I started to understand my behavior as I started to work on early childhood abuse. I found that my exhibitionism was a recapitulation of those early experiences in the "shed." I realized that my inability to say no to women came from my family experiences. Women could intrude on me and I felt that I had no right to say no. This resulted in very convoluted relationships. I took three years before dating. I became self-sufficient and realized that I was okay being alone. The desperation was gone. I found that my profound friendships in SAA became even more durable and valued. When I started to date, my friends watched me like hawks. When I made choices they disagreed with, they let me know. Their opinions were in synch with my children. They all agreed that one woman I dated was a good match. I resisted my friends, my children, and the woman for a number of years. And then came the realization that this was a new frontier. I would have to risk my new-won self-sufficiency and make myself vulnerable to this woman. Now I would have to finally learn how to be true to myself and be in a relationship with her. We started going to a fellowship for couples. I crossed the line and committed myself.

It has been a wonderful marriage. There is no volatility, no ache to be out of it, and no preoccupation about alternatives. I don't think I would have ever gotten there without the help I received. Most importantly, I am grateful that I took the suggestion from my sponsor to take time out so that I could finish the work I needed to do. My greatest learning is that I never stopped finding the program central to my life. It always seemed to offer what I needed, long after sobriety stopped being the main challenge.

There were other challenges. I did three complete and thorough Fourth and Fifth Steps. Each taught me important lessons, and each was a very different experience. The steps are always there to help us in our process. I have friends who stopped going to meetings and moved on to what they thought were other forms of personal growth. A couple of them have had relapses, which were very costly to them. What I have found for myself is that to live the discipline of a twelve-step way of life is an enduring challenge that keeps on giving back. There is a saying in SAA that recovery does not mean that you stop having problems. Rather, you get to have problems that are not sexual ones.

2.

A PHONE CALL SAVED HER LIFE

In retrospect, what I experienced classifies as a miracle. At the time I thought I was merely having a bad day.

I was restless, lonely, thirsting for escape. I had phoned seven different people from my twelve-step list but contacted none of them. Couldn't that effort count as "going to any length to stay sober"? Hadn't I earned a slip?

The world outside of me was blissful. However, inside of me a storm brewed. Rage thundered and lightning flashed in arcs of fear. Outwardly my face registered nothing; inwardly, sadness fell in torrents. What at the time I believed to be a breaking apart, I would subsequently come to see as a breaking through. The lightning jolts of terror I registered then, I would come to understand as Higher Power surges shocking my heart back to life.

In retrospect it was the smallest choice, the choice to attempt one more number on that list, that shifted the course of my life in the right direction. On that eighth call I reached someone; more importantly, I reached out to someone. Amazingly, the person I contacted was uniquely qualified to help me with a problem more primary and life-threatening than my alcoholism; he was to help me with a problem I then did not know I had. No bells. No whistles. No aura of bright light. I was at the pivotal point in my life, completely blind to signs of Grace operating.

On the eighth call I got an answer. The last one I expected to be home was a friend whom I will call R. I imagined he would be boating, sailing, water-skiing, fishing, or luxuriating at his "estate." But he was home. He was free. We met at a Vietnamese restaurant in Minneapolis. Over egg rolls, I outlined for him what I saw as THE problem: there was something wrong with me. Over fried rice, R. dispensed the typical program support. His actual advice at dinner has not stayed in my memory. Rather, what I remember vividly is that the mere presence of a friend in recovery was help enough. I would, I believed, always be "faulty," but I would, because of R.'s presence, stay sober, if only for that night. That was all I expected from our encounter. I would be given much more.

R. suggested that we take a walk around Lake Harriet. We chatted while we walked and, eventually, he asked me, "So what's going on in the rest of your life?"

The ordinary instinct: to deflect the question. A second life-changing event: I told him how it actually was.

How was it? I led a double life. Helping professional by day, crazy woman by night. At the time I had eight sexual partners. That number was typical. My sex life was a chess game played at high speed. One of my partners at the time was paying me for sexual favors. He was not the first to pay me for sex. The real prostitution taking place, however, was the prostitution of my integrity. The real "pimp" was my sexual compulsion. My private life belied the person I believed myself to be. I was a decent person living an indecent life. I felt trapped in a labyrinth of secrets and desolation. I related these facts to R. We completed our round of the lake. As we approached the parking lot, he asked if I would go around the lake with him again. This time he told me how it was with him. His story paralleled mine but included an important difference. He told me of a small group, newly formed, of men supporting each other in recovering from what he called sex addiction. This group's wisdom and support were offering him a map out of his own addictive labyrinth.

R.'s story moved me. The moon cast our shadows before us: twin brother and sister, hands held, with affection forged by secrets shared and by shared secrets. My life was transformed from that point on.

He got back to me the next week. A woman joining the group of twelve men was an "issue" with which the group felt unready to deal. I was to wait until more women could get the word.

I waited four months.

I experienced both joy and hope from knowing that the sexual chaos of my life had a name and that the name held in it the potential for recovery. I knew that sexual addiction was a humane description of what I was experiencing. In 1980 the women's movement was still in preschool. Its message had not permeated into the popular culture. In society, the men with whom I had sex would be considered, at worst, Lotharios or Don Juans. The terms were naughty but normal enough, perhaps even "cute." Just one of the boys. As their partner, for the same behavior, I would have been called a whore or a nymphomaniac, these terms implying hopeless degeneracy. To other women I would be considered a pariah. Sex addiction equalizes those afflicted. It is a metaphor for hope: one works a program and with others' assistance is helped out of the quicksand.

While I awaited the formation of a women's group, I found that I had no sense of what sexual sanity looked like. I balked at finding out. I began to drink again, losing a three-year period of sobriety.

R. called to tell me that three more women had been found who wanted an SAA group. He and one other man from his group met with the three women and me. The men told us how their group ran, how they handled newcomers, how they dealt with confidentiality, etc. Then they left. We were on our own.

I eyed the women at the table. One woman had traveled from another state, a four-hour drive. A second was doubtful that she belonged; the third worked in a factory and regularly had sex at the workplace with different coworkers. I, the fourth, was a drinking alcoholic.

Within a month, the group was down to one other woman and me. We still met. I sobered up. By spring we were eight women strong. Two of those original eight women became, and remain, my best friends.

That spring of 1981, SAA had reached the point of needing an intergroup to coordinate service work and deal with issues of policy and ethics. At the first intergroup meetings there were five members: one from each of the men's groups, one from each of the two co-addict groups, and me. Things were beginning to coalesce. How was it possible that SAA would grow by the tens of thousands to become the international organization that it is now? What God had bestowed to Bill W. and Dr. Bob in 1935 was a gift that kept on giving. Such a legacy!

For me, beginning in a women's group was a godsend. Being in a same-gender group stabilized me in the adjustment phase of my early recovery. I would not be alone in this belief. As a woman with experiences of child sexual abuse and rape, I had a fear then of perpetrators, even recovering perpetrators. I also feared seducing or being seduced. Any of these could have caused me to flee. Starting in a women's group not only helped me to avoid a negative situation, but also created a positive opportunity. In the women's group I got a chance to see that my own brand of junkie male chauvinism amplified my addiction. Up to that point I valued men at the expense not only of myself but also of other women. Other women were either the competition or the condemners.

In my first years of SAA, my sisters, all peers, strove together to transform the chaos of each of our lives and reestablish integrity. From them I realized that honest sharing, with no need for sexual barter, was the prerequisite for intimacy and committed love.

Getting into SAA was not all that easy. The stigma of being identified as a sex addict could keep prospective members from seeking a group. Those desperate or courageous enough to seek out a program often confronted barriers designed to protect present members. For its first three years the women's group met in private homes.

The growth, stability and cohesiveness of the women's group depended on the commitment of present members to the newcomers. We were exquisitely sensitive to a woman's special needs as she was introduced to SAA.

Early on, group wisdom made clear to us that compassionate handling of the initial contact was crucial. Whether or not a woman came to a meeting and whether or not she stayed seemed to rest on her impression of the first women she met. For women the question of "who" is extending a hand usually supersedes the "what," "how," or "where" of the task undertaken. Careful guidance of the beginner made the women's group viable. Two members met with the newcomer and shared how it used to be, what happened, and how it was improving now. The women's group was distinctive in what followed that initial contact. The two members accompanied the woman to her first meeting and volunteered to be her temporary sponsors for the first six weeks. More importantly, each of the sponsors used those early weeks to teach the new member how to use sponsorship. Membership in other twelve-step fellowships did not necessarily mean that a woman knew how to use a sponsor, especially in dealing with sex addiction. With the newcomer's approval, her sponsor would call and check on how things were going until the new one felt comfortable about calling her sponsor as needed.

This one-to-one connection created a sense of trust for the new member that was a prerequisite for facing and sharing her First Step. The friendships she formed would keep her coming back. Coming back exposed her to the use of the tools and the steps of the program. Employing the tools and the steps led her to abstinence. Her abstinence sustained her in connectedness with other recovering addicts. That connectedness provided a safe haven in times of personal crisis for her. In gratitude she could then reach out and help to carry the message.

Through my intergroup contacts with men in SAA, and later in mixed group meetings, I learned that brotherly support looked different from sisterly support and that both worked. The men showed me how to confront my addiction head-on and how to be more forthright with the women I sponsored. The women's group taught their brothers about gentleness. Gentleness was an alternative to addiction; it was also a method to re-enter the program following a relapse.

Energy and synergy flowed throughout the Twin Cities Intergroup of SAA in the early 1980s. Men and women members created a viable support system to reach addicts in other cities. In the early years, I handled most of the out-of-town contacts from women. Some needed help in establishing a group in their community. Others needed to find a therapist in their community with an understanding of sexual addiction. Others, more isolated, worked the program through other fellowships, but needed an SAA sponsor to deal with the specific crises and "secrets" inappropriate to share at those twelve-step meetings. On one occasion I had a long-distance phone call from Los Angeles during which I listened to a woman's Fifth Step.

In 1983, SAA was one thousand strong (about one third women), large enough for us to employ a full-time staff person. He was a wonderful man, a brother in recovery, with superior administrative skills. Maybe his was the first SAA voice you heard. Subsequently the organization blossomed. Literature committees expanded. Books and pamphlets were published. Speaker meetings happened. Group retreats were organized. A national directory of meetings emerged. Handbooks were written on how to start a meeting in your own community. Permanent communications were established among various regions' intergroups. National conferences were held. The word was out.

SAA's first formal contact with the media had occurred in 1982. From then onward we relied on the Twelve Traditions, just as AA had always done. Anonymity was reverenced by us and respected by the media. I participated in several TV, radio, and magazine interviews on behalf of the women in the program. My story became a means of reaching others. Thus the pain and humiliation of my acting-out days became transformed into something meaningful and life-enhancing through the alchemy of recovery.

During one of my TV interviews, I appeared with a psychiatrist who gave the best description of sexual addiction I've heard. He said that sex was like swimming. An addict sees others enjoying it, dives in at the deep end, nearly drowns, drags himself out and dives in yet again, with the scenario repeating itself over and over. He observed that addicts would never think to look for the shallow end, let alone take lessons.

In early 1987 a few of us appeared on a network TV talk show. I attended a small SAA meeting in the city that same evening. A man entered the room and related that having seen the show that afternoon, he had decided that SAA was exactly the group he needed. At that moment I had an uncanny sense of being of use to my Higher Power, rather than the other way around. It was a watershed year for SAA. The show received over a thousand letters the next week, responding favorably. This represented more correspondence than they had had from any previous broadcast. The Twin Cities Intergroup was deluged with calls. In 1989, I was a member of a research team on sex addiction, collecting data from over one thousand individuals from around the country. Part of my duties was to conduct extensive personal interviews with 150 of these individuals. This proved to be a singular experience and stands out as the most gratifying work that I've ever done.

My participation in this project taught me again and again that "all is one." Not only does unity exist among all the different faces of addiction, but there is also an integrity existing within each addict. The moon has a dark side as well as a bright, but is still one moon.

The longer I'm in recovery, the more clearly I see through my delusion about being unique. Addiction is only one facet of being human. It merely makes me special like everyone else. SAA is just a safe place to find this out and to learn to live a better way. In SAA I can also work on increasing my tolerance for joy.

So what has twenty years of SAA brought me? My proudest achievement from my program is the claim to a normal life. Mine is no longer the stuff of soap operas or X-rated movies. The program takes me beyond personal limitations into frontiers of creative development and deep-rooted friendship. From the women in SAA's early years I learned new skills of intimacy, and recovered the old value of my integrity. The group as a whole helped me out of my sexual quagmire. I came to define my abstinence as sexual contact limited to relationships with men that I share a deep intimacy with, and to whom I can commit myself. I abide by that now.

From the major miracle of recovery so many minor miracles arise, like the surprising bud-like burst of color blossoming within a fireworks bouquet. I had one recently. I know a man to whom I am strongly attracted. Around him I feel trust, intellectual challenge, joy. He is not available. The miracle: I do not manipulate the situation but honor him and honor what I know to be my values. "Not available" are the operative words that dictate my conduct. That's abstinence. Trust in my (and his) integrity allows me to enjoy the activities we work on together.

That's recovery. Several months after meeting him, I shared with him the low points of my life. He asked me, "When did you first feel that things were turning around for you?" I have no hesitation in stating when that moment was: that bright August day when I decided to call the eighth person on my list. In retrospect I have no hesitation in knowing that that was THE golden moment. At the time, though, I thought I was just having a bad day.

3.

BECOMING WHOLE

I am the person who proposed the "three-second rule." This is the rule that if you stare at the object of your addiction for more than three seconds, you endanger your sobriety. Three seconds was right for me, and I find it comforting that three seconds has proved right for others.

A professor, I was turned in by one of my graduate students for propositioning her in 1978. For two years I lived in horror because of the shame I felt. Then a kind colleague told me about a group she had heard of, and I was interviewed by a member. I "passed" and was then passed by the group. We were very secret then, and I was overjoyed to be called by someone else I knew who was already in the group. I went to my first meeting, and I had gotten to the right place, but at the wrong time. I sat in a church parking lot for an hour. Then group members began to appear. When I recognized the person who had called me, I got out of my car and said hello. The last two years had been endless, and that hour I waited seemed endless too.

I was at the end of my rope. I was suicidal with shame. My acting-out behavior had been serial affairs while I was married. Given that all the affairs had been with graduate students, I knew that the word was out about me. I did not kill myself, because I had two children whom I loved dearly, but sometimes that did not seem enough of a reason.

My mother had sexually abused me until I was eleven. I had called a halt to the abuse, but felt permanently damaged. The abuse must have started in my infancy but I had no memories of the early abuse, only that I felt different, enclosed in a glass bubble that had separated me from other people ever since I could remember. I drifted, rather than plotting my life, because everything seemed artificial in the world. I saw the world through the screen of my abuse.

I was fairly good at maintaining a façade. I was a high school athlete and was accepted by an Ivy League college. I was sexually active with a fifteen-year-old girl when I was fourteen. It was the era of going steady, and we went steady, always sexually active, until we graduated from high school. I was never really intimate in the relationship, and I broke up with her when each of us went to college.

I had a series of sexual encounters with a number of women in college. It was what I knew how to do. I went into the military after graduation. The military, in its wisdom, put me in signals intelligence—a role I was suited for because of my disinterest in anything real and my interest in the formal interactions between individuals. While I was in the service I felt a freedom I had not felt before, and I believed I could overcome my past. I married an extraordinarily beautiful woman. I was twenty-three and she was nineteen. She was a foreign national and I immediately lost all of my security clearances. It didn't matter. I left the service soon after being married. I returned to school, this time to graduate school. I earned a Ph.D. at another Ivy League school and joined the staff at the university where I made my career. At first I was the soul of enthusiasm and did well, being promoted quickly. Then I returned to what seemed to be my real self, a self I had never lost. The center of that self was self-hate. I began a pattern of serial affairs. I let my work slip. I was passed over when I applied for administrative jobs.

Increasingly my only solace was the mistaken belief that I was beating the system. Flirting and sexualizing were the amusements that kept me going. I had no sense of the power I abused in acting out with graduate students. I felt like a child and could not see that I was abusing my academic children. Now I say to people that if you think you are beating the system, you misunderstand the nature of the system. It is not in the nature of systems to be beaten.

I joined the SAA program full of anger at being turned in and at having to do something about my shame. I was never going to have any fun again.

My first group was a powerful one. It was the very first SAA group, and we invented some things as we went along. When a group member would give an inspired step talk, we would smile and say, "The spirit moves." I had a sense that the group was right for me. But I had a terrible time with the first three steps. I solved that problem by saying that I had messed up my own life and that admitting powerlessness, coming to believe, and turning over my will certainly couldn't be worse than what I had tried to do on my own. I came to trust the group.

I even had intimations of spirituality, such as driving alone in my car, looking for a radio station I could stand, and discovering that I could listen to an intelligent sermon without immediately spinning the dial. It made me smile.

I was encouraged to do a Fourth and Fifth Step by my sponsor and the group. I plunged into the Fourth Step and then, in something of a panic, called the minister whom I had chosen to hear my Fifth Step. I told him that I already had forty-seven handwritten legal-size pages and was afraid I'd never be ready for the Fifth Step. He was a good man. He told me to use a certain pamphlet that only gave a little space to write each response, and to limit myself to that space.

Doing my Fifth Step was a deep emotional experience for me. I cried at length for the first time in forty years. Now I cry a lot, mostly about what I'm reading or what I hear in meetings. I tell people that I'm just making up for lost time.

The Fifth Step allowed me to go back and do the first three steps in a better way. I was opened up, and for me that was the secret of spirituality. I did the Sixth and Seventh Steps with the help of retreats sponsored by the group. I did the Eighth Step and acted upon it in the Ninth Step. For eight years I did a daily moral inventory. I joined five other group members to study meditation with a Zen priest, meeting with him weekly for meditation and lectures. I said to him early in that year and a half we spent together that I had been doing baby meditation but that I could recognize that this was big time. He laughed and told others what I had said.

I stopped meeting with the priest when he suggested that he had done what he could without having us move toward conversion. By that time I had become a believing Christian thanks to a group member who introduced me to the writings of some modern Christian mystics. I parted from the priest affectionately and he gave me his cup with a Zen inscription on it.

I am still aware of my flaws. I have to tell my story and do the steps over again to approximate the man I want to be. I get so much out of meetings. The members of my second group are often inspired.

But here is the strange part. Because of the program and my spiritual practices, I began to feel almost a whole man. I have come to enjoy the company of men. I now think that my military experience, from which I always fled before, was the most important thing I ever did. Like my father, I plan to be buried with the flag and my medals. We both had "distinguished" civilian careers (yes, I resurrected mine) and yet now it is the soldiering and my family that seem the most important things. I am reintegrated into society as a man. My second wife regards me as I regard myself, complex and somewhat difficult, but basically a good man. I love my children and my grandchildren. They love me.

Strange that with the raw material I brought to the program I should feel so whole. That is the gift of the program, available to all.

4.

MAKING A CHOICE

For as long as I can remember, I knew I was "different." It took years to understand that the difference was the fact that I was gay. Being a male attracted to other males, and growing up in the 1950s and 60s, left me with no positive role models. My religion told me homosexuality was wrong, so I prayed. I had people lay hands on me, speak in tongues over me, and attempt a host of other "cures." The pain, loneliness, and feelings of inadequacy were unbearable. I tried almost everything to ease the pain. I even tried marrying a woman, thinking that would redirect and satisfy my sexual desires.

During my marriage, I set a pattern of being in a relationship while acting out anonymously. Although I tried to stop acting on my feelings, I could not sustain a period of sobriety longer than three months. I always felt terrible afterward and vowed to myself that I would never do that again. I was never able to keep that vow. The guilt, loneliness, anger, isolation, and fear just escalated. After six years of marriage I was acting out multiple times daily. I thought this was because I was oversexed, or just needed to be with a man instead of a woman. I divorced my wife without any explanation, and certainly did not give her any choice in the matter.

I had several different relationships after my divorce, all very short term, lasting only a few days or weeks. Then I began a relationship with a man who was very much like my ex-wife. During our relationship I began acting out again. I justified it because he was not able to satisfy me sexually. No matter how much I rationalized my actions I still felt guilty and afraid of being caught. After a year and a half I ended that relationship, blaming my partner for not meeting my sexual and emotional needs.

After several months on my own with no relationship, and acting out without guilt, I met a new partner. I began the relationship with a lot of fear that I would repeat my pattern of being with someone while still acting out anonymously. This relationship has been through much turmoil, but has lasted fourteen and a half years and is stronger today than ever. The first ten years were a lot like my other relationships—trying not to act out. The feelings of guilt, isolation, loneliness, and fear of being found out were overwhelming to me. I was angry that I couldn't control my behavior and confused by why I was still acting out, when I had what I wanted at home. I certainly did not understand addiction or powerlessness, so I blamed my partner. I thought he must be the reason I wanted to act out. He was not as experienced sexually as I, so he could not satisfy me. If he would just reach out emotionally, I would not have to seek out other sexual partners. I felt that my acting-out partners would surely know what I needed, and yes—the next one would save me!

In the first ten years of this relationship I was stopped by police officers twice for having sex in a public place. These were humiliating events, but not as bad as when I was arrested for the same behavior. (Ironically, I was not actually having sex when I was arrested—we were only talking about it.) My partner was aware of this arrest and stood by me. I believe I somehow made it his fault so I did not have to take responsibility for my actions. I did appreciate his support and yet I still could not stop acting out.

Word games were how I survived when talking to my partner. If he asked me if I were being monogamous I would always throw the question back to him. "Why do you ask? What are you trying to project on to me?" I would never answer the question, but I would create enough of a smoke screen that he would stop asking. I never accepted responsibility for my behavior. There was always someone or something that caused me to act out. I justified acting out to myself and lashed out with anger, self-pride, and condemnation to anyone who questioned me. My acting out became progressively more dangerous and time-consuming. Virtually all my waking hours were taken up with planning how I could get away and when I could act out again. I was on a spinning wheel and could not stop—my life was truly out of control. I was miserable, but I had to keep numbing the pain. Sex was my drug of choice. I did not want to use alcohol or drugs and lose control of my senses. So I felt totally in control by having sex. I did not have a clue how powerless I was.

Then it happened. I hit bottom. One Sunday evening in May of 1994, I was driving home after taking my son back to his mother's. I was feeling a lot of pain, loneliness and guilt, so I stopped by a familiar acting-out spot to ease the hurt. After all, my partner was at church and would never know. During my acting out the other man pulled a razor or a knife, I'm not sure which, and sliced my throat open. He left me to die, bleeding on the restroom floor. I was able to stagger to my car and drive myself to the local emergency room. (Talk about a Higher Power doing for me what I could not do for myself!) In the emergency room I made up a story about what happened because I could not tell anyone the truth. I did not want to take any responsibility for this situation. After all, I was the victim here. I felt I was completely innocent. Although the police did not believe my story, I stuck to it. My partner thought it sounded a little bizarre but did not question me further. It was my counselor a few days later who confronted me after I told her my story, and asked me what really happened. I broke down and told her the truth. She helped me come clean to my partner about my acting out. I was able to admit I needed help and was directed to SAA.

My partner stood by me to see what I would do. Was he being supportive or just too shocked to leave? I didn't care; I needed recovery for me. I couldn't predict if my relationship would last or not—ten years is a long time to deceive someone and be forgiven. But I understood that I was powerless and needed SAA recovery, regardless of anyone or anything else in my life. What a relief not to have to carry around that secret anymore. Everything was out in the open and I did not have to hide or feel guilty. It was a strange and wonderful freedom.

My life is much different in recovery. I have found a satisfaction in my relationship with my partner that I never thought I could find. We talk about everything now. We discuss feelings and what we each think we need in order to feel fulfilled. I have found that although rigorous honesty is not always easy, it is the key to my sobriety. It has taken a lot of work to learn to be honest with myself—I lied to myself for years. Honesty with my partner takes work as well, but certainly pays off in the long run, as we are able to understand each other and share when something is not right.

I have learned that recovery is a choice and that I can make that choice each day. I know I must take responsibility for my choices, and that this requires honesty and a daily inventory. I can choose to dwell on addictive thoughts and images or I can choose to focus on recovery. I have discovered that I am not the center of the universe. All of life and other people's actions are not related to my sexual desires.

Working a recovery program is not easy. It takes continuous work, and I have found that what worked for me last month may not work this month. People don't always say or do what I want them to, but only I am responsible for my actions and reactions. I can choose what is right for me and my recovery, not falling back into old behaviors. For me, attending meetings on a regular basis, doing service work for the group, helping with twelfth-step calls, and supporting other group members with understanding and feedback are all parts of working the program.

My partner got into recovery about a year after I did. That was a scary time because I thought he would "get healthy" and leave me. What I have found is that as we grow in recovery we are much better at communicating our needs and feelings. We can support each other without trying to work each other's program. Now we can spot old behaviors and call each other on them. I am able to laugh at myself now when I am trying to manipulate my partner into taking responsibility for my actions, and he stops me to let me know that it is not his issue. Laughing at myself is essential to my recovery.

I now have four and a half years of sobriety from bottom-line behaviors. I have a much stronger relationship with my partner. I am honest with him and have found the intimacy and love I had been searching for. It was not "the next one" that saved me—it was recovery! I am grateful to my Higher Power for protecting me through my bottoming out so that I could truly live. I have found peace. History does not have to repeat itself in my life. I have choices!

5.

HER DREAMS ARE COMING TRUE

I am a woman committed to health. I am a lesbian. I am a recovering sex addict. When I look at my life today—its balance and the many dreams that are coming true—it is hard to believe that there was a time when I did not want to live. I felt then that there was no place on earth for me where I could be fully the person I am and where I could be at peace with myself.

I grew up a very sensitive child, filled with fear, and was encouraged to be excessively dependent on my parents. I was touched in inappropriate ways and was not given permission to have my own emotional or physical space. I was invaded in the context of love and care. My free and defiant spirit, though misdirected for many years, has been a catalyst for much searching and wholeness in my life. Although I still struggle with the depth and details of incest in my family, I am coming to take my reality more and more seriously.

It has been very difficult for me to accept myself as a lesbian and to embrace my sexuality as a beautiful part of myself. For years I "tried" to be heterosexual. It was as though I wanted assurance that I was attractive to men and that I fit as a woman in this society. Yet most of my fantasies and attractions involved women.

My early life as a lesbian was tormented with alcohol and other drug abuse, sex with a series of partners, and an intense dependency on sexual relationships. I was obsessed with whomever I was currently involved with, and I had great difficulty concentrating on the other parts of my life. I knew inside myself that I was desperately seeking from sexual partners the stability and meaning I needed to find within myself, yet I could not face my emptiness. I was incapable of true intimacy with others because I was running from any kind of intimacy with myself, my feelings, and my needs. My life felt like a continual drama where I confused instant intensity in a relationship with the intimacy I longed for. Although I appeared very successful in many parts of my life, my inward desperation was unbearable. I sought relationship after relationship, and neglected friendships, family, and many of the activities I loved most. Also, I used masturbation as a way to comfort my loneliness, soothe my fears, diffuse my anger, and simply "feel better."

Thirteen years ago I began my recovery from alcoholism and a long journey of therapy, through which I discovered the depth of my sexual addiction. My sobriety from alcohol was a first step toward health; yet in spite of several years of recovery and much therapy, I continued to endure an inner desperation and an inability for healthy sexual intimacy. My values spoke of a desire for a lifelong commitment to one partner: a relationship equal in respect, power, and love, and a bond that would nurture the many special parts of me. I could not begin to know the reality of this vision until I took responsibility for my sexual addiction and began working the SAA program. That was six and a half years ago.

As I have maintained my commitment to recovery, to dealing with the many issues from my family of origin, and to nurturing my spirituality, I have become capable of and gifted with a committed relationship. When my partner and I met seven and a half years ago, my focus was on bettering my own life, not on finding a partner.

My spiritual growth has been at the heart of much of my healing. I have struggled with my sense of God. A profound turning point in my recovery happened when I faced and embraced the pain of the emptiness I felt inside, which I had tried to fill with so many fixes. It began when my partner decided to take a few months' space from me soon after I began in SAA. I had been resisting some of my therapy work and was becoming overly dependent on her. She decided that she needed to separate from me for a while to take care of herself. Although this time left me in deep despair, I see it now as a crucial part of my recovery.

I had to face myself and my desperation in a deeper way than ever before. I remember actual physical pain in my abdomen as I cried and hugged myself, choosing to not avoid this pain. I had a sense that God was in there somewhere and also surrounding me as I cried. And I somehow moved through it.

I continue to struggle with trusting the wisdom and safety of this God spirit. To look within and embrace the many parts (sometimes fragments) of myself rather than looking for my definition in others has been an important process. I know that I am on track spiritually when I am able to be honest with myself and be present both with my feelings and with the moment at hand, no matter what it is. At these times my thoughts toward myself are like those of a loving friend.

When I'm spiritually uncentered, I don't want to slow down or be alone. I am internally compulsive and out of touch with my senses and feelings. Life seems continually overwhelming.

In seeking to become a whole person, I have been given the opportunity to grow in relationship with my partner, who is committed also to her recovery. The healing that has occurred in my sexuality is miraculous. My sexuality is integrated into my entire being, not simply into my genitals. I have developed appropriate emotional and physical boundaries. For example, I can acknowledge myself as a sexual person more often, having attractions to others without being manipulative, flirtatious, or seductive. I have learned to get to know people slowly rather than quickly and intensely. I am able to express myself sexually with my partner in a variety of ways, not only by making love. I do not use sex as a way to fix my feelings or get reassurance as a person or a partner. Instead, my expressions of sexuality come from my fullness as an emotional, physical, and spiritual person. A mutual respect, equality, and pure closeness happens. This includes times when my partner needs her own physical space and does not want to be touched.

Also, I do not expect sex always to be a "perfect, passionate experience." It is about the overflowing of my love for her, for myself, and for life, a celebration of our growing love and of my humanity. My sexuality enhances the rest of my life—it does not leave me in shame, secrecy, or pain as it once did.

I am not trying to say that my life is perfect or that my relationship is always smooth. I am saying that my tools are working. I seek love and support from a variety of people as well as myself, and I am growing into many of my dreams. Success is still difficult to accept, but I'm getting better at that too. Through my own work and my God's blessings, I am no longer sabotaging my life or my sexuality.

6.

A NEW WAY OF LIFE

I have always had a strong fascination with nudity and sex. I have memories of sexually charged incidents that go back to my preschool days. My obsession has been centered around voyeurism and fantasy. I have never gone as far as looking into people's windows, but I have always been alert to any voyeuristic opportunities in daily life.

As a child I never was able to fit in with my peers, so I isolated myself physically and socially from them. I created a complex fantasy world in which I was respected and looked up to for my wisdom and abilities. I created characters and scenarios that were developed and replayed for months on end. There was always a component of nudity and sexual play in these fantasies. When I discovered masturbation, my fantasy world became even more sexualized and I masturbated almost daily. At the same time I was very shy and reserved around girls.

About the time I entered high school my life took a significant turn as I got involved in church and became a Christian. I was attracted to all that Christ stands for and the life lived by many of the people in the church. They had something I desperately wanted. I became very active in the church, attended Bible college, and entered the Christian ministry.

All the while my fantasy life and masturbation were continuing. I did have some inner boundaries that saved me from the worst that my disease could have produced. I made a commitment to refrain from sexual intercourse outside of marriage, to set firm boundaries on sexual behavior I would engage in outside of marriage, and to consciously avoid behaviors that would reveal my preoccupation with sex. I would not purchase pornography, but whenever I had the opportunity to view it, I would.

My strategy worked pretty well. I was a virgin when I got married. I have been faithful to my wife. I have raised two daughters in a sexually safe environment. I have avoided any close encounters of the sexual kind outside of my marriage. I think I have a good reputation in my church and community.

However, over the years I brought erotic materials into our marriage. Occasionally I would buy a pornographic magazine. There was a cycle where I would collect these materials and then get rid of them, have a more or less extended period where I wouldn't use pornography, then I would get more, and go through the cycle again.

In 1998 I discovered how to access pornography on the internet, and my addiction took hold of me. In a very short time it affected our sex life, and my wife asked me if I was using pornography on the computer. I confessed, and went through over a year of reading, counseling, and seeking accountability with some close friends. In January and February of 1999 I had two relapses and confessed when questioned by my wife again—I had encouraged her to ask about how I was doing.

In the introspection that followed I realized several things: 1.) I was addicted to sex and I was powerless to control viewing pornography if given the opportunity to do so. 2.) I enjoyed the rush the pornography gave me and I did not want to give it up. 3.) My addiction to pornography on the internet was progressing, and would continue to progress until it would impact my life and the lives of others in devastating ways. 4.) I would lose the things I valued most if I did not find a way to change the direction in which I was heading. 5.) All of my knowledge, all the counseling, all of my spirituality (as it had developed to that point), and the awareness of all that I had to lose, still could not keep me from acting out if I remained in isolation. 6.) I couldn't promise that I would remain free of pornography, but I thought I could make a commitment to working a twelve-step program. 7.) The most painful realization was that I was a hypocrite, a play actor, someone who appeared one way to most people and who was something else on the inside. That really rocked me because I had consciously worked very hard at being a person of integrity.

When I realized how I had been living a lie, even to myself, I felt devastated. I immediately shared what was going on with one of the elders of my church and with three of my fellow ministers who were long-time friends and prayer partners. I questioned whether I should resign from the ministry. I was encouraged to continue and work for recovery.

I called the number for Sex Addicts Anonymous. God surely has a sense of humor. In my first meeting was a young man whose parents are members of my church. After the meeting he approached me, welcomed me, and assured me that my anonymity was safe with him. That was a wonderful gift!

Since entering the program I have not violated my inner-circle boundaries of using pornography and masturbating to pornography, but that is only the beginning of how things have changed for me. I have a group where I can talk openly and without shame about my addiction and learn from others who suffer from the same affliction.

My wife is the most loving and supportive friend in my life, but I can not and should not depend upon her to provide the kind of accountability and impartial feedback that I need. My SAA friends help me to not only keep my inner-circle boundaries, but to understand and learn from middle-circle issues as well. When someone talks about their experience, strength, and hope around issues that are important to me, I learn a lot about myself and how to respond to similar situations. In the group I know that if I am having a hard time with something, or even if I have a relapse, there will be no relational fall-out. All I will hear is, "Keep coming back!"

Before I got to SAA, I made many efforts to find support and accountability in battling my sexual obsession. I attempted to practice the spiritual disciplines of my religion in a variety of different formats and different times. I mentioned my obsession with sex in private counseling on more than one occasion, only to have the subject overlooked. (I grant that I may not have mentioned it as strongly as I thought.) I was part of a prayer group for over ten years in which I shared my struggle with pornography. They were loving and supportive, but did not seem to understand how pervasive it was for me. They seldom brought it up and I felt uncomfortable bringing it up. The result was that I could let the matter slide. I read numerous books on character development and sexual issues, but increased knowledge was no help against the desire to act out.

This program is the only place I have where there is a single-minded emphasis on gaining freedom from sexual addiction. That is what I needed all along.

Not only have I remained free of my acting-out behavior, but I have greatly improved in the area of my middle-circle behaviors. My fantasy life has been strongly curtailed. I consciously avoid surfing the TV for sexually stimulating programs, and I have renewed my commitment to not get cable or satellite TV. I seldom scan department store ads for lingerie advertisements. These and other similar behaviors have been dramatically reduced because of the constant reminders and helpful ideas that I receive in the program. I never had that kind of focused support before.

Another gift of the program is the emphasis on developing a new way of life through a spiritual awakening. I am encouraged to focus, not so much upon not acting out, or even avoiding middle-circle behaviors, as on practicing a new way of living that brings wholeness and integrity to everything I do.

I am thankful for the structure of the Twelve Steps and the Twelve Traditions that make this a safe place for all of us. A challenging place to be sure, but a safe place. I appreciate the discipline of Tradition Ten: SAA has no opinion on outside issues; hence our name ought never be drawn into public controversy. The principles of the program remind me to talk about my own stuff and listen as others share their experiences. It is freeing and healthy to focus on my own story and my own recovery, in the knowledge that I can help others only to the extent that I gain what they might want. And I am working to take that same attitude into other areas of my life as well.

7.

NO NEED TO FIGURE IT OUT

I could not stop acting out in ways that put me at risk for disease, arrest, and bodily harm. I knew in my heart and soul that what I was doing was self-injurious and toxic to the soul. I wasn't so concerned with it being morally wrong, although I wasn't proud of it, but I could sense the destruction and injury I was inflicting on my own spirit. Still, I simply couldn't stop doing it. I saw this as hard evidence that I was a defective, weak, and probably worthless human being.

I remember a night I spent trying to chase down a sexual massage. My "regular" was no longer in business, but her friend had taken over. After obsessing about it all day, I arrived and found she had given me the wrong address. Wounded and desperate, I scoured the internet for an alternative. Within an hour I found myself in a dark and dingy apartment, greeted by a woman with an eerie smile. She offered me an "aperitif," and I took a small sip of it. I nearly passed out. I'm certain she was trying to sedate me and take my money. I fled from there. But I wasn't finished. After more searching on the internet and frantic calling, I ended up in a seedy side street, ringing the doorbell of a person who never answered. There I stood at midnight, alone on the street, overwhelmed with futility and self-loathing.

That was a bottom of sorts, and I tried to "get a handle" on my acting out, yet continued to do so sporadically, in search of the elation, the "high." The persistence of that illusion was astonishing. The urge would often take over when something positive was happening in my life: the prospect of a new job, a new girlfriend, a new direction. It had reached the point, after ten years of such behavior, where acting out wasn't working for me like it used to. I craved real intimacy, real human contact, real risk, but had no idea how to get it. Much as I prized my own intellect, I found I couldn't think my way out. I wanted to stop spending so much money, wanted to stop hating myself and feeling so alone.

Not only did I act out in massage parlors, but I also used phone sex, the internet, pornography, and even occasional visits to S&M parlors, where I would pay women to beat and humiliate me. That seemed to be the best solution when my spirits were low and I needed a "lift": soul-crushing visits to shadowy places where I received the opposite of love and affection. I had somehow become attracted to dark, hostile attention (which after all, was better than none), and had sexualized my yearnings for intimacy and human connection.

I hit another bottom when, one day, after successfully finishing a new creative project, I found myself feeling compelled to return to an S&M parlor. I hated this place, but it was almost as if I were hypnotized by a force of evil. I rationalized it as a "reward" for my efforts. In truth, I was powerless and defenseless against this insane urge.

It had just stopped raining. I withdrew my money from the ATM machine, walked dolefully toward my destination, the perfect slave to a ruthless disease. I noticed that people in the street were smiling, looking skyward. What were they noticing? A rainbow spanning the sky. The sight of it, after a long, cold rain, seemed to make people giddy. My mind, alas, was chained to other things.

I thought it was a sign of my failing that I couldn't "figure out" a way to stop this insanity. Fortunately I was attending some twelve-step meetings dealing with codependency at that time, because of some alcoholics in my life. I was actually abusing alcohol myself—alcohol and acting out were perfect companions. Finally another member of the program persuaded me to go to meetings for my drinking. After a hard-fought struggle, I surrendered alcohol to a Higher Power who, I felt vaguely in my heart, wanted to see me happier, and free.

I acted out two more times in early sobriety, and the demoralization was too much to bear. I saw myself differently sober, and I also saw the women I acted out with in a different, more human light. They were no longer manipulative goddesses, capable of rescuing me from on high (while deviously taking my money and self-esteem); they were, in fact, just people doing the best they could. They struck me as lonely, confused, and quietly desperate, in that they subjected themselves to degradation for the sake of money. They did not seem happy. I realized that I was actively participating in their demoralization as well as mine.

A friend had offered to take me to Sex Addicts Anonymous, but I procrastinated and put it off until, when the pain was too great, I walked, terrified, into my first meeting. The atmosphere could not have been more friendly or welcoming. I felt at ease immediately, found indescribable relief in finding a group of spiritually minded people who welcomed me without qualification, and shared so much of my story. Tough as it was to move some of my core behaviors into the "inner circle" (acting out with prostitutes, erotic massages, phone sex, and S&M parlors), my spirit, that which had craved consolation, gradually became my guide.

It was difficult surrendering my prime weapon—my intellect—but not as difficult as suffering the hell of active addiction. I sensed that recovery was a spiritually based experience of active surrender, not something to be figured out. God guides me with the light of his compassion, though it is I who move my feet.

I might never have surrendered had I not wanted what I saw in other SAA members: abstinence, humor, a connection to a Higher Power, real relationships, and a great deal of warmth and kindness.

I am completely powerless over addictive sexual behaviors. Because I attend meetings, help newcomers, and apply twelve-step principles to my daily life, I have been able to find freedom from obsession, isolation, and despair. Freedom, too, from the need to "figure it all out." What has replaced it—a sense of usefulness and belonging, of being needed and wanted and loved, and a newly empowered understanding that puts humility first—is a much better solution to my problems than I would ever have guessed.

8.

A NUN AND A SEX ADDICT

I was the youngest of nine, in a Midwest rural Catholic farm family, growing up in an environment that I thought was healthy. I was later to realize that both my parents were adult children of alcoholics. My mom did not talk about sex, but said, "Put down your dress, you dirty little thing." I don't remember my childhood before the age of ten. Then I remember playing prostitute and trying to masturbate through my clothing. That lasted a year, after which I suppressed all my feelings. It seems that feelings were never validated in my family.

I dated in high school, but I decided to enter a convent at the age of eighteen. I took my first vows of obedience, poverty, and celibacy in 1961. The vow of celibacy was a commitment not to get married, not to express my sexual urges with another or with myself. I had no problem with that until I was thirty-four years old. At that time I was the principal of a grade school, and a colleague started to be sexual with me. I began to masturbate. A female staff member was also sexual with me. I was very confused, and I continued to be sexual with her and another woman with whom I was living. This went on for a year. I tried to stop this sexual acting out many times. My most desperate attempt was when I used a razor blade to cut crosses on the inside of my thighs to remind myself that I was breaking my vow.

I went into total denial of what I was doing. I wouldn't let myself think—I only lived in this fantasy world where I could do anything that I wanted without consequences. So I continued to have unprotected sex, until my pain, guilt, and shame began to break through my denial. I made a geographical change by asking to be transferred. At my new mission, eighty miles away, I continued to masturbate and at one point I had a passing thought of suicide.

During the next six years, I moved four times. I went to Africa to teach in a secondary school, and struggled with culture shock. I used masturbation to cope with my feelings. I was not able to express anger or even to feel it. The Sister that I lived with knew when I was angry, because I was silent or I cried. Then a priest started to be sexual with me. It felt as if I attracted men in this way because I had no boundaries. There was a one-night stand with a professor, who was drunk. I had gone to bed praying to God "to send me a man" as I masturbated myself to sleep. At midnight he came. The day that I was flying back to the states because of my mother's death, I had unprotected sex with the priest—a man I had resisted for a long time. Once on the plane I thought, "Thank you, God, for getting me out of there, because I don't know how to say no to men."

While in the states, I asked for help to deal with my anger. I was sent to an outpatient program. At intake, I knew that I had to be totally honest. When asked if I was sexually active, I had to acknowledge that I was. When the therapist said, "It sounds like you were compulsive," I suddenly felt hope, that maybe there was help for me.

It was there that I became aware of the twelve-step program and attended my first Sex Addicts Anonymous meeting. It was made up of all women. Two women had "twelfth-stepped" me before the meeting. They told me their stories, and I shared why I thought that I was addicted to sex. One of the women offered to be my temporary sponsor and I accepted this. I was not working at the time, so I read program material during the day, wrote in a journal, started to feel my feelings, and went to outpatient treatment at night. I learned that boundaries were to keep me safe, not to keep me out of trouble. More of my rigid, negative attitudes started to change with group therapy, the feedback of my therapist, my SAA sponsor, and my SAA group. "If you want what we have, you need to be willing to go to any lengths" inspired me to let go of the idea that "I can never change." My sponsor told me to be gentle with myself, to let the program work. The feeling of total acceptance from my SAA group was new and validating for me. They never used "You should do this" statements. They offered only their experience with the issues at hand.

I had agreed with my therapist that my bottom-line behavior was not to be sexual with men or women. I made a commitment not to contact my former partners, to tear up past letters and photos from them, and to get rid of gifts I had received from them. In other words, I was to break all ties. It was painful, but my acting out with them had been more painful.

At my SAA meetings I saw the serenity that these women had; I heard their stories and I wanted that same peace too. I realized that I had no control over my sexually compulsive thoughts—they just came. I asked my Higher Power to take them from me. I kept asking, and within the first two years of recovery, they lessened. Every time they came, I just said, "God, I can't handle these thoughts, you have to take them from me."

I changed sponsors after two years because mine was over-committed and asked me to find another one. I admired her for taking care of her own needs. It was during this time that I also changed my ministry. I went back to school and became a physical therapist. To accommodate my new work, I made another geographical change. When I began to attend mixed meetings, I noticed that I felt very scared. I started to have flashbacks that I was sexually abused as a child. There might have been just one other woman at those meetings, but my Higher Power used the men in that group to heal me. Some of them had been incestuous fathers.

A local treatment center asked us to start a meeting at the hospital for SAA. I volunteered to do this with another man. It was at one of their meetings that the healing started to take place, when an incestuous father described how he was trying to make amends to his daughter. I started to cry, because it was like my own father talking. My father had been dead for ten years at that point.

. From the beginning, service has been a strong recovery tool for me. Coming to the meetings a little early, helping to set up the room, taking charge of the literature, being the trusted servant, making a step presentation at our meetings, being a sponsor—all these were simple to do. I attended the intergroup meetings and the national conventions during the first five years. I seemed to get back more than I was giving. Setting up the meditation rooms with an emphasis on feelings was my gift to the program. No one knew that I was a nun; I had my anonymity. But in 1997, I felt the call to share my story, and did so at an international convention. By that time I had eleven years of sobriety from my bottom-line behavior and two years from my struggle with masturbation.

I used to masturbate to the point of pain. When the desire to do it arose, I would try to think it away, or do other things, but then I'd think, "Well, I can't stop, so I might as well give in and get it over with." In recovery it was the constant asking of my Higher Power for help that enabled me to choose not to masturbate when the thought arose. Now, even the desire is gone.

Honesty was another tool that I needed to use. I was surprised at how dishonest I was with myself in my active addiction. When I realized that, I began to ask daily for the grace of honesty, acceptance, and surrender.

That continues to be my prayer today. Lying was a partner to dishonesty, because I had to cover up my secret life. This weakness of mine still shows its head now and then.

After I came back from Africa, I felt a strong a desire to return there. Two years after I was out of PT school, I returned. It was a challenge to be away from SAA, and to be back in the same area where I had acted out. I had just finished two years of incest survivor work when I knew that I needed to return to the states. I was depressed and felt like a failure. I went into a therapeutic community for eleven months. Two years later I asked to return to Africa and was told "No". I felt devastated! In therapy I discovered that my drive to return to Africa came from the ten-year-old inside me. I thought that I was responsible for my incest and had to make up to God for it. An African missionary visited my school when I was a child, and he emphasized how hard it was to live there. That is how my desire to go to Africa originated. When I realized this at the age of sixty, it felt like a huge weight was lifted from me. For the first time, I choose what I want to do with a new freedom. I am still a nun, and I am a grateful, recovering sex addict.

9.

FREE IN PRISON

I'm a gratefully recovering sex addict who is currently serving a five-to-fifteen-year sentence for Criminal Sexual Conduct. So, how did I end up in prison? As I reflect on my past, I realize that I've been working towards this all my life. Like the majority of sex offenders, I was molested as a child. It was then that I first experimented sexually with children my own age. By the age of thirteen I was obsessed with sex and became compulsive. Masturbation became routine on a daily basis, sometimes as often as four times a day. Just being around girls my own age or older gave me an erection. This always embarrassed me, giving me feelings of guilt and shame. From childhood I had the impression that sex was dirty and wrong. Since I always thought about it, I always felt dirty and wrong. To avoid having an erection I increased masturbation, but also felt guilty about that.

I also developed a serious problem with drugs and alcohol. I found that if I were high enough or drunk enough I wouldn't act out as much, or at least I wouldn't have the negative feelings that came with it. It wasn't until I came to prison that I learned that the brain produces a similar chemical high with sex as the heroin user has. All the drugs did was to slow down my acting out until my tolerance increased for drugs. And then they were not enough.

At the age of twenty I was completely out of control. I would have sex at any opportunity, and not only did the drugs and alcohol numb the guilt and shame, but they helped me get sex.

I instinctively turned towards religion in a desperate attempt to regain control of my life. I enrolled in a seminary and was able to abstain from everything but masturbation. I rationalized that all I needed was a wife as a constant supply of sex. I finished seminary and became a minister for a short time. My addiction was still with me. I realized that God was not going to be my codependent, so I left the church before I acted out in some way.

About a year later I fondled a friend's daughter and was promptly turned in to the police. I was sentenced to one year in the county jail. My wife divorced me and moved away with my son without a forwarding address. Upon release I enrolled in a sex offenders therapy group. Being fearful of looking any worse than I already did (as if anything could look worse than being a convicted pedophile), I played along. They mentioned SAA to me, but no way was I going to admit I had a problem. After all, I had only been caught once—I wasn't an addict. After eighteen months of therapy I was released from probation.

I found another good woman to marry, so I figured that having her, along with alcohol and drugs, meant I was doing just fine. The fear of being imprisoned kept me from acting out. I still masturbated almost daily, even though I was having intercourse almost every day, and often more than once in a day.

Seven years later, in spite of using drugs, alcohol, acceptable sex, religion, and counseling, and in spite of one year in a jail cell, I fondled both daughters of an acquaintance. At that time I ran into a friend who attended a twelve-step program for his addiction. He told me where to find an address to contact SAA who, in turn, would contact someone in my area to help me. That is where I met my sponsor. He shared his experience, strength, and hope with me. In the ninety-five days between being charged and sentenced, I attended three meetings a week.

My SAA friends gave me the moral support and courage to endure coming to prison. In prison the only thing lower than a pedophile is a snitch, and snitches are abused and even killed occasionally. In my state there are six prisons of this security level. 85% of their populations are sex offenders. Many of these men can't see where they might have a problem with sex. As for me, I am a sex addict who is gratefully recovering thanks to a loving Higher Power and SAA. I am still in a physical prison but I am free from a far worse prison. Someday the physical will catch up to the spiritual and mental. I continue to recover one day at a time.

10.

SEXUAL ANOREXIC

I was born in Germany in 1942, during the Second World War. Living close to Frankfurt, the bombings must have had a big impact on me. I think the constant fear and terror of my mother during pregnancy and after birth strongly affected me without my having any memories or awareness.

My dad was seductive and my mom rigid, cold, and sulking. Once in a while she would mention how disgusting sex was. At the same time she was preoccupied with sex, reading cheap magazines like the tabloids and getting upset about the filth happening in the world. There was some talk about prostitutes, and later on I realized that it was a familiar world for my father until he died at the age of eighty-two.

I have few memories of my childhood, mainly happy ones from holidays and vacations. I seem to have repressed most sad and traumatic memories; the events are gone, the feelings still in me. I do remember some physical beatings with a rod, and one time they went on for a long time because I did not give in. For my "stubbornness" I got more punishment.

I first had my period at age ten in summer camp. I was afraid that I was going to die of cancer, since I couldn't explain the blood in any other way. A nun at camp asked me if I wanted kids and when I said yes, she answered that I would bleed every month from then on. I had no clue what all this meant. My parents were notified, but they decided not to visit me, and nobody ever mentioned anything to me about having a period, not even my mom.

I rarely slept alone. Either I shared a single bed with my sister or slept between my parents in their bed. This continued until about age eighteen. I didn't realize that this was unusual, since it was the only life I knew. I don't remember having any sexual feelings. Once my father tried

145

to touch me sexually in bed. I pushed his hand away and lay frozen for many hours, not daring to move or leave.

I perceived my sister, who was six years older, as pretty and popular with boys, whereas I perceived myself as ugly, uptight, and non-sexual. My sister started having mental problems at the age of sixteen. She spent some time in a mental institution getting shock therapy. Many years later I read the most heartbreaking pages from her journal that revealed her pain and desperation. At age twenty-eight she committed suicide and took her two-month-old baby with her. For many years in my family, the focus was on my sister. I felt neglected, rejected, and jealous. At the same time I felt guilt and shame for not having more empathy for her and my parents. It took over twenty years before I could cry over her death and start mourning.

When I was about fourteen years old I started having physical problems: intense abdominal cramps and sometimes passing out. These cramps continued until about two years ago when I became aware that these pains were related to terror about possible sex. I struggled with that problem for forty-four years.

As I grew older, I experienced more negative reactions to anything sexual. My sexual encounters with my boyfriend (later husband) were accompanied by intense anxiety that sometimes led to hyperventilation, to the point of my body feeling totally frozen. The only body part that I could move was my head, and I was able to talk. These experiences were very frightening for my husband and me.

I started dating my future husband on and off when I was seventeen. We got married six years later. For the next thirty years I played victim, not knowing that I have choices. Fear of sex, aversion against sex, feeling obligated, pretending, picking fights at night to avoid sex—I had all these feelings and behaviors without being aware of what really was going on with me. Shortly after the birth of our second son I started therapy because of depression and rage. I feel shame over the amount of therapy I had, altogether about twenty-two years of seeing psychiatrists, counselors, and group therapy. I am sure, though, that it was helpful and led me towards recovery.

Fourteen years ago I started eating compulsively, which brought me to a twelve-step program, and my journey of recovery began. From there on I was guided to fellowships dealing with codependency and incest. I'm sure all these stepping-stones were beneficial and part of my journey, and at the same time it was an extremely slow, painful process.

I became aware of the nature of my problem about seven years later. We were on vacation, and my husband was taking a nap in a mountain cabin while I sat outside in a recliner. I couldn't enjoy anything. I felt mesmerized by the door, waiting for him to come out, worrying that he might want to make love. I was watching him all the time to figure out what he wanted and when. That's when it hit me. "I am not living," I thought. "I am in a horrible self-made jail." Later I was standing in the kitchen and my husband came up from behind in the middle of an argument and embraced me sexually and I snapped and screamed, "Stop that!" He was stunned. I finally blurted out the truth about behaviors that had been bothering me for years.

My husband's reaction felt so incredibly painful to me that I didn't think I could handle it. He turned off and did not talk to me for several days. This was unbearable, combined with my fear of rejection and my lack of awareness of any choices. Several counselors and couples therapy followed. None really worked. There was something missing in my recovery.

Two and a half years ago, a friend suggested Sex Addicts Anonymous to me after I shared about my sexual fears. That was the beginning of healing and tremendous relief. I always had friends to share my feelings with, but nobody ever close enough or trusting enough to talk about sex. There was a whole world of terrifying, disturbing feelings bottled up inside of me. For the first time I was able to talk about that stuff, cry, laugh, and share my fears, my terror. The relief is tremendous. I go to two or three SAA meetings a week.

I read a book about "sexual anorexia" and I knew that it was talking about me. I felt at home when I read that book; almost everything fit me, and for the first time in my life I saw myself being described. My confusion about what was going on was over.

I made amends to my husband and took responsibility for my part. I always believed that if my partner wouldn't need sex so much I would be fine. I realize now that my avoidance of sex is compulsive. Here are the feelings I struggle with: jealousy, possessiveness, wanting to control everything, suspicion, fear of betrayal, fear of abandonment, anxiety, rage, guilt, shame, and fear of rejection.

I used to lash out at my husband and punch him. He would immediately restrain my hands and it was over. On a couple of later occasions he hit me back. It was our secret for over thirty years. We never discussed it. The shame for both of us was unbearable. I finally had the courage to bring it up at SAA meetings. We are dealing with it openly now and there have been no more occurrences for over a year and a half.

A counselor pointed out to me that I dissociate a lot. I didn't even understand what she meant and only slowly became aware of my checking out, "being gone." I believe that I must have shut down any sexual feelings from the beginning of puberty on. I completely shut that area off from my awareness pretty much to this day. I do not want to feel sexual or turned on. It seems frightening to me, not safe. I have fears of getting punished, raped, or killed if I let go and feel sexual. My body tightens up, my chest feels heavy, my head hurts, and I am close to vomiting. My fear and disgust is that big.

My addiction circles around my obsessive thinking. For someone who hates sex, I spend an awful lot of time obsessing about it. It goes around and around in my mind. Through working the program I've become aware that my feelings are part of me. If I can learn to embrace them, all of them, then I don't need to spend so much energy pushing the sexual part of me down. All of my life I put others down, and it was really me. I need to accept myself as a sexual being—a frightening thought. Would I still be safe? How would I protect myself? I understand that I pushed my sexuality down in order to protect myself when I was a little girl and a teenager. I had to do that to survive. It worked then, but does it work now? Do I still need that protection or can I feel sexual and feel safe? Yes, I can feel sexual and feel safe. I feel anxious about what I will learn and I feel hopeful at the same time.

My shortcomings include jealousy, possessiveness, and suspicion. By taking responsibility for these shortcomings I have made some progress. They are part of my addiction, I am powerless over them, and my life is unmanageable. It is easy for me to admit that my life is unmanageable. It always was. Steps Two and Three give me hope and show me the way to recovery.

I enjoy doing the steps. Working the Fourth Step and then sharing the Fifth Step with my sponsor was a healing experience. I keep doing inventories and sharing them. I continue to work the steps in SAA. This program gives me hope, love, and compassion—compassion for others and myself.

I will never be "done" with my recovery. By getting out of the victim role I take responsibility for my actions. It also diminishes the rage and physical abuse towards my partner. Self-awareness allows me to make conscious choices for my benefit, and I am less in a reactive mode. I am developing compassion for those who suffer, like I did, from the disease of sex addiction. I am grateful to have found SAA, and I treasure the fellowship. I keep growing and changing one day at a time.

11.

STILL GROWING SPIRITUALLY

I remember little of my childhood. What I do remember is feeling lonely and feeling less than the other boys. And I felt uncomfortably close to my mom. I think she always wanted a little girl. Every time one of my younger brothers was born, major disappointment was expressed.

Once, when I was about twelve, I was asked to baby-sit for neighbors living behind us. After they left for the night, I remember rummaging through the dresser, looking for female underwear, feeling excitement and fear. Perhaps that was my first secret.

At about the same time, I fondled a girl a few years younger than I. Behind a garage, while trying to cleverly distract her with conversation, I touched her genitals. Again, that excitement and fear kicked in. My sexual addiction was beginning to blossom.

Later I began spending weekends with a girl I knew. We slept in the same bed, and I would try to touch her without waking her, slipping under the covers to see what I could see. This friend's mother was alcoholic. She would occasionally come home late and fall asleep totally nude across her bed. Her bedroom was on my way to the bathroom, and so back and forth I would go during the night, stopping to look at her.

Once, this girl was visiting my house and had to use the bathroom. I peeped into the window from the porch, but she saw me and yelled at me. I felt more shame and excitement.

During that time, I met a girl and while visiting her one night, I was masturbating her when her parents came home. I had to leave by the window and jumped into my friend's car (they were waiting for me). I felt pumped up and ready to explode with excitement.

At college I met the woman who was to become my wife. My cousin had brought her to a party, and I fell immediately in lust over her. She and I spent the whole evening dancing, and I made a promise to spend a lot more time with her.

I would call her compulsively, drive halfway across town from campus to pick her up at her school, buy her gifts, and try to win the affection of her parents. We began petting before exams, because I wanted the medication of a sexual experience.

A female friend of the family was going to be home alone, and her parents and mine agreed I should stay over to protect her. They trusted me. I suggested to the girl that she would sleep better if she took something. This was my first experience of drugging someone for sex. I molested her while she slept.

My disease almost never took a rest. My girlfriend had twin female cousins, and I was sexual with one of the girls, later writing passionate letters back and forth for some time.

I graduated from college, married my girlfriend, and took a job that ended up becoming my hide-out. It was my source for acting out, power, resentment, and dishonest actions, and my statement of who I was. It was where I had an extramarital affair, my place to go after being with a prostitute, and a place to sexualize and objectify applicants and subordinates. This lasted a long time. I became an addict with no boundaries. I felt my pleasures were well earned and deserved, and that I was too clever to be caught.

My wife got pregnant soon after we married. We were both excited and proud. One of her twin cousins came to visit and spent the night. I lay in bed with my pregnant wife on one side, and fondling her cousin on the other side of me.

Our first son was born, and two years later our daughter. My lust for neighborhood women grew. My satisfaction with normal bedroom sex was replaced with a desire for what I thought was more interesting sex. We drifted apart sexually.

I was sexual with a young baby-sitter, and I still feel shame when I remember my six-year-old son walking in on us. I had no control. The pleasure outweighed the consequences. As our daughter grew up, I would objectify her visiting girlfriends.

Later my wife and I went to a marriage encounter. The weekend was full of feelings and sadness. We wrote letters to each other and then read them silently to ourselves, crying together. It felt spiritual. Perhaps it was a beginning. Yet my disease was still progressing.

I remember a trip to another state, driving the station wagon, my wife in the front seat next to me and my arm reaching back to touch my daughter's leg in full view of my youngest son. One night I told my wife that I was having sexual feelings toward our daughter. I must have been desperate for help, but wasn't willing to ask for it directly.

I would climb into the attic to peep down vents and fan spaces to see my daughter undressed. I would unlock bathroom doors and peep in while she showered. I drilled holes from the closet into her bedroom to see her. I would touch her inappropriately.

When she began dating, I had strict rules about what time to return home, and once when she was very late I yelled at her. I said that I didn't want her to get in trouble with these young guys. Actually, I was out of control with jealousy.

Our oldest son got involved with drugs, and my wife and I began a drug abuse program for parents. We were introduced to the Twelve Steps, sponsorship, rigorous honesty, and other principles of the program. I became very involved, running meetings, fundraising, even counseling others. But my acting out was near a bottom.

One day my daughter broke down at school and told her teacher that her father had fondled and kissed her breast the night before. This had truly been the farthest my disease had taken me, and she had had enough. The school called my wife, my wife picked up our daughter, and then they returned home that night with a deputy sheriff. My wife came into my bedroom, sat at my bedside and said, "I know what you have been doing and you better get help."

Everything went black inside. I could not say a word, and every thought left my mind. This was the worst and the best moment of my life. I remember putting on slippers and a bathrobe, going downstairs, reaching for the yellow pages, and calling a toll-free number for child molestation. I cried and confessed to what I had been doing and they made an appointment for me to see a counselor the next morning.

I knew that I had no control. And I needed to know this if I were to have any chance of getting well. I questioned nothing. When I was told to be at a certain address at a certain time, I was there. When I showed up, I withheld nothing, telling anyone that would listen what I had done. I see now that I had no boundaries. Yet it served me at the time. I needed to have all illusions of ego and control removed.

My wife and I met with a therapist. Then we met with my daughter, and I was told a very important thing. I had to accept all the responsibility for what happened, even though I wanted to believe my daughter was a willing participant. I agreed to accept this responsibility. And that was very important for me.

My wife and I decided to try to stay together. I returned to the addiction program we had found for our son, although I withdrew from any leadership position. God was good to me. I needed help. It would still be three years until I was led to Sex Addicts Anonymous, but miracles surrounded me.

I decided to share my experience with a counselor. I cried, she cried, we hugged and then she told me of a friend she would like me to meet. We met the next day at a coffee shop, and he told me about a meeting of four or five people that he ran in his office once a week. They read from a book about sex addiction. This man shared his sexual story with me. My trust was slow to come, but I showed up weekly at the meetings in his office and also met him at many twelve-step meetings, where he would keep a seat for me.

Things at home were strained. I began to get numerous phone calls from other addicts, and my wife felt left out and annoyed. Once or twice she left me angry notes saying she was finished and could not stand it any more. I would read these notes and feel terrified of abandonment.

I called my therapist and he said to do nothing. Was he kidding? So, I sat on the couch, wrapped in a blanket, crying and shivering. And then I would continue as I did before, going to meetings and getting calls and doing what I had to do to stay alive. My way was clear. Make calls, read recovery material, go to meetings of any twelve-step kind, go to therapy, retreats, workshops.

Then I heard about SAA. I went to my first meeting in 1987. I felt at home. I shared my story that night, and the fellow next to me, a newcomer, told me afterwards that he never thought he would hear another person share about the same things he had done. I knew then that God had intended for me to share my story to help others.

Afterwards, another addict told me that I belonged there, and I liked hearing that. Funny, isn't it? Who would want to belong at a sex addicts' meeting? But being with others, knowing I was not alone, being accepted in spite of what I had done, and seeing these people laugh and joke, told me I was being led by a Power greater than myself.

I got a sponsor. He had something I wanted, and that was humor. He asked me to call him daily for thirty days and read three pages a day in the AA Big Book. At the end of thirty days, he told me that few had kept the commitment as I had. Slowly I was able to find a little humor inside myself.

The one meeting each week split into two, and soon we had choices. Slowly, more people would show up, and with them different variations of the addiction. The phone lists grew, and intimacy grew. We would use the Big Book of AA and simply replace the word "alcohol" with "sex" or "compulsive sexual behavior." We knew what we meant.

God's plan is perfect. I refer to his messengers as "angels." And I have met so many. The Twelve Steps became a continuing theme in meetings and began to penetrate my resistance. For years I had heard that until I cleared the wreckage of my past, I would be likely to repeat my behavior. Now I finally wrote my Fourth Step and cried all the way to my sponsor's house to complete my Fifth. Giving the shame away by sharing it worked for me. I also had to divorce my mother on paper, with the guidance of my therapist. The enmeshment had to end. I had to grow up.

As I took all these risk-taking steps, I had a place to share about them, and sometimes another person would gain from them. And often I would gain from the sharing of others. So, in recovery, I was left with feelings. Feelings I could no longer act out over. Prayer, writing, and the power of the group would be my source of strength when I thought I would die from the feelings. And by learning to say what I thought and felt, I began to be okay with having them.

A funny thing happened along the way. Someone actually thought I had something he wanted, and he asked me to sponsor him. Yes, God is most generous. And now, years later, I celebrate ten years of abstinence, one day at a time.

My three circles were drafted and refined with the help of my most recent sponsor. I work my program as if my life depends on it, even today. Some say I work too hard. But I am still abstinent and I feel that if I do my ninety-eight percent, God will do the rest. And God has.

I love SAA. My best friends belong to the fellowship, men and women. I have loving, intimate relationships with others now. I can have a relationship with my wife like never before. And with my children, too. Because I am present and without secrets.

Still growing spiritually, I am now working on the Ninth Step. My amends list is long, and I am willing. My life is richer today than ever before, and the family will never be the same, THANK GOD.

12.

TRAGIC CONSEQUENCES, GREAT REWARDS

I'm a recovering sex addict. I've been introducing myself that way for the past eleven years, since my first sponsor advised me to be gentle with myself and recognize my first step into the rooms of recovery as the start of my journey, no matter how rough the road has been since taking that tentative beginning step.

Like many sex addicts, my story begins with a history of abuse. First my mother used me to satisfy her need to have a daughter by ignoring my true gender and treating me as her daughter. She still says she treated me that way because I wanted it that way, a classic example of blaming the victim. This was also the first instance of my perceiving the needs of others as greater than my own and doing everything, including sacrificing my self, to meet those needs. Later, at age eleven, I fell into the same pattern with my older brother, who promised sex education in exchange for sexual compliance. His abuse continued until I stopped it at age twenty-one.

Long before that, I learned that there were many others outside of my family who would give me love and acceptance in exchange for meeting their sexual needs. It never occurred to me that I might be loved for being myself, believing that I was unlovable unless I sacrificed my entire being and subsumed myself to the desires of anyone that asked.

It's impossible to tell when my history of abuse ended and my addiction began. Over the years, I learned to trade sexual favors for acceptance in gay bars, then bookstores, then cruising parks, bathhouses, and finally from prostitutes. I even engaged in sex with other relatives and friends and neighbors, thinking I was finally getting true love because these were people I knew, rather than total strangers. But my use of prostitutes, and my prostitution of myself, became the lowest point in my acting-out history. Seeking to pick up hustlers in a porn shop, I was arrested for solicitation and had to spend three thousand dollars in attorney's fees to strike a plea bargain that saved my career. Nonetheless, I failed to stop, even returning to the same location. In hiring prostitutes, I felt I could control the situation and become more in control. Yet I found myself paying prostitutes and then failing to get them to do what I wanted to do, instead reverting to my old pattern of meeting their sexual desires rather than my own.

I put my life in danger time and again, getting robbed and beaten, spending way too much money, even having to end a vacation early because I spent all of my money on prostitutes. I combined this with alcohol and drugs, and found myself waking up from blackouts, not knowing where I was or how I got there.

Eventually I was hospitalized for depression following a severe beating and robbery in a homeless camp, with no memory of how it happened. Then, while in the hospital, I asked for an examination of my wounds from the beating. The doctor came and told me bluntly that I probably had AIDS, and drew blood for a test. When I got the results a few weeks later, they were positive for HIV. Fortunately, I found a physician who explained that I did not have AIDS, that I was only HIV-positive. I had to bear this devastating news alone, just as I had the details of my earlier arrest, because I didn't have a support group to help me deal with it. The only way I knew to deal with feelings of this magnitude was to act out, which, sad to say, I continued to do over the next several years. Although I tried to use safe sex, I wasn't always able to stop myself from acting out when I didn't have a condom readily available. I'll never know how many others I infected, because my partners were always anonymous. Since I showed no symptoms, I convinced myself that I must have been a false positive, but a nagging doubt always remained.

Three years later, I tested again, and was stunned to get a second positive test. Now deeply shaken, I had to face the fact that I had infected others. I was overwhelmed with guilt. I was a caring person! How could I have acted so callously?

Through what I now believe was God's intervention, I had been transferred to a city where there were AIDS services, good SAA recovery and meetings, and a coincidental connection with a Catholic nun who had gotten me involved in studying to convert to Catholicism. Intensely involved in this study and in my spiritual quest, I could no longer reconcile my sexual behavior with my deepening sense of values. I became despondent over this seemingly unresolvable issue and sought help at an AIDS service agency, where I informed them that I was planning to commit suicide.

Assigned a counselor, I told her that, should I decide to live, the only two possible courses of treatment I could accept as helpful would be either aversion therapy to kill my sex drive, or sex therapy with a surrogate partner who could help me learn to enjoy sex. Fortunately for me, she smiled and suggested I attend meetings of Sex Addicts Anonymous. I immediately knew she was right. I was a sex addict! That explained why I couldn't stop, even when I wanted to and had every reason to stop. Even so, I was scared when I went to my first meeting and saw over fifty people inside through the windows. They were laughing and looked happy! Didn't they know how awful and tragic being a sex addict was?

That first meeting was a blur. I don't remember any of it, except that at the end I was astonished to see the people hugging each other and talking about how much they loved each other. It seemed so fake! How could they really care so much, when they were supposedly not having sex with each other? I was extremely confused and bewildered.

After a few meetings, I went on a business trip to another city, where something strange happened. First of all, I didn't act out, which had never happened at a conference before. But a more amazing miracle occurred. In my Catholic studies, I had learned to pray a novena, which is a prayer said every day for nine days for a specific need. On the ninth day, the answer is received, and is followed by nine days of prayers of thanks for the answer. I decided to make my first novena a request for physical, spiritual, and emotional healing. No sense asking for a minor miracle! On the evening of the ninth day of the novena, I had a dream. In this dream, I was in a hospital bed, when a figure in white approached me. I was irritated, and asked the figure, "What do you want?" A gentle voice replied, "I am healing you." I felt an instant sense of reassurance, knowing that I was already being healed and that the process of my healing had begun even before I had asked for it. On awakening, I realized that I had received the answer to my novena on the ninth day, as promised.

The eleven years following this beginning of my recovery journey have been amazing, and filled with ups and downs. On the down side, I became addicted to work and nearly killed myself with that behavior, which I now realize was part of the continuing problem of a lack of identity that had fueled my sex addiction. I also progressed into full-blown AIDS and had to retire and go on disability. I struggled with sexual sobriety for many years. I became more estranged from my family and experienced years of loneliness.

Each of these things has brought an equal amount of blessing into my life. My work addiction allowed me to seek in-patient treatment, which also addressed my history of abuse and sex addiction as well as depression. My retirement has given me the opportunity to live work-free and receive an income that sustains me, while giving me time to make amends to the community for the damage that my acting out wrought. My loneliness ended when I met, fell in love with, and married a wonderful life partner, which has now led me into dealing with relationship issues in a new way.

Throughout all of these ups and downs, I have had one huge blessing. Unlike when I had to deal with my arrest and my initial HIV diagnosis alone, I have had the loving support of the SAA fellowship. I never have to experience great joy or great sorrow alone again. I finally learned that I did not have to give up my self, my identity, my sexuality, or my money to have the love and acceptance I had sought for so long, in so many painful and isolating ways. My Higher Power works for me through those with whom he has surrounded me. While I live one day at a time, I am so very grateful that, when my life comes to an end, I will not have to take that final step alone either, for my Higher Power will be there to receive me from the loving embrace of my friends in recovery, my true family.

13.

THIS IS WHAT WORKS

The best way to describe my active sex addiction is that it was like water flowing down a hill. My behaviors always seemed to take the path of least resistance. There were times when my main venue of acting out was with street prostitutes. Other times there were adult bookstores and adult phone party lines. Indecent exposure, swingers clubs, personal ads, and the internet were all a part of the scope of my active sex addiction. It was usually a combination of these behaviors. If I was low on money, I might drive up in my car and expose myself to street prostitutes or to an unsuspecting woman in the car next to mine. If I had time constraints I might take a quick trip to an adult bookstore. If I had the day to myself I might act out three or four times. I acted out most of the time, given the opportunity. To this day I don't know how I never got arrested.

My inner-circle behaviors are any sexual act outside of my marriage, indecent exposure, voyeurism, phone sex and cybersex. The first item on the list encompasses many behaviors.

There are some actions I identify as my middle-circle behaviors, such as flirting and purposely driving by sexually oriented businesses and areas where prostitutes congregate. These middle-circle behaviors tend to give me a small level euphoria without the danger and rush of acting out. When I engage in such behaviors I share this with my sponsor or bring it up at a meeting. Ninety percent of the time I engage in middle-circle behavior, it is because I am angry about something, my ego is damaged, or I'm on a "pity pot." Working through this with my sponsor or another member of the program gets to the roots of what's really bothering me and clears the way to a healthy life. These boundaries, my inner and middle circles, deal with behaviors and not thoughts. If I were to put thoughts within my boundaries, I would be setting myself up for failure.

Over the years my sex addiction got worse because it took more outrageous and risky behavior to give me the euphoria I was seeking. When I sobered up in SAA at the age of thirty-four, I had had sex with more people that I can count, acted out with hundreds of prostitutes, missed career opportunities, and spent over fifty thousand dollars because of my sex addiction. In addition to this, I left a trail of a lot of hurt women, time away from my children and marriage, and lost productivity in my job.

I was fifteen years sober from alcohol when I joined Sex Addicts Anonymous. I had actively participated in a twelve-step fellowship, worked the steps many times over, done service work, regularly attended meetings, and had sponsors and sponsees. But my double life of sex addiction was slowly wearing me down.

The last time I acted out was two and a half years ago. I told my wife I was going to a hardware store. I went to a "health spa/massage parlor" and acted out. On the way home I made the decision to join a sex addiction twelve-step program. I did a web search, and SAA came up first. Three days later I made my first meeting. By the end of the meeting I knew I was in the right place. It wasn't what people shared, but how they shared it. I knew I was with people who were serious about getting better.

Shame and guilt had nothing to do with my decision to recover from my sex addiction. I was not thinking of the people I hurt, or even how I was hurting myself. I made the decision to recover because I felt like a mouse in a treadmill, stuck in a vicious cycle. I had to finally admit that I was addicted to harmful and compulsive sexual practices.

Since I joined SAA, I have not engaged in my inner-circle behaviors. Recovery in SAA has been simple, but it has also been the most difficult thing I've ever done. I have contact with my sponsor at least twice a week. I also attend the same SAA meeting every week, rain or shine. I am active in the local intergroup, and have sponsored many men. I've done three formal First Steps; the last one took two ninety-minute meetings to get through. My program is by no means perfect, but I slowly make progress for the better and have kept within my boundaries, even though sometimes I let my toes touch the edge.

Just as my active addiction was progressive, so is my active recovery. I am a better spouse, father, employee, friend, and citizen of the community. I take good care of myself physically, mentally, and spiritually. Even though I am not a member of any religious organization, I am on a spiritual path where I have conscious contact with God. As a member of

SAA, I am equal with all other members, regardless of education, social status, and length of abstinence. The person who just walked in the door is just as much a member as the man or woman with over a decade of sexual sobriety.

If you are new to this fellowship, it's my hope that you stick with it. You will find that a life without acting out is a much better life indeed. If I can do this, you can too. Attend meetings, even after you "get better." Trust in God, clean house, and help others. This is what has worked for me. As I see it, SAA is about learning to use simple metaphysical tools, connecting to a Higher Power on a daily basis, and living a life free from addiction. These are things we can't learn from reading books. We recover best by doing.

14.

LIVING AMENDS

When I was about four years old I was introduced to sex by my brother, who was over seven years older. I liked the attention he gave me. He continued to experiment with my body until I was about fourteen. I began masturbating right after my initiation to sex, but was very anxious about being found out by my pediatrician. I tried to stop, but couldn't. I remember masturbating in grade school, thinking that this was hidden by my desk. I even masturbated while watching TV with my family. I would just claim to be cold and pile blankets on top of myself so that no one could see what I was doing. In kindergarten I began exposing myself to boys—again, liking the attention.

My teen years were spent engaging in sex with other teens and men—adults who were often twice my age, and one who was four times my age. I felt ugly and dumb, and disliked by my schoolmates. I found I could find approval and acceptance from men if I would be sexual with them. Even though I started therapy in eighth grade and tried to control myself, I kept having sex, alone and with others, and I hated myself. I had no boundaries and was so sexually indiscreet that my closest girlfriend scheduled me to "de-virgin" her younger brother as a service to him. My promiscuity was viewed by my peers with a nonchalance that sickens me today. I tried to keep it a secret from my parents.

I began seeing a twenty-seven-year-old man when I was fifteen. I had previously had sex with a dozen men, but being with this man alienated my friends, nearly destroyed my family, and almost drove me to suicide. He beat me and cheated on me. He raped me once when I was too sore for intercourse, and once immediately following an abortion. I tried to leave him but couldn't, so I stopped eating for a month. No one at work, home, or school seemed to notice my drastic weight loss, and I felt alone and terrified. I don't know what power finally broke my four-year addiction to him, but one day I felt as though I had fallen out of a trance, and I left him. Unfortunately, by that time I was addicted to controlling my weight. I graduated from high school with a D average and no plans for my future.

My twenties unfolded with a series of low-paying jobs and a multitude of exploitative relationships. I experienced more and more self-loathing, and one thoughtful boyfriend took me to the outpatient clinic affiliated with the teaching hospital where I worked. I was immediately admitted to the psychiatric ward for evaluation, which was awkward, since I worked there. Upon discharge my addiction escalated. I was living a bizarre, polarized life, spending my entire discretionary income on therapy and all my discretionary time having sex with strangers, friends, coworkers, and even my gynecologist. I engaged in sex in public places, exposed myself at work, in a national park, in bars, and once on a city sidewalk during Halloween. I was using street drugs to amplify the intensity of acting out. Although I was hospitalized four more times for depression and suicide attempts, I didn't realize that I was sexually abused as a child, and no one asked. When I asked my psychiatrist what he thought of my extreme sexual behaviors, he told me that I was "just hypersexual."

In my late twenties, I married a man with whom I didn't want to have sex. Since there was no physical attraction, I felt safe with him, but I tried to control every aspect of our lives together. We quickly had a baby, and then completely stopped being sexual with each other. My use of fantasy and masturbation escalated to injury level; I developed acute tendonitis in my wrist and ignored my infant's needs. I received cortisone injections, but kept acting out with myself.

My addiction escalated even further when I left my husband for a "cute" neighbor. Fortunately, that man demanded I acknowledge that being sexual with my brother was abusive to me. I joined a twelve-step group for incest survivors, broke through my denial, and recognized that I had been molested as a child many times. I realized that my family had been sexually inappropriate and that my grandfather had had multiple affairs. I worked the first eight steps of recovery and stopped hating myself. However, my neighbor exploited my sexual addiction and used it to control me. My deepest regret is the amount of neglect my son endured while I was enmeshed with this man. I was sicker than ever, despite having been in therapy for twenty years.

After years of painful breakups, followed by highly sexualized reconciliations, my neighbor casually stated that I was a sex addict.

The moment I heard the words "sex addict," I knew that I had found the missing piece to the puzzle of my insanity. I looked up Sex Addicts Anonymous in the phone book, called, and had to leave my number for a return call to learn where meetings were held. It seemed an eternity of waiting for that return call.

When I went to my first meeting, I knew I was home. For thirty years I had felt different, flawed, weird, and hopeless. Here was a room filled with people, nice people, who were addicted to sex, just like me. I was overwhelmed with hope, and I cried as I had never dared to cry before.

I wish I could say that all was happily ever after, but I can't. What I can say is my life steadily improved, with some serious bumps in my path. Withdrawal was terrible for me, and looking back I realized that I had either masturbated or had sex with someone every night for the last two decades. Now I couldn't sleep, and felt as though I had the flu. Every joint ached. I was irritable, forgetful, and weepy. I attended every meeting we had (only two a week), got a sponsor, wrote out my three circles, and started reading everything I could find on sex addiction and recovery. The first six months were intense and painful, but also hopeful and joyous. I had friends in recovery, and I broke up with the neighbor.

Eight months into the program I violated a middle-circle rule and told a married man, who was not in SAA, about my addiction. Within twenty-four hours we had sex. Even though he was in an "open marriage," what I had done was inner-circle for me, and I was so angry with myself that I became suicidal and quit eating. My huge hope for recovery burst with my relapse, and I crashed into despair. For about a year I relapsed with this man, went to meetings, lost several sponsors, went to therapy, lost and gained weight, and somehow kept my lousy job. I was terribly depressed and terrified that the Twelve Steps weren't going to work for me. Most of the men in the program didn't understand the relationship element in my addiction and were frustrated with my relapse. In our city I was the only regularly attending woman in SAA at that time. But I kept going to meetings because it was the one place in the world where I felt safe. Even though the men in the group may not have fully understood me, they listened when I shared, and I was growing to love them and myself.

My acting-out partner left his wife, and our relationship now met my sobriety requirements: sex with a committed monogamous partner. He became my boyfriend. We engaged in both unhealthy and healthy sex as I slowly learned to set boundaries. I still struggled with masturbation and moved it in and out of my circles several times. I kept attending meetings.

A crucial event in my recovery then occurred. Out of a desperate need to find sponsors, five men and I formed a "co-sponsorship group." We met once a week to read our step work, go out to dinner, and attend a meeting together. With the support of my co-sponsorship group I presented my First Step to the fellowship, four years after joining SAA. During my preparation for my First Step I had a transforming spiritual awakening, actually feeling a physical and loving presence of God in my life. Newly motivated, I eagerly continued with my co-sponsorship group working Steps Two, Three, Four, and Five. I was sexually sober, getting emotionally healthier, and going to college. There was joy and laughter and hope in my life, replacing despair and loathing.

Then I found out that my boyfriend had been cheating on me for years with three different women. My life shattered. I became suicidal again. I wanted to give up on life, believing that I had failed at recovery. I developed acute post-traumatic stress syndrome, quit eating for weeks, and became borderline psychotic.

I believe the members of my co-sponsorship group and others in the fellowship saved my life at this time. I wanted to die, and felt unable to continue. They cared for me, taking me to their homes to sleep because I felt too suicidal to be alone.

I went to two twelve-step meetings a day for seven weeks. I wasn't trying to set a new record for attendance. I just couldn't tolerate being alone, and I was too sick to go to work. I went to an outpatient treatment center for a one-week intensive therapy program. It was there that I safely processed my rage about being molested, addicted, and betrayed. But as I left the center, I drove out into the desert alone, wanting to commit suicide because I was still miserable with grief. In desperation I stood in the middle of a huge open, mountainous desert and begged for God's help. At that moment I completely turned my life over to the care of God, as I had been unable to do before.

When I came home I started taking anti-psychotic drugs to help me get better. I started working at living God's will, not mine. I continued with two meetings a day, and participated in a four-month therapy program that taught me life skills. I realized I had spent so much time in fantasy and masturbation that I hadn't developed healthy techniques for managing the normal stress of life. I continued with my co-sponsorship group, reworking Steps One through Five. Although discovering my boyfriend's infidelity had seemed catastrophic, through that experience I learned true compassion, for myself and for others. I was learning to let go of being in control and being right. I was becoming a loving parent to my son. I was turning to God for help.

My boyfriend returned to make amends for what he had done. I was still in love with my boyfriend in spite of what he had done, and I was able to forgive him, although the forgiveness took years. Allowing him back into my life initially caused a great deal of conflict with my friends and family who had supported me during our breakup. Some felt that I was acting out by being with him. Fortunately, I continued to pray, meet with my co-sponsorship group, and work the steps. It took time, but I finally realized that I had been hiding from the general fellowship and meeting only with my co-sponsorship group because I too was conflicted about reconciling with the man who was about to become my husband. I kept struggling with a lingering depression that I feared I had brought on by being with him.

Over time I returned to full involvement with SAA. I got a new sponsor, went to the International Convention, got married, and reworked the first seven steps. With Steps Four and Five I realized I had been depressed since early childhood. Using Steps Six and Seven I could see depression as a character defect (or as I prefer to say, as "ineffective behavior") and ask God to remove it. With God's help, I am now rarely depressed and have an arsenal of tools to work through depression if it does arrive. I forgave the SAA members who had judged me, realizing that I had judged myself and had drawn them into my shame. I am now in the midst of thoroughly and formally working Steps Eight and Nine.

I have made amends to my parents about the terrible times caused by my relationship with the twenty-seven-year-old boy friend. I told them how sorry I was to have attempted suicide at their house. While I have made a living amends to them by caring for my father's mother for five years, speaking words of apology about specific events has changed me forever. I am no longer afraid to make or admit mistakes. I have made numerous other formal amends and have found each one to be a truly freeing experience. Although I'm not yet done with Steps Eight and Nine, I work Step Ten daily.

My self-hatred is absolutely gone now. My parents and I are closer now than ever, and I am so grateful to have done this work while they are still alive. My son and I are as close as a sixteen-year-old and his mother should be. I have good boundaries. I adore my husband. We share a spiritual practice and have the best intimate relationship I have ever had.

My weight is stable. I have loving friends and good health. And through God's grace, I'm returning to finish college.

I express my gratitude to SAA by working with others. I have several sponsees. I started a meeting and serve as its secretary. I volunteer with the local intergroup and am doing service work with national outreach. I do these things because I owe this program my life.

Before hearing about Sex Addicts Anonymous I thought I was an anomaly, alone in the world. Here in SAA I found the answers that had eluded me. I am grateful to be a recovering sex addict.

15.

TWO WORLDS COLLIDE

I grew up in a middle-class family in a small Midwest town. We had a family business, a nice home, were active in our church, and looked from the outside to be an ideal family. I learned from a very young age to protect and promote that public image. This was the first instance of developing two separate worlds that would later become a big part of my sex addiction. You see, behind those closed doors was rampant alcoholism, verbal and emotional abuse, lots of tears, and lots of unhappiness. But this the outside world must never see.

I was the fifth of six kids. The first four were much older than I, and well into their teens when I was a child. They gave my parents all the trouble, and then some, of typical teenagers. As the stress of the family dysfunction mounted, I soon learned my role in the family: I was the funny one. Whenever voices started to be raised or conflict mounted, I ran in to break the tension by cracking a one-liner, playing a practical joke, standing on my head—anything to distract from what was happening around me. I also learned to numb my emotions. I was naturally a very emotional child. But I soon learned that anger was never tolerated in my household, except my father's. Tears were reserved for my mother only. And only "happy feelings" were okay to be shared with others. "I'm fine," plastered with a fake smile, become my motto.

I discovered masturbation by accident one day when I was eleven years old. What a wonderful feeling! What an incredible distraction from the tension and dysfunction of our household! It quickly became a compulsion for me, every day, many times a day, to the point of making myself sore.

I eventually showed this newfound activity to a friend of mine and we began some mutual exploration. Nothing too serious, nothing too often. Looking back, it probably was pretty normal childhood exploration. But what I do remember now is that I was very much more interested and sexually excited by this than he was.

One common thread throughout my addiction is that I quickly became bored with whatever activity I chose. I needed more stimulation; eventually I needed more risk. So after compulsive masturbation, I turned to pornography. Although we never had this in our home, the fathers of kids that I babysat had ample stashes, so it was easy for me to use. Occasionally I would steal some from the local drug store. After this no longer provided me with enough stimulation, I started masturbating in places where there was a slight chance of getting caught. I remember masturbating in a dark movie theater with a coat over my lap or in the back of a car while someone else was driving. Once I remember masturbating on the balcony of a hotel from the twelfth story, partly hoping someone would see me. All of this occurred while I was still a young teen.

As an older teen I became seriously involved with a girl in my class. This relationship quickly became sexual. There was not a lot of give and take in our sexual relationship. It really was just another form of masturbation for me. We both grew up Catholic and believed that sex outside of marriage was a sin. We went through a pattern of being very sexual, being overcome by guilt and stopping for a while, back to being very sexual, then the guilt returning, and so on. I came to associate sex as synonymous with guilt and shame.

Shortly after high school this girlfriend became pregnant and we married. I was eighteen at the time and had just turned nineteen when our daughter was born. We were both very young and not mature enough to be married. We divorced after only one year, and I received custody of our daughter. I was nineteen years old and a single parent of an eight-month-old little girl. I needed to grow up very fast!

Looking back today I know that nearly all of my masturbation fantasy has been about males. It's odd that I never wondered whether or not I might be gay. Homosexuality was simply so unacceptable in my religion, my small town, and my family, that I couldn't even let myself wonder. I just knew that being attracted to women was the right thing to do.

Once during that young marriage I had a homosexual experience. I found an adult bookstore in the town where I was attending college. I was naïve and did not even know at the time that people met there to have sex. I went into the booth and was watching a gay adult video for my first time. It was extremely sexually stimulating for me. Then an older gentleman offered to perform oral sex, and I let him. I ran from that building in shame, fear, and disgust. The smell of that small booth stayed with me for weeks. I drove over one hundred miles that evening trying to process the experience. I eventually went home and showered for over an hour. I was so full of shame. I couldn't believe I had done something so horrible. I was sure at that moment I couldn't be gay. After all, I would have enjoyed it and not been so repulsed. The disgust lasted a few weeks, and then fantasies about men slowly began to return. I didn't go back to any place like that for a long time. But the memory and fantasy remained.

I eventually graduated from college, got a good job, and remarried. My job often took me away from home. My addiction progressed to include adult bookstores and strip clubs as well as heavy alcohol use. One day I was driving home from my travels when I stopped at a rest area along the highway. I started reading the graffiti on the restroom walls. Now, I'm sure that all that writing has been there my whole life, but I simply never noticed it before. This time the suggestions of male sex sounded very stimulating to me. I could not get the thoughts out of my head. For the next year I found myself in these restrooms reading the walls, fantasizing, driving from rest area to rest area masturbating along the way. Some times I'd even expose myself to vehicles that were higher than mine or bicyclists that could see inside my car.

The funny thing is, during this period, I didn't actually act out with people in the rest areas or bookstores. I wanted to. I knew they were there. But I was too scared. I discovered that it is not the sexual release that is the real "drug" for me, but the pursuit. I got a huge high off of cruising for sex and imagining the possibilities, rather than the sexual activity itself.

One day while on a business trip, I crossed the line from cruising to acting out with someone else. I don't even know how we hooked up. I was very drunk by the time a group of us went to the bar that night. The last thing I remember is buying a round of shots for the whole group. No one wanted them, so one by one I downed eight shots of tequila. I don't remember much after that. I came out of my blackout in my hotel room in the middle of a sex act with a very muscular man who was sniffing some type of drug. I was still drunk, but extremely terrified. I didn't know who this was or how we ended up together. I hadn't been around drugs very much either. I tactfully got him out of my room as quickly as I could. I'm sure I didn't sleep at all the rest of the night.

I felt like my life was out of control at that point, and I thought I knew the reason—alcoholism. My drinking was out of control. I had high moral values, and I was quite certain that if I didn't have the alcohol in my life, my values wouldn't allow me to continue my illicit sexual activities. I started going to meetings for my alcoholism, and have remained sober ever since. But as far as my sexual acting out, I was in for a real surprise.

The next two years were pure hell for me. All of the time and energy I used to split between my acting out and my alcoholism, I now devoted exclusively to my sex addiction. I started acting out with men in rest areas, bookstores, parks, and other public places. I spent more hours each week cruising than I could ever have imagined before. Each time I would act out, I'd instantly be filled with shame and remorse. I'd race home to my family and promise myself that I would NEVER do this again! The next day, I'd find myself back in that same situation.

I remember once cruising all night, falling asleep at the wheel and putting my wife's car in a swamp. My most regretful memories have to do with my children and my wife—such as sneaking out of our motel room in the middle of the night to have sex with a stranger in a bookstore and crawling back in bed with my wife like nothing had happened. The most painful memory of all is coming out of an adult bookstore where I had left my two young children asleep in the back seat in the middle of the night. They had awakened and were looking for me. My daughter saw me and yelled "daddy" and a couple of bookstore junkies, who had been trying to help them, sarcastically said, "You really think he's your real dad?" That was such a low point in my life. In every other aspect of my life I was the epitome of responsibility. Look how low my addiction had made me stoop!

The rest of my life looked from the outside to be pretty normal. I really had two separate worlds. One was the dark, secret part of my life that was my sex addiction. No one knew about this person. I kept him well hid. The other world was one of a devoted father and husband, a man who was active in his church and community. I had a great career that was going very well. We owned a beautiful lake home. We looked like the ideal family. But on the inside, things were not as ideal. My wife believed something was wrong. She knew something was wrong. She just didn't know what it could be, and her questions to me fell on deaf ears.

In all other aspects of my life I was an extremely honest person. I remember driving ten miles back to a convenience store because I had accidentally taken the pen I had written a check with. I prided myself in telling the clerk at a store that she had given me too much change. I was impeccable in my business dealings. Honesty was extremely important to me. I surrounded myself with people who were honest and direct. I believed deep in my heart that I was an honest person to the core.

Yet, when it came to my sex addiction, I was as far from honest as I could get. No one can spend so much time cruising without making up lies about where they were. I had more flat tires, car trouble, friends in crisis, etc., than you could ever imagine. The worse my sex addition got, the more lies I had to tell. I spent time that I was supposed to be working or at conventions acting out. I spent work money on strippers and wrote it off as business meals. When it came to my addiction, my integrity was nonexistent. It got to the point where I couldn't remember which lie I had told to whom, and I had to think fast on my feet to cover my discrepancies. This happened mostly with my wife, who often had to wonder if she was losing her mind.

I juggled these two worlds almost flawlessly for a long time. My whole goal in life was that the two worlds would never meet. But it took a terrible toll on me personally. I suffered from depression and anxiety attacks. I lived my life in constant fear. I feared that I would be arrested and my wife and kids would be publicly humiliated. I feared that I would lose my family, that I would die of AIDS, that someone would beat me up in these public acting-out places. And then the most unthinkable began to happen. My two worlds started to collide. I received a phone call at work from someone I had acted out with. Someone I knew saw me coming out of a bookstore. My main goal for all these years had been to keep these two worlds apart, and now I felt completely out of control.

The fear of humiliating my kids as a result of my addiction was one of the strongest. Up until that point in my life I never really considered suicide, even in the worst of times. But now it started to seem like the most logical option. After all, wouldn't it be much more humane for my kids to lose their father to death, than for him to be arrested and my name be splashed across the newspapers? (I had a high-profile job and was quite certain that my arrest would be news.) Or wouldn't it be more humane for me to kill myself than for them to have a father in prison or dying a long, lingering death from AIDS? I made a decision at that point to commit suicide. I had tried over and over to stop my acting out and knew at this point that it was hopeless. I promised myself each time that I would never, ever, do this again. But I always went back the next day. Suicide seemed like the only logical answer left.

Up until that point I had never told anyone about my sexual problem. It was a dark, dirty little secret that I kept buried deep within. In a moment of desperation I remembered one counselor I had seen many years prior that I thought maybe, just maybe, I could tell this to. I decided that before I killed myself, I would tell this one person, in the small chance that there could be some help. I called and made an appointment.

When I met with her I had nothing to lose, so I told the whole story. It was the first time I had ever heard these words out loud and it was quite scary and painful. She got up from her chair, walked over, and gave me a badly needed hug. She told me there were lots of people like me, and she gave it a name—sex addiction—and referred me to another counselor that specialized in this disease. The other counselor introduced me to Sex Addicts Anonymous. Some people go to their first several meetings trying to decide if they are actually sex addicts. I was not one of those people. From the very first time I heard someone tell their story in a meeting, I knew! As each person followed I was totally convinced. I felt at home. It was so comforting to know that I was not the only one. It even angered me that I had kept my secret so long, when there was help and understanding available.

Through the help of my group, my fellow sex addicts, and my Higher Power, I was able to stop my cruising and acting out. I was able to shed the shame and remorse that was such a big part of my life until that point. I was able to come to terms with myself as a sexual human being rather than sexuality being a dirty little secret. I can't say that recovery has been perfect. There have been a few slips along the way. The biggest was when the internet became so popular, and I discovered how to cruise the electronic highway. But today I'm doing well, and my life, as a whole, is phenomenally better than the day I walked into SAA.

The biggest gift recovery has given me is honesty. Today I no longer live in my two separate worlds. I have been slowly able to bring them together as one. I have been able to stop the lies and deceit. I don't have to cover my tracks or try to remember which story I've told to whom. This has given me a freedom I never knew possible.

Another gift recovery has given me is the opportunity to explore my sexuality. I've had these fantasies my entire life but never allowed myself the opportunity to question my sexual orientation. In recovery, without acting out, I was able to explore those feelings. I was able to use words like "bisexual" and "gay" without cringing. I finally came to understand that I am indeed a gay man. I spent seven of the eleven years I was married in couples counseling trying to solve a multitude of mysterious problems. The truth is they were not real problems, nor were they mysterious. I was a gay man trying to live a life where my insides would never match the actions I was portraying. That conflict was killing me, and I had to let go. I came out to my wife and kids. We separated and eventually divorced.

I began a new awakening that is not that dissimilar to a teenager. Even after acting out all those years, I really didn't know what it was like to be with a man. Yes, I spent ten-minute intervals on my knees in rest areas. But that didn't teach me anything about intimacy with a man. I learned what it's like to kiss, hug, cuddle, touch, pray, and share myself completely with another man. I felt whole for the very first time.

I have to tell you, I'm eight years into my recovery, and I'm happier today than I've ever been in my life. I still have personal struggles. Things don't always go my way. But today I live one honest life, and my insides match my outside. My recovery and the fellowship of the men and women of SAA have given me the biggest gift imaginable—my life!

16.

ANOTHER DOOR OPENS

As I think back on where I've come from, I can't help but feel a sense of relief. Yet at the same time the storm clouds are still on the horizon, there's a killer twister in the next county, and a hurricane is brewing in the Pacific of my mind. I hold my six-month-old baby and marvel at how much she has grown and changed. Where does addiction begin? Is it in the genes, or from an abusive upbringing? My baby is already learning some healthy ways to comfort herself. We try to allow her the opportunity to put herself back to sleep. It's a fine line between love and smother, between independence and neglect. But being a sober recovering member of Sex Addicts Anonymous, I can and do walk this line. Without my abstinence and recovery, I would be torn to pieces by the tornado and blown away by the hurricane. The success of my recovery determines the quality of my life.

My disease progressed over the years from isolated incidents of extreme sexual arousal in inappropriate situations, along with weekly masturbation, to cruising, stalking, manipulating victims, and masturbation with obsessive fantasy three times a day.

I had my first powerful, adrenaline-charged experience with sex when I was about twelve. My friend and I, on vacation with our families, were in a hotel swimming pool. We had met a thirteen-year-old girl who was friendly to us in a daring way. We started chasing each other, and one time she pulled at my bathing suit. Once she did that, both my friend and I felt like she'd given us permission to do the same. When I began masturbating about a year later, I returned to this memory, embellishing and rearranging the scene in whatever way that brought maximum sexual pleasure. All I knew was that recreating that scene in my mind during masturbation really "worked."

Another formative experience also illustrates the powerful payoff and the lack of regard for others that were to become a destructive way of life for me. It was movie day in my seventh-grade cooking class. When the lights went out, I leaned back in my chair and bumped the shy girl who was sitting behind me. She didn't seem to notice or care. I put my hand on her knee and left it there. She looked nervous but didn't react. Throughout that thirty-minute movie, my hand remained on her leg. My heart was pounding throughout the entire experience, but the girl never pushed my hand away. She just looked too scared to say anything. This experience was imprinted on my mind forever, and I would refer to it many times in fantasy. It seared a path in my brain, body, and soul that is open and receptive to inappropriate sexual behavior. I had created the sex addict's drug and learned to access it through acting out.

I tell the following story to illustrate the beginning of my tendency to live a double life around relationships and sexuality. By the time I hit seventh grade my father was in a state of dangerous, physically violent alcoholic insanity on many days of the week. The normal fears and insecurities of any adolescent male were surfacing, but at the time I had no place to go with it. Home, a safe haven for most people, was often the scariest place in the world for me. As a result, I believe that my normal fears of associating with the opposite sex were compounded. I'd already had a girlfriend for the entire year of the sixth grade. She was the prettiest girl in the school, and I was the most popular and all-around athletic guy. I was confident and outgoing. I felt like a true "Master of my Universe."

This came to an abrupt halt in the seventh grade, just about the same time my dad's alcoholism and spiritual and mental illness flared up. I went from an outgoing, confident boy of eleven to a shy, self-conscious, frightened adolescent of twelve. My girlfriend broke up with me over the summer, and I was alone, a seventh grader being hunted by abusive eighth graders looking for someone to trash. Fear, loneliness, and self-consciousness were my constant companions. On top of that I was stricken with mononucleosis and had very little energy for almost the entire year.

At this time someone told me that a popular and very pretty eighth-grade girl liked me and that they would set her up with me at a dance. I was excited and afraid at the same time. I went there hoping that I might get up the courage to ask her to dance. When I got there I found that I barely had the courage to go inside, and when I saw her, I froze. I could barely even look at her, let alone ask her to dance. I never did talk to her that night. I just sat in my chair glumly, unable to move, scared of a pretty girl. When I left the dance, I swore at myself, berated myself for having been so weak and frightened. It was a painful experience, and did a lot to discourage my pursuit of healthy social and sexual relations.

By the time I was sixteen my parents had divorced, my dad had moved out, and I was free to do just about anything I wanted. I started to bring girls home from school during the lunch break or from parties or from anywhere. I had sex with these girls mostly to satisfy my ego. I had never stopped masturbating. Throughout the next several years between high school and my graduation from college, my addiction to alcohol and drugs became my guiding force, and my sexual acting out was mainly disguised as "doing what boys will do." After I got sober in a twelve-step program in 1987, my sex addiction flourished despite my efforts at recovery. This was when I began to revert back to the behaviors of childhood, which would have serious consequences.

It was barely six months since I began a coaching job, when I "stumbled" upon the open locker room door. I was using an adjacent equipment room to change clothes so I could go from substitute teaching to coaching. I had been using this same room for months, but for some reason on that day it was different. I was single and lonely and bored, so maybe acting out presented an opportunity for some excitement. I do know that on Valentine's Day of 1989 I heard the girls entering the locker room and slamming locker doors, and the idea came to mind to try the door that looked in to where the girls were changing. At the time it seemed like a brilliant idea. I know now that it was the epitome of insanity, an insanity that would all but destroy my career dreams.

Many sex addicts know the feeling of adrenaline rush that comes with doing a high-level dangerous activity for the first time. I suppose that even a person who wasn't sexually addicted might have taken a look. But for me, that look led me into a progression of increasingly risky and value-violating behavior. Within a few weeks I was leaving in the middle of practice to take a peep through "The Door." I felt guilty to be so blatantly neglecting my duties, and I remember feeling grateful the time my best player asked me to hit her a bucket of balls just as I was about to "escape" again. I really enjoyed working with this girl, so I was able to turn away and leave The Door alone. Sometimes I would see swimmers going to shower, and that became a major trigger because I knew that they would undress completely, providing my addiction a powerful adrenaline rush. Finally I got so out of control that I even set up some of my own players and tried to peep on them. I knew I was violating a basic trust, but in the face of the addictive payoff I didn't care. One day I was peeping within four feet of where the swimmers were dressing, when I took a break because I had to go to the bathroom. When I came back, the floor was wet where I had been only minutes before. A swimmer had come in to turn on the showers, and avoided knocking me over only because I had left moments earlier. I wish I could say that this near discovery stopped my behavior, but it didn't.

The Door was what helped me get into recovery. At the time I had been sober from alcohol for years, and I knew that we are only as "sick as our secrets," so I had been confiding all my transgressions to my sponsor. At first he was amused and even envious, but when I continued he began to forecast doom, and tried to get me to use the steps to stop the behavior. I tried, and I was okay for a few days, but then I failed. Finally I shared about what I was doing in a closed men's meeting. A guy came up after the meeting and suggested three things: to be careful who I shared this with, to try attending twelve-step meetings that deal with addiction to sex, and to get rid of the key that gave me access to The Door. The third suggestion was certainly a good idea, but at first I could only think of all the reasons I should not give it up. Finally, when the pain, remorse, and fear became too much, I was willing to take his suggestions. I found a way to dress somewhere else, and I began attending the meetings of another fellowship that talked about addiction to sex. The importance of open-mindedness became very clear. When people give suggestions, many of us use our addict minds to rationalize why they won't work. The principle of open-mindedness asks me to carefully consider all sources and try some of the suggestions, even if they seem difficult or I don't think they will help. I thank God I was able to apply the principles of the steps well enough to at least get me into an "S" program and get me away from The Door.

I eventually lost my teaching credential as a result of my damaging sexual conduct in the classroom. At the time I knew I was in trouble, and I had made the transition to SAA several years before. I was checking in with my sponsor daily before and after work. I was talking to friends who were also battling to recover from sexual addiction. I was praying and meditating for fifteen minutes a day, exercising, and trying to live a healthy, spiritual life.

Despite these efforts, and the knowledge of almost certain consequences, I failed to stop myself from victimizing a student. That day I thought I was feeling okay, except for a vague feeling of irritation. I was maneuvering around the classroom, signing students up for a project. I had learned that I needed to regulate both my proximity to students and my visual perspective, because peeking at girls' breasts had been a trigger for me.

I did not intentionally sign students up in order to be in this position. Rather, I failed to recognize it as possibly placing myself in a vulnerable position in regard to my sex addiction. I was also angry and worried at the time because the lesson wasn't going well, and some students were rebelling against the assignment. When I went to sign up a student in the second row, I handed her the clipboard, and I could see her breasts from the position I was in above her. I knew it was absolutely against my boundaries and sobriety to look any further, but the temptation and craving felt too powerful for me to resist. I knew from my past experience that voyeuring students was very risky for me and could lead to worse behavior, but at the time I was easily able to push aside that wise thought in favor of the adrenaline rush produced by acting out.

This is the type of insanity that defies all logic and good sense. I had a career I'd worked for eight years to build. I had a secure job and a loving wife who was almost one month pregnant with our first child. We were financially secure with no evident difficulties. Yet I was willing to risk it all for a peek down a teenager's top. In other areas of my life I was responsible and even thoughtful. I paid all my bills on time. I paid my taxes and made a conscious effort to live by the principle of rigorous honesty. I never had an affair. I volunteered to help my community and was deeply involved in helping "at risk" students at school. The irony is apparent, but the important point here is that in most of my activities I was responsible and honest, with a deep desire to be useful. Yet I engaged in a behavior most people would have little difficulty in controlling, and which runs contrary to all of the positive efforts I had been making.

As a result of my actions I faced charges of molestation, paid thousands of dollars to lawyers, lost my teaching credential and an excellent job referral, and am now, one year later, earning a third of my former income without sick pay or medical benefits. But these consequences are minor in comparison to the damage I have done to others. I had already foreseen these consequences. I had great knowledge of my addiction. Yet it had failed to stop me from acting out.

I have come to know that my sex addiction is extremely powerful. I cannot restore myself to sanity, so my recovery and my life depend on a combination of surrender, footwork, and grace. God gives me guidance in my life if I look for it. I am surrounded by God's blessings at all moments of my life. If I can slow down and open my mind and heart enough, I will see these blessings. I can get access to God through a myriad of ways: phone calls, exercise, sincere prayers, meditation and reflection, connecting with people and nature, listening with my heart in meetings, experiencing emotions, braving long-term therapy, taking care of and loving myself with showers, baths, oils, and flowing water, rocking my baby, sharing with friends, holding my wife, petting my cats, and working the Twelve Steps with my sponsors. I can be renewed when I am able to see the world through others' eyes, admit my faults, take advice, or let go of something that wasn't mine in the first place. I need to set boundaries and work on maintaining the willingness to set them. Breathing exercises help me lose the sexual craving. Self-reflective, creative, and purposeful writing also help me a great deal. When I look at my own defects, instead of just blaming others or rationalizing, I am often restored to soundness of mind and spirit. None of these recovery efforts, which are outlined in the Twelve Steps and Traditions and in other SAA literature, works all the time. I have to apply them continuously so that I can live happy, joyous, and free of my obsession to act out sexually.

I have found some new tools that seem to help. I know that for me a successful program must have an approach that is multifaceted: physical (my body), mental (my thinking), emotional (my feelings), psychological (my psyche), social (my relationships), and spiritual, which I believe embodies the combination of all the above. At the recommendation of my therapist, I am now taking antidepressant medication. Treating my depression doesn't guarantee my abstinence, but it helps prevent a lot of the thoughts and images from taking hold and turning into craving and insanity. I am in group therapy specifically for sex addicts. I got an additional sponsor. Now I have one sponsor whom I consider my spiritual sponsor and close friend. I meet with him weekly for lunch. The other sponsor is guiding me through the steps in a rigorous manner. We are in the middle of the Fifth Step now, and I am practicing daily the habit of asking God to remove my fears, and trying to look at people who hurt me as spiritually wounded. I believe it is helping.

I sponsor two recovering sex addicts, but with some trepidation, because my own continuous abstinence has been so tenuous. I try to stick to sharing my experience, strength, and hope, and reading the SAA literature together so that it's a learning experience for both of us.

I hope I have shared my story in a way that can be helpful to others suffering from addiction to sex. I thank God for recovery in SAA and a chance to live again.

17.

AN END TO ISOLATION

I worked the Twelve Steps seven years before I came to SAA. I admitted my powerlessness over alcohol, had a spiritual experience, and was given back my life. Three years later I was at college in my hometown in England and discovered pornography cartoons on the internet. On a number of occasions I spent hours looking at these cartoons on the university computers, the more unusual and abusive the better. A year later I moved to London and lived in a shared apartment where there was a computer in the front room. Despite its non-private location, I stayed up on a number of work nights for hours on end, searching for and looking at pornography.

My use of the internet became more compulsive when I moved to the U.S., where I had my own apartment and laptop, and where hardcore porn of many types was easily available. I also discovered the internet newsgroups where S&M and cross-dressing material was easily available, and the "cybersex" chat rooms and sex shops. I would stay up entire nights, browsing through print and internet porn and engaging in cybersex. I also experimented with self-abusive masturbation, such as auto-asphyxiation. I was ashamed when I went into work to think of the pictures I had been looking at and the things I had been doing, but at the same time I looked forward to just locking myself in my room and living in my fantasy world.

I was still going to meetings for my alcoholism and trying to work the Twelve Steps, but knew that I was going backwards spiritually, physically, and emotionally. I hoped that by praying and working my program my Higher Power would reduce my lust, which I considered a defect of character, or at least make me ready to have it removed. But my acting out was getting worse rather than better, and I became alarmed at how the porn I was browsing was getting more and more extreme. At the start of each week I would promise myself that I would control myself more, but by the end of the week I had inevitably let myself down.

Eventually my sponsor said that I was so out of control that I had to get outside help, either from therapy or a fellowship like Sex Addicts Anonymous. By this time I had moved back to England. I ordered all the SAA literature from the website and most of the tapes. I realized that I needed to admit that I was as powerless over pornography and the internet sex scene as I was over alcohol.

I was lucky enough to be introduced to another sex addict who was seeking recovery. I shared the literature with him, and we started an SAA group. Soon, a third and fourth member came along. It is through my home group that I do my steps and service. This provides a foundation for my sexual sobriety. Since the day I admitted my powerlessness and unmanageability, and put my problem in the hands of my Higher Power, I have remained sexually sober. This was almost two years ago.

My use of hardcore pornography was utterly compulsive. On my own, I could not imagine ever being able to resist it. However, by admitting that I would never be able to resist, and using the steps, I have found it easy to not act out. It has not been a struggle. It is amazing to be protected from such an intense compulsion. It demonstrates the power of this program.

My image of women changed as I stayed sexually sober, and I began to date and feel part of the normal world of men and women. I stopped feeling isolated from the world of families and relationships. I was no longer disgusted with myself for what I was looking at on the internet, and no longer felt too ashamed to be part of the normal sexual world. Eventually I met a woman and we began a committed relationship that continually teaches me more about myself. I am able to grow spiritually again, grow sexually, and grow as the partner of another person. I am happier and more stable than I have ever been.

18.

MANY HURDLES TO JUMP

My father would spend his weekends in the garage with his power tools and a bottle of vodka. He complained so much about work that I assumed his mood swings and rage attacks were due to that. Fear quickly became a huge part of my childhood. I was afraid of my father's rage. I was also afraid of my classmates at school, and of my teachers. I was afraid of everything, including God. The depression I suffered from was believed to be only "shyness." All I knew about love was that it had something to do with Dad yelling at Mom, and control. In my family, sexuality was never discussed. There was an unspoken unease about viewing each other's nakedness, even just partly. However, my mother felt it was important to subject my brother, sister, and myself to frequent thorough washings of our genitals and occasional bedtime inspections by flashlight of our anuses for worms.

As soon as I could, I escaped into fantasy, starting with the boys in my kindergarten class whom I was too afraid to play with. I felt joyful when I would make them my "imaginary" friends, believing that in reality I was not good enough for them. Television also became a big source of escape for me. Because I felt so ugly, shy, and unworthy of male attention, I enjoyed the control I had over what I could experience with my imagination.

One day at school I discovered that by climbing the ropes in the gym I got a really good feeling. When they took down the ropes, I found I could get the same result by climbing a pole on the monkey bars in the playground. So I kept going to the gym or to the playground as often as I could. I had discovered masturbation. The only orgasms I ever experienced happened by masturbating this way, or in my sleep. Nothing else worked. Later, aggressive thoughts started entering my fantasies. I combined climbing ropes or poles with thoughts of bondage and aggression. I tried to play games involving abduction and bondage with some of my girlfriends.

At sixteen I had my first sexual encounter, with a guy five years older than me. It never progressed any further than foreplay. He also got me drunk for the first time. I discovered the love affair between sex and alcohol. Alcohol let down all my defenses and gave me the courage and the fire I needed to seek out men. I didn't know what it meant to be "in love." I thought it had something to do with being "high." If I met a guy who was attractive enough, could fulfill my sexual fantasies, liked getting drunk, and was willing to spend money on me, he was the right one. Since no man ever came close to fulfilling these requirements, I began taking out my rage on God, the way I understood him at that time, blaming him for bringing me such "losers."

By the time I was in college, I was spending nearly every weekend in bars picking up strangers and having sex with them. It didn't matter where we did it. Usually it was at his place, but frequently it was in the car or out in the woods nearby. I never remember a guy being willing to pay for a hotel room. If I weren't looking in bars, I'd go to parties or visit my sister at her college to cruise for men. My health spa was another potential place to pick up men. So was my college, where I acted out with a teacher. The next morning after acting out, I always felt ashamed, guilty, and worthless. But the next day I was ready to start looking again, living in the delusion that I could find "the right guy" eventually. Some of the high that I derived from these experiences was from the power and false sense of self-esteem that I got from seducing and winning over so many men. I would remember how rejected I felt when I was younger, and somehow this made up for it, until the next morning when I felt rejected again.

By this time my fantasies included rape. My sadomasochistic preferences were shameful and embarrassing to me, so I would never ask for it outright. When I looked at a man, I saw only an object. I never saw him as a spiritual being. Nor did I care what he was feeling emotionally (though I would pretend to). They were all selfish creatures to me. All the things I was incapable of giving, I needed from them.

Every once in a while I had a "boyfriend." This was someone I was with for more than one night. I used birth control pills and cigarettes, which helped keep my figure slim. I always wanted to be the most attractive woman in my social circles. Jealousy was a part of my obsession. One jealous obsession over a coworker lasted ten years.

After a fling with a student at my sister's college, I contracted a sexually transmitted disease. It damaged some nerves and made sex painful. I spent years of anguish and hundreds of dollars going from doctor to doctor trying to cure it. Nothing worked. I believed I had finally received the ultimate punishment for my sins. God was surely angry with me. Despite this and the fact that I had never learned to have an orgasm with a partner, it didn't stop me from acting out. It became evident that if I just allowed enough time between the times when I had intercourse, the pain was not as bad. Suicide became a frequent temptation.

A man whom I worked with started dating me, and we eventually married. We would drink together and he bought me gifts. This impressed me, but I went through sexual withdrawal in my marriage to him. Not only did he fail to meet my impossible expectations, eventually he stopped having sex with me entirely for nearly five years. I was terrified at the idea of cheating on him or ending the relationship, because I thought that meant that I would deserve the same treatment back, and God would punish me. I clung to the hope that I could still change him.

Behind all this, I believed that the true source of my misery was a God who was ruthless, cold, and abusive. By some act of grace, I found myself, in total confusion one day, surrendering to the lame, useless Higher Power I believed he was, out of complete desperation. I had nowhere else to go. Soon after, I found myself at a twelve-step meeting. It finally occurred to me that alcohol might be the problem. I started attending regularly. My chances for recovering my marriage and sex life seemed within reach. I started feeling physically well again just a month into my sobriety. But several months later my brother committed suicide, and I was the one that found him. Shortly after that, my husband and I separated and divorced. My obsession with sex took on a new dimension. Since I had modified my concept of a Higher Power, I became convinced that God's will for me was to find the right man and have my fantasies come true.

My bottom in my sex addiction came after meeting a man in a meditation group I had started attending. It wasn't long before the hugging became foreplay, the foreplay became intercourse, and then I was sending him to the hardware store to buy "enhancements." We turned his bedroom into a sexual torture chamber. My fantasies were finally becoming fulfilled. My partner seemed willing and eager to try anything. That is when the obsession took full hold over me. Alcohol had never given me the high that sex with this man was giving me. Whatever real relationship I had with the God of my understanding at that point had disappeared. Sexual obsession had once again become my Higher Power. This is what I thought I had always wanted. I lost all desire for anything else. Anything that came between me and my "drug" sent me into a rage. My job started suffering. It became intolerable. I was overcome with jealous paranoia about my partner seeing other women, and became obsessed with proving that he was cheating on me. After being with him at night, I would go to work feeling hung over. This finally became the clue. I could no longer deny that I was hitting another bottom.

I fled back to the meetings. I worked a Fourth Step with a sponsor that clearly revealed my sex and relationship addiction. I got involved in service. My sponsor set a boundary of no dating for a year, which I followed, still fantasizing about men all the while. Gradually I began to see a side of men that I had never seen before, and that there was a part of me that had spiritual needs that had never been met. I was being attracted to people by their depth and honesty more than by their physical appearance. My need to flirt was disappearing. It was as if the physical urges and emotional sickness I had experienced throughout my life had overshadowed the deep desire I had to relate to people on a spiritual level, causing me to rush into sex too fast. When I first realized this, a deep sadness came over me. Not only had I denied myself my real needs growing up, I had denied myself the opportunity to know God. This new relating to men was now letting me see men for who they really were, not just as sexual objects. And through this experience, I was developing a whole new relationship with God and myself for the first time.

At this new point in my recovery, I realized that I was not feeling lonely anymore. My life felt rich and fulfilled. Why then, was I still having the fantasies? They were as present in my mind as they were from the beginning. They threatened constantly to destroy the new and healthy friendships I was making. My first slips occurred about two years after I returned to twelve-step meetings. I acted out with four different men friends. Each time, it had started out by just playing and wrestling around. Several friends had suggested that my physical urges needed to be honored and that perhaps I was healthy enough now to have normal sex. I lost all four of these friends after trying to be sexual with them, and I felt myself slipping back into obsessive thinking. My fantasies did not decrease as a result. I noticed that my interest in God started fading. It felt like a vacuum.

I didn't think about getting help from a sex addiction recovery program until Thanksgiving of 1997. A friend suggested that what I needed was more sex, but somehow I knew that what I really needed was to talk to another sex addict. I had heard about some twelve-step programs for sex addiction and decided to try one. That wonderful hopeful feeling came back to me when I sat down in my first "S" meeting. There were people in there who were speaking my thoughts, wrestling with the same demons, and completely understanding my frustrations. Nobody tried to convince me to have sex. Instead I was advised to decide on a bottom-line behavior for my abstinence. I knew this was something that my Higher Power would reveal to me. He made it clear that I needed to keep the bottom line of abstinence and no masturbation that I had already been trying to follow in recovery. I needed to keep working the Twelve Steps and maintaining celibacy, so I could relate in a more healthy way to people.

Several months into the program, I moved to a different state and started attending Sex Addicts Anonymous meetings. I now have a home group and a sponsor who keeps me focused on the steps. It has been several years since I have acted out under my bottom line. Fantasy still plagues me from time to time, but has decreased over the years. And with the help of the program, I don't act on them.

There have been many hurdles to jump in all my years of recovery. Some bad episodes of depression tempted me to thoughts of suicide again. One of these times landed me in a mental hospital for several weeks. Several years after my father sobered up, he suffered a disabling stroke. I learned a tremendous amount from him in his struggles, and witnessed some real miracles. We were able to make our amends to each other before he died. I have discovered that my understanding of my Higher Power has grown largely because of what I have learned from my sufferings. My relationship with God and myself comes first, then my relationship with others. But all three work together in strengthening each other.

Today I choose abstinence. In SAA I've learned that I have a choice to follow whatever path is right for me spiritually. "Choosing" was never an option for me in the past. Even though God eventually answered an old prayer, and recently gave me the option to remarry, I was able to make a healthy choice for the first time in my life and decline gratefully. Instead I have chosen a marriage to myself and my Higher Power and the intimacy that I find in friendships. This is not an easy road. Learning how to have a healthy relationship with God, myself, and others has involved as much work as a marriage. I still have to keep my side of the street clean and pray for God's help constantly. Working the steps is the key.

Oftentimes I have to pray to God not to let my addiction ruin a great friendship. Recovery has also meant being willing to let go when it is necessary and set some boundaries. It may take the rest of my life to learn this, but I am willing. If somewhere down the road it becomes clear that my spiritual path should include a sexual relationship again, I am free to choose that, but I always pray for my Higher Power's will for me first. Then I go on intuition. And what I have discovered here is that God is not shaming and does not expect perfection from me. He has truly become my best friend over the years. I think he only hopes that I will continue to grow in my trust in him.

I am grateful to SAA for helping me to accept my sexual addiction, providing me the fellowship I need, and keeping me focused on the steps and my sobriety.

19.

A HIGHER SOURCE

I didn't want to say the words. I didn't want to go to the meetings. I was addicted to phone sex, but I was certain I could deal with the problem by seeing a psychologist. This was a private matter that I would handle privately. I knew about twelve-step programs because six years earlier I had gone to a fellowship that dealt with drug addiction, and I successfully stopped smoking pot. But being a pothead carried a certain glamour—it was hip—and I was able to admit to that addiction before a group of strangers. Sex was different. It was unsavory to think about discussing my sex habits with anyone but a paid confidante.

The twelve-step meetings had inspired me. I went for several years and never slipped. I liked the honesty and down-to-earth candor of the participants. I made friends and looked forward to sharing. The group solidarity helped me enormously. I made commitments and, ever since my first meeting, have honored my commitment not to drink or drug. My marijuana obsession lifted. But I never got a sponsor and never worked the steps. I was able to achieve sobriety without working a rigorous spiritual program. After my third year I stopped going to meetings.

Sex was something else. As an adult, sex had been an issue since the 1970s, when I talked my wife into an open marriage. Our agreement was that we could date, even have affairs. Though our sexual relationship had always been one of the strongest and most exciting aspects of our marriage, I felt restless. Gay liberation was in the air, and I wanted to explore. I went wild. For five years, I had sex with men as well as women. I didn't take seriously the fact that I had been molested by my uncle when I was a teenager. During this "open period," when I myself molested my teenage nephew, I didn't see the connection with my own history. I wasn't conscious of violating boundaries. I ignored the pain and confusion I was causing my nephew. I didn't want to see, didn't want to think about the catastrophic consequences of my actions. I didn't allow myself to feel the damage.

Meanwhile, my freewheeling sexual encounters grew in number. My only guide was physical pleasure. On certain nights, the city seemed to call to me—the fragrance of the air, the party lights, the action in the clubs—and all resistance collapsed. I wanted what I wanted. And I wanted it more and more. When a counselor warned that I was taking dangerous risks, doing grave harm, and that I was, in fact, on the brink of losing my wife and children, her words shocked and frightened me. I vowed to stop all extramarital encounters.

I did. I didn't have person-to-person sex outside of my marriage in the 1980s, but I did masturbate more frequently, and I did purchase pornography, and I did find myself living in lust—lust for men, lust for women—even as my sexual relationship with my wife remained surprisingly good. In retrospect, I see that nearly every sexual encounter was fueled by dope. The relationship between sex and drugs was something I took for granted and never challenged.

In the mid-1980s I was confused enough to go into psychoanalysis, thinking it might give me clarity and, at the very least, help me stop smoking pot. It did neither. I went four days a week, often arguing with the traditional Freudian analyst about why I had to remain on my back on the couch while he lorded over me from his high-backed chair. I questioned the hierarchical relationship between therapist and patient. I wondered whether I was addressing my real problems. After fifteen months, I quit. At the start of the 1990s, I concluded that I could not give up marijuana on my own. Even with my career progressing well and my marriage intact, I felt the drug both draining and over-stimulating me. After going to meetings, I got a glimpse of the spiritual heart of the program but stopped short of embracing that heart. I had achieved sobriety, and sobriety was enough. What else was there to do? My sexual habits, my excessive masturbation and flirtation with pornography were not, I rationalized, the worst thing in the world.

Late in my third year of sobriety from pot, I discovered phone sex. I kept hearing the voice of my mother from somewhere in my remote childhood saying, "Push down one addiction and watch another flare up." Phone sex flared up like fire. Its anonymity, its availability, its variety—everything about phone sex conspired to hook me and hold me in its grip. This was clearly my "drug of choice." Even though I was stunned by its power and the vast sums of money I spent on the indulgence, I wasn't quite ready to see it as an addiction. It was simply something I overdid.

I masturbated while engaging in spoken fantasies with other men on the phone. The fantasy and play-acting became more extravagant. The more I did it, the more I wanted to do it. It was progressively taking over. Whenever my wife left me alone in the house I was on the phone.

In front of a therapist that my wife and I were seeing, I admitted my problem and said it was something I wanted to address with a therapist of my own. I found that therapist, and I continue to work with him today. He heard me discuss my troubled relationship with phone sex. I told him how angry my wife was, how angry I was at myself, and how all these issues muddled my mind. I told him that someone had suggested a twelve-step group focused on this issue, but I didn't want that. He didn't argue. He was content to listen to me.

It took over a year. Our discussions invariably turned to phone sex. For short periods of time—two weeks here, three weeks there—I was able to stop. But then I would start up again, and I was unhappy about it. I was doing it when I didn't want to. I was acting compulsively and, in time, acting recklessly, toying with the idea of arranging rendezvous with the men I met on the phone. I was also living in lust, hammering myself with questions about my sexual identity. Was I hetero, homo, or bi? And how could I escape this state of habitual desire and confusion?

My therapist and I dealt with the ways my inner voices undermined my sense of worth. I slowly started to isolate and identify those voices, to strip them of their masks and many disguises, to see the ways in which negative messages—brutally self-destructive assaults—were wired into my emotional system. The task of understanding those compassionless voices goes on.

Despite all this good therapy, though, my addiction did not abate. Phone sex raged on as an obsession and source of conflict. I loved it; I hated it; I wanted to stop; I couldn't stop. Pledges to stop were broken time and again. The act itself, dialing the numbers, cruising the connections, finding still another make-believe partner, had become a supercharged ritual I couldn't resist.

"It's nothing I want to discuss before strangers," I kept telling my therapist. "It's something I want to deal with here."

My therapist let me go my own way. But one day he said, "Secrecy only serves to fuel obsessions." The statement struck me. I didn't want to consider its wisdom, but the words wouldn't go away. My addiction, born in secrecy, remained shrouded in secrecy. Confessing to a therapist didn't change that. My wife assumed I had stopped when I hadn't. Outside my therapist's office, no one knew how my preoccupation with phone sex was ruling my psyche.

I rationalized: I wasn't physically touching anyone other than myself; I couldn't get AIDS; I could afford the phone bills; there were far worse addictions; I wasn't harming anyone. This last rationalization rang the most hollow. I knew I was harming myself. I thought of my spiritual life and felt stifled and stuck. Smiling and sighing at the same time, I remembered a line from a movie, "Are we making progress or just beating off?" I knew I wasn't making progress. I knew what I had to do.

Before doing it, though, I spent Yom Kippur, the holiest of Jewish holy days, the day reserved for the repentance of sins, indulging in an orgy of all-afternoon phone sex, while my wife sat in a synagogue. The next day I called information and asked for the number of sex recovery groups. The first number I was given was for SAA. As my fingers punched out the numbers, I thought of all the times I punched out numbers for phone sex. The next day I went to a meeting, nervous and angry and still not entirely convinced I had the guts to go through with it.

I went through with it. At my first meeting, I swallowed hard and said I was a sex addict. I had worried that the others in attendance would be creepy characters from the underbelly of society. I was surprised and heartened to see that they were much like me. The meeting wasn't as bad as I had feared. And a few days later I was back. I listened more intently. I liked what I heard. The honesty was inspiring and courageous. The honesty had me saying things in public that I had never said before. I kept coming back. I was moved by the stories I was hearing. My therapist suggested that I had found my core addiction. I agreed.

When my work required travel early in my recovery, I took some phone numbers and called people in the program from my lonely hotel rooms. The calls made all the difference. I didn't act out. When I had gained a good understanding of the concept of the Three Circles, I decided to put not only extramarital sex in my inner circle, but masturbation as well. After all, phone sex, the behavior that crushed my spirit, was a form of masturbation. I didn't want to flirt with disease. I wanted serenity and recovery.

I got a sponsor. That wasn't easy for me. I don't like authority. I resist being told what to do. I'd rather give than take advice. I like to play the part of senior statesman. The fact that my sponsor was younger than I presented a challenge. But he had been one of the first to offer his support, one of the people I called when I was out of town. I was drawn to his seriousness and devotion to the program. He was open-hearted and eager and hungry for recovery—for others as well as for himself. He was generous with his time and tough-minded in his approach. At first I resisted his lead. I wanted the upper hand. Like so many addicts, I wanted to direct and control my own recovery. As I argued, he talked about the beauty of surrendering.

I argued with God. I argued with the concept of God. These were old arguments, stale arguments, but arguments that continued to haunt me and hurt my program. They were necessary arguments, though, that needed to be worked through and voiced out loud at meetings. At meetings I also needed to say what I had done to my nephew. After a few months the arguments began to dissipate. I admitted that my spiritual life had been an unmanageable mess. I recognized the need for a Power greater than myself to free me from the prison of my addiction. I surrendered. All the while I tried to remember the overriding principle of my program—abstain; don't act out no matter what.

Following my sponsor's lead, I decided to approach my recovery aggressively. I formed a feedback group. I made a habit of going to many meetings. I shared. I took commitments. I called other addicts and encouraged them to call me. I forged friendships. I began a practice of morning meditation and prayer. I strove to understand the program's original purpose and plan. I sought to know the source of its inspiration.

Miraculously, my obsession started to lift. I was no longer in a perpetual state of lust. The issue of my sexual identity ceased to be a burning question. I was more patient and emotionally available with my wife than ever before. Our physical relationship grew happier and healthier. My wife agreed to attend a couples group, where the only requirement is that one member of the couple define himself or herself as a sex addict. The group hasn't always been easy. Anger and resentment still linger, but the forum is open and honest, and, best of all, the secret is out. There's something liberating about sitting in a room announcing to others, while my wife is by my side, that I am a sex addict. It's critical for me that my wife, the love of my life, has become part of my recovery.

All the tools help. I speak to my sponsor almost every day. At first I hesitated about appearing so needy. Now I worry less about my image and more about my abstinence. I allow myself to go to as many meeting as I like. I've also allowed myself to voice my enthusiasm and love for the fellowship. The meetings provide a deep and satisfying connection to others, reminding me of the emotional connections I sought but never found in phone sex.

I see my recovery as nothing more or less than my daily life. Listening more attentively to others is part of my recovery. Writing this story is part of my recovery. When I was deep into my addiction, my mind was fogged over. My spirit was in disrepair. Abstinence has blessed me with a degree of clarity, even a measure of calmness. Calmness has allowed me to see what I really want and need. In my morning prayers I ask that kindness be my guide, not apprehension and fear. Last week my wife and I bought matching plants and placed them outside my office door. In the early morning my eyes are drawn to the plants. With their leaves reaching to the sky like open arms, the plants absorb sunshine from a higher source. They receive the warmth required for growth. I seek that same source, that same warmth.

20.

TWO SURRENDERS

My first memory of acting out was at age six. I remember urinating into bottles and burying them under the house. By the age of eight, I would get a rush by going through my mother's or grandmother's drawers and touching or smelling their underwear. When I was ten, I acted out with the teenage boy across the street. We only acted out together once, but he continued to seek me out and I continued to want him to be my friend for months.

At age twelve, my addiction seemed to take off. I don't think it's a coincidence that that was when we moved out of my grandparents' house and got our own. I would climb out of my bedroom window and stand on the wall and try to see the neighbor ladies undress. This was my first memory of the rush—the adrenaline pump that became so familiar to me. By the time I was thirteen, I would go to the local dairy and get a charge out of sneaking up on the cows and pulling their udders. At fourteen, I had my bedroom walls covered in porno centerfolds. To this day, I wonder why my parents allowed this, but I remember getting in trouble in school, and the punishment was that I had to take the porn off my walls.

At fifteen, I had sex for the first time. I still remember my orgasm as lasting ten minutes. Of course it didn't. I thought I had found the answer to the business of living. I proceeded to have sex with as many partners as many times as I could. I sought out mostly undesirable women because I believed nice looking women wouldn't have sex. I was obsessed with sex from the age of fifteen to twenty-two. I would find women who were willing to have sex with multiple partners, and bring my circle of close friends together for that purpose. I felt like a big shot for doing this. I now understand about my own self-esteem and feeling of "apart from." A few times, I remember my dad handling calls from irate parents whose daughters were pregnant. When I was twenty, I was arrested for indecent exposure. I was drunk in a parking lot, got out of my car, urinated, then exposed myself to the girls in the car next to me.

At twenty-one, I was arrested for statutory rape. The girl was about fifteen. Around this time, one of my semi-steady acting-out partners became pregnant. I manipulated her into giving up the baby for adoption with the intention of bailing. Well, the addiction pulled me back to her, and she got pregnant again. This time the guilt was too strong—we got married. As dysfunctional as the marriage was, I thank God for it, because it probably saved my life.

At this point, I made what I know now was an addiction switch. My obsession became work and money. For the next fifteen years, I only acted out once outside of my marriage. However, I would sacrifice my values, my self-respect, and my dignity to have sex with my wife. I was very controlling and tyrannical during the marriage—God bless my now ex-wife. The only real power she had was sex, and so a power struggle was the norm.

At this point, the family started to fall apart, and the pain started to return. Although my drinking was always in the background, now I started to drink heavily. (I am sober now—thanks to God and the Steps). I was burned out on work—the booze wasn't enough—so I had sex with my first prostitute. The feeling was exhilarating. I was free at last. I was no longer trapped in a power struggle with my wife for sex. Within six months, I was acting out twice a week. In a year, it would be about four times a week.

The run I was on lasted five years, the last two years of which I acted out every day. I had unprotected intercourse with over four hundred street prostitutes—mostly in my car, occasionally in a motel, always accompanied by cruising.

Some of the consequences of my acting out were that I wrecked my car twice chasing prostitutes, got crabs about ten times, had gonorrhea twice, and had chlamydia once. I remember I brought crabs home to my wife and convinced her it was her fault. When I brought gonorrhea home, I passed it off as just a slight infection and called her gynecologist and convinced him that I would stop what I was doing if he could cover me just this once. He somehow did.

But when I brought chlamydia home, I was busted. I admitted to sex with several prostitutes, and the marriage was finished. I ended up losing the marriage and the relationship with my children. Then came divorce. The monetary losses were staggering.

The insanity continued. All of these things only put a dent in my acting out. I tried everything I could to control and enjoy a little acting out. Some of the things I tried were swearing off my addiction, acting out on weekends only, acting out on Tuesdays and Thursdays only, prostitutes with large breasts only, prostitutes with blond hair, etc.

Nothing worked. I went to a therapist and would act out before a session. Sometimes I would act out after. This lasted for about a month. I contacted another twelve-step program dealing with sexual addiction and went to a couple of meetings. I knew their program wouldn't work for me.

I thought I was doomed. My spiritual awakening came on a day when I got up and felt strong and resolved not to act out that day. By five p.m., I came home one more time and realized I had done it again. I got in the shower and felt like taking the first layer of skin off with a wire brush. I got out of the shower crying and fell on my knees and cried out the only prayer I had left: "Oh, God, help me."

Nothing much happened right away. Then about a week later after a twelve-step meeting, I went to coffee with a friend. I told him what I was doing. He told me what he had done. He told me about a bunch of guys on the other side of town that called themselves sex addicts and if I wanted to go, he would go with me. About a week went by and I called him and we went.

I have been hanging out with these guys now for six years. By the grace of a loving God and my SAA group, I haven't acted out in my inner circle for four and a half years. That is truly a miracle. I can say that SAA saved my life. When I got here, I was helpless. I knew I was going to die of AIDS. The first year and a half was a struggle for me. The first seven months, I couldn't seem to get more than a few days. Then I received enough grace to put together eight months. I then slipped and went on a three-month bender. I just couldn't seem to get back to the meetings—too much shame, humiliation, and pride. I thank God today that I got back to the program on June 9, 1989. I slipped again on the tenth; got back to a meeting on June 11, and have been abstinent until today.

About this time, I made the single most important discovery I have ever made right up until today. I discovered that if I asked for God's help to stay abstinent in the morning, checked in by phone with another addict in the middle of the day, and went to a meeting of SAA that night, I didn't act out. God gave me the willingness to carry this out for a little over a year. It is now my foundation.

My abstinence took two surrenders, really. I had to surrender my disease to God and then surrender myself to SAA. My deal with God is simple today—he takes care of the abstinence; I take care of meetings, phone, and asking for help. In a way, I had an improper use of will for a long time. Trying to will myself not to act out never worked. But what I could will myself to do was to go to meetings, pick up the phone, and ask for God's help.

Almost two years ago, my obsession to act out was removed. I don't think it was a coincidence that this took place about halfway through my Ninth Step. I love the results of applying the Twelve Steps in my life, because the more I do, the better my life gets.

I have dreams today that are coming true. I have recently moved to the beach area—something I have dreamed about for a few years now. Prior to this, I had a chance to live alone for the first time, and the experience was great. I got a chance to furnish my apartment from the ground up. I am getting in touch with what I'm like as a person and taking the action to have a nice place.

I am in a committed relationship with a wonderful woman today. I never knew I could have a person in my life who was loving, caring, understanding, nurturing, and supportive. I never knew I had these same things in me to give to another person. I have all this today.

I have received many blessings in recovery. I go to meetings about twice a week and have a great time. Sometimes I even learn something. I have changed my work situation. I realized that the choice I had made for a career did not suit me. I stopped doing that work. I still don't know what I want to do when I grow up, but I'm having a good time looking. My life has abundance today—even some money in the bank too. SAA saved my life, and I am eternally grateful. When I came in, I was in a hopeless state of mind and body—chronically addicted. If this program can work for me, it can work for anybody. Keep coming back. God bless.

21.

OUT OF THE PARKING LOTS

I was a late bloomer in my sex addiction. Once I got started, though, I made up for lost time fairly quickly.

I don't like to spend a lot of time dwelling on my parents and my upbringing. I will say that I grew up in a blue-collar neighborhood on the east coast. My mother was a mean, abusive alcoholic whose disease grew worse over the years until it finally killed her. We had been close up to a point, and then her alcoholism created a wedge in our relationship. My father, who held a couple of different blue-collar jobs over the years I was growing up, almost never drank; yet he had serious problems with rage. I was terrified of him. Later in life, I spent a lot of time trying to get my father, in the guise of men who resembled him, to love me.

I really craved the attention of men. I remember when I was about six years old our family went to Niagara Falls. A man standing next to me at the falls started a conversation with me. At one point my mother told me to be careful not to get too close to the railing, for what would happen if I fell in? The man said, "I'd go right in after you." That sort of display of caring from an older man was completely foreign to me, and I still remember it to this day.

One of my happiest childhood memories was of being taken under the wing of a man who lived across the alley from me. He was an avid chess player and would take me to his matches on Saturday afternoons. I wanted more physical closeness with him, and at the same time I was happy to get the attention I was receiving from this older man whom I liked and respected.

While I was a child I learned to voyeur from the underwear ads in the department store catalogues. In high school, I was the manager of one of our high school sports teams, and I quickly figured out that the manager position gave me a chance to voyeur the guys on the team when they took their showers, under the guise of handing out towels to them. I could have easily left out the towels for them to retrieve on their own. Mostly, however, I was attracted to several of the gym teachers, and was always looking for excuses to go into the office where they changed clothes and showered; my efforts were rewarded whenever I caught one or another of them naked.

I was very much a loner all through my school years and knew little about sex. Even though I was accused on occasion of masturbating in the bathroom, the truth of the matter is, I didn't even know what that was or how to do it. I didn't learn until I got to college in 1969 and heard my friends talking about it. Even then I couldn't believe that what these guys in my dorm were describing could possibly be correct because it sounded so undignified. It was not until I was a junior that I even gave it a try. I was immediately hooked. I had changed dorms by then, and would masturbate in my upper bunk bed several times a day. My roommate, who must have known of my activities, never said a word about them, so I believed that neither he nor anybody else in the dorm knew what I was doing.

Eventually I got to be a little more discreet about my masturbating, and my addiction went into a semi-dormant phase until my fifth year of grad school, which is also when I came out as a gay man. I was working on my dissertation and had a very unstructured schedule, only teaching class two hours a day, three days a week. So I would work on my paper "all day" and then figure my reward was to go out to the bars at night. Since I didn't have a car, it took some time to walk to the bars and then of course time to walk back, so I often didn't get home until four a.m. or later, which meant that I wasn't getting up until late in the morning. So I wasn't working on my paper nearly as much as I had convinced myself I was.

Accordingly, I didn't finish my paper on time, and my teaching job at the university ran out. So I took a full-time college teaching job in another state. I still only had to work three days a week. It didn't take me long to discover the acting-out places, and it was at this time that I started to have sex with men on a semi-regular basis. I'd walk to the acting-out area, a couple of miles away, and pick up a man who would bring me back home. We would have sex and then he'd rush out the door. Many of these guys had told their wives they were going out for groceries or some such thing, and so, between that and the shame I judged that they carried, there were no pleasantries either before or after the sex. I had also started attending a local church on Sundays and on

Wednesday evenings; there was a family who would come and pick me up and take me to church, and I would do the family routine when I was with them. So I was living a real double life.

My most shameful moment that year happened after I finally bought a car. I drove to the local acting-out spot and picked up a man who turned out to be a student at the college where I was teaching. He wanted me to perform oral sex on him; I didn't do it, although the shame was almost as great as if I had actually gone through with it.

My job at this college lasted only a year. It could have gone on longer, as there was still a vacancy in the department that I could have filled. But I was not asked to stay. I've always suspected that students had seen me frequenting the local gay bar, and word had gotten back to the dean of our college, who was also a minister for a conservative denomination in the town.

In the fall of 1979, I came back to the town where I had gone to grad school, still not having finished my dissertation. I got a full-time job, and in the evenings I was more interested in hanging at the bars than in working on my paper. Eventually I discovered a much bigger city in the same state where I discerned that the acting-out opportunities were greater, so I moved there.

My acting out increased for a while, as did my drinking, and then slowly I moved into another semi-dormant phase. I got to a point where I was only going to the bars once a week. The rest of the time I was isolating. I'd tape the daytime soap operas and spend my evenings watching them. I felt that the characters in these soap operas were my friends, and so I didn't need any flesh-and-blood friends. In the meantime, my addiction was doing push-ups, as I was soon to discover.

Back in the 70s, before I ever owned a car, CB radios became the rage for a while. It seemed every car had one. By 1985, when I got a CB radio put into my car, they were something that once again were mostly the province of truck drivers.

In mid-1986, I went out of town for the weekend to visit the town where I used to live. I still had a lot of friends there and would go on occasional visits. Driving back, I had my CB on, and about thirty miles short of getting home I heard a truck driver soliciting sex. I immediately answered him and arranged to meet him at the rest area where he was sitting. That was the first time I had ever crawled into the cab of a tractor. Besides being of course a blue-collar male, the driver called me "buddy," which pushed a lot of my buttons. I felt like this man was accepting me, and of course being accepted by a blue-collar, masculine male was the thing I had been craving all my life.

We had sex, and for the rest of that evening and all the next day I was floating. I felt like I had finally found what I had always wanted. My CB radio became my own personal play toy, and any time I was hungry, angry, lonely (that was a big one), or tired, not to mention any number of other things, I'd be out there in my car, only now I was the one doing the hunting. I had a fairly good success rate, and even though I had to put up with a fair amount of verbal abuse, I figured that came with the territory. I would wake up in the middle of the night, figure I had to go to the truck stop or rest area even when I didn't want to, because I might miss something, and then stay out the rest of the night, just barely dragging myself to work on time.

One night, after about a year of this, a truck driver who heard me on the radio lined up a couple of cops, set himself up as the decoy, and the cops caught me. They shamed and humiliated me, asked me if I had AIDS, laughed at me, and put me in the back of their squad car. For some reason, they chose not to haul me in, and instead warned me that if they ever found me out there again, I would go to jail. As I got back in my car and started it up, my CB radio automatically came back on. Even though I had been with the cops for a good ten or fifteen minutes, the driver who had served as the decoy was still on the radio laughing about the fact that he had helped catch a queer. This was without a doubt the most shameful night of my life. And all I learned from it was that I had to change my modus operandi.

Around this same time, I ran across a book whose title caused me to wonder if I had a problem with sex addiction. I eventually called the number for Sex Addicts Anonymous in the phone book, and the man who returned my call asked me if I was a sex addict. I told him I didn't know, and he suggested a book that I should read. Once I had read it, if I thought I was a sex addict then I should call back. I read the book and there was nothing in there about truck drivers, so I figured I must not be a sex addict. Some six months later, things had gotten bad enough that I decided to call the hotline again. This time I said yes, I was a sex addict, and the man I was talking to gave me the times and locations of two meetings.

In the meantime, one of the new ways I had discovered for finding truck drivers was to run personal ads. I eventually hooked up with a man who lived about forty miles from me. I went over to his house full of excitement, and ran through my whole sexual repertoire with this man, hoping to snare him. When we were finished and he expressed no interest in getting together with me again, I was crushed. That's when I figured I had better get to a meeting. This was in April of 1991.

I stayed in SAA for a few months, and things went well until I did a formal First Step in front of the group. Everybody but one man applauded after I finished it—of course, he's the one I focused on. This man came up to me after the meeting and told me that we don't talk about our parents in meetings, and other discouraging things. Believing this man's assessment that I wasn't a sex addict and didn't belong there, I left SAA for what turned out to be about a year.

During that year, my life became much worse. On one occasion, I picked up a hitchhiker at a truck stop and brought him home with me. After one night of sex, I was convinced we were going to be together forever. He left a few days later while I was at work, taking about six hundred dollars worth of my personal belongings with him. I really felt violated by this theft. My response, after spending a Saturday replacing all my missing stuff, was to head out to the truck stop, saying to myself, "This is all I have; it has to work, it just has to." I was more indiscreet than usual that night and was stopped by another cop while I was cruising the parking lot. I lied about why I was out there, and he ran a search on me that turned up nothing. So he let me go, and I headed the fifty or so miles back home. This was the last straw. All the way out there I had been saying to myself, "This has got to work," and now I was saying "This has got to stop." Even though I didn't recognize it at the time, in many ways that hitchhiker did me the biggest favor anybody ever has.

The next night, I was back at the SAA meeting where I had done my First Step a year earlier. I'm convinced that there are no coincidences— the man who had lambasted me so severely the year before was there doing his First Step. Not only that, but I came in a few minutes late and right when I walked in, he was talking about his parents! So I figured this was where I was supposed to be. I'll admit that it did take me a while to let go of that particular resentment, however.

A few weeks later, a man offered to sponsor me, and we worked the rest of the steps. I was starting to get active in SAA and was coming out of my shell. For several years running I opened up my house at both Thanksgiving and Christmas to those members of SAA who chose to spend the holidays with other recovering sex addicts.

I had worked my steps, and things were going fairly well, certainly much better than they had in a long time. I even remember the day I got in my car to drive to a truck stop and then turned around and came home after deciding on the way that I didn't really want to do that. Still, I had gotten to a certain point in my recovery, and couldn't seem to get past that. I would be okay during the week, and late on Friday and Saturday evenings I would go to this trucker bar, have a couple of beers, and sometimes pick up a driver or get picked up by one. Most of these men had rooms at the hotel to which the bar was attached. The majority of these liaisons ended without incident, although in a couple of cases, once the sex was over the man got angry and even threatened to become violent. I especially remember one man who accused me of "targeting" him, and told me while I was quickly getting dressed that he had military training in making people "disappear." He went into the back to get some tool to help him carry out his threat. I didn't know if he was bluffing and didn't plan to stay around to find out. Somehow I managed to keep my wits about me, got my shoes on, and got out of there, replying to his statement "Don't go; we're not finished yet" with a polite and terrified "Good night" as I hurried out the door. Obviously the issues of this man and the others who threatened me were being triggered big time, but that would have been small consolation had I ended up in the hospital or the morgue.

I didn't give up on SAA, though, and in fact I went to my first convention in May 1995. I had made my plane reservation so that I would be leaving for home early Monday morning, thus missing the last speaker and the closing ceremonies. However, I had such a great time all weekend that I called the airline Sunday evening and had my plane reservation postponed. I haven't missed an SAA convention since then, and have been involved in the planning of two of them. Still, the memories of that first convention are very special to me.

A couple of months later, an SAA member, in response to my sharing about getting drunk over a Labor Day holiday, suggested that I look into my alcohol issues. So I started going to twelve-step meetings for my drinking as well. I began drinking only soda at the trucker bar and found that I could no longer approach men for sex. Up until that time, I had no idea how unmanageable alcohol had been making my life.

During the next several years, I spent a lot of time working with men in alcohol and drug rehabs. Many of these places being open late, this gave me something to do later in the evenings when I had lots of time on my hands, time that I would have otherwise spent drinking sodas at that bar. I would still show up at the bar occasionally, and even though I wasn't acting out there any more, God saw fit to do for me what I couldn't do for myself—within a couple of years the management of the hotel decided to close the bar for good.

Obviously I couldn't make direct amends to the many truck drivers I had harmed over the years. So instead God laid it on my heart to get involved in a truck driver ministry at one of the local truck stops, which I did for about four years.

I remain very active in SAA service, particularly in the areas of literature and prison outreach.

I think that the single greatest reward I have received from SAA, and twelve-step recovery in general, was to learn that I had a lot more to offer others than my sexual repertoire. I have returned to some of the things that interested me back before my sex addiction took over. I continue to spend time working on myself, meditating, praying, and giving back. I'm fifty-two years old now; when I was younger I wondered if I would still be sitting on barstools when I was in my 70s, or if the cops would one day find me with a bullet in my head in the parking lot of some truck stop. I'm happy to say that my life is better today than it has ever been, and SAA was the catalyst that started me on that journey of fulfillment.

22.

STAYING ON THE PATH

I have been a sex addict for sixteen years, fifteen of which I've been married to the man I'm still with. I joined SAA because my life had become completely unmanageable. Even though I risked alienating my children, contracting AIDS, and losing my husband, I continued to act out sexually. My acting out consisted of giving myself sexually and emotionally to anyone who showed an interest in me. I had no boundaries.

I now realize that my addiction stems from what I went through as a child. I was a victim of incest by my father from birth to twelve years of age. I feel that I never have had a healthy sexuality. Incest was a violation of my sexuality, my being. When my sexual boundaries were violated time after time, I lost sight of them. My innocent child's unconditional love for my father made me confuse love with sex. I only felt lovable if sexually desirable. I had to be a good sex partner or else I would be rejected and abandoned. I grew up and lived with shame that fueled my sex addiction, which created more shame.

Going to SAA was a turning point in my life. Working the Twelve Steps, hearing my group members share their experiences, and consulting with them when I needed help have given me much strength and direction. After I stopped my acting-out behaviors, I was able to define and embrace what my personal values really are. Here is some of what I learned:

Before: Other people's needs were more important, even when they infringed on mine.

Now: I have a right to make my own boundaries and stay within them.

Before: I had to be sexual to be liked; it was the price to pay.

Now: My sexuality belongs to me. I can say "No" to anyone who tries to cross my boundaries.

Before: I sought out sexual partners to give me a temporary good feeling about myself, but afterwards I'd just feel ashamed and worthless.

Now: I can value myself as a person, raising my self-esteem by affirming my strengths and having compassion for myself.

Before: Although I wanted to be married, I was powerless to be faithful. I was sexually addicted and out of control.

Now: With the love I have for my husband, I want to keep my marriage commitment, and above all, I want to remain monogamous.

Before: I was a compulsive liar, an expert at deceiving others. I needed to protect my addiction above all. I even fooled myself.

Now: I want to be honest in all parts of my life, to others and especially to myself.

Before: Sex addiction was my Higher Power. I didn't think I could live without it.

Now: I feel I can't be sexually healthy without being spiritual. Knowing that God (my Higher Power) is there for me makes all the difference.

I think I've always had a sense of what my values were, but as an addict I rationalized my values to protect my sex addiction. Adhering to my personal values still allows me to be sexual, but in a healthy, self-affirming way.

Even though one of my values is to remain monogamous with my husband, that doesn't mean my sexuality will be naturally healthy like I want it to be. I need to remember certain things:

When I feel the hurt, needy child within me come out (the one who grew up without a nurturing, emotionally present parent and the one who confuses love with sex), I need to nurture her. My natural instinct is through sexual means. When I feel this way I need to identify it and tell my spouse aloud, "I am not feeling sexual right now. I just need to be close, to be hugged, and to know you love me just the way I am." I used to take it for granted that he should know how I'm feeling, even when I didn't always know myself. Then when we were sexual, even though I would enjoy it, I would end up in tears and not have the faintest idea why.

I do not allow myself to fantasize about other people when I'm being sexual with my husband. Fantasizing was an acting-out behavior within my marriage. For me it added to my unhealthy sexuality.

For right now, masturbation is not a part of my life unless it is shared with my partner. Masturbation played a large part in my sex addiction. Until I become more aware of why it was such a compulsion for me, I've eliminated it.

Sometimes I identify a certain touch at a particular time with the sexual touch from my father. This is a dangerous situation for me to remain in—it's like a flashback. I need to center myself by realizing the present time and who I'm with.

Before recovery, my feelings after being sexual were completely different than they are now. While acting out I would feel good, like a "high" feeling, but afterward I would feel isolated and lonely. I would have shame attacks and go into a depression until the next "fix." Now I feel a real connectedness within myself. I feel much love for my husband before, during, and after being sexual with him. I choose to be sexual by desire, not out of neediness. My self-esteem grows after our sexual beings come together and share each other.

I know I'm on the right track to becoming sexually healthy. I don't always know the answers, but talking with my SAA group always helps me stay on the right path. I need to share about problems I'm having and how my progress has affected my life and family. For me it is immensely helpful to receive feedback from other sex addicts. I know I won't be judged because we all share a common goal: to become sexually healthy.

23.

GROWING UP

I never thought that there was anything wrong with my obsession with sex. As an adolescent, I reveled in dreams and fantasies of encounters with people I knew. Finding a stack of pornographic magazines in my father's dresser fed my frenzy—it felt so bad, so wrong, and yet so pleasurable to look at illicit material. At the age of twelve, I got an early morning paper route and used the opportunity to fantasize, expose myself, and masturbate outside. Of course, there was always the terrifying possibility of getting caught, but somehow the chance of humiliation only made me bolder.

Masturbation quickly became a way of life for me. Although frightened that I might be caught, I took ever greater chances. Taking risks made me feel alive, and this prompted me to take more risks. At fourteen, while spending the night at a friend's home, I had an encounter with another boy. I was anxious that I might have contracted AIDS, but was too afraid to take an HIV test. My fear fed my addictive cycle of acting out as a way to feel safe and secure.

Toward the end of high school, I found myself in my first real relationship with a girl. She was a wonderful girl, and she knew absolutely nothing about sexuality. I took the opportunity to "educate" her in every way I knew how. I clung to the idea that I would be a virgin when I was married, but I considered virginity to be only applicable in the strictest sense. As long as intercourse was not involved, I was still a virgin. So for two and a half years, I pushed my high school girlfriend to do more and more that she did not want to do. I was voracious—willing to take risks that terrified her, such as having encounters at school. And after a while, I decided that it was okay to supplement my physical relationship by fantasizing about other women, although I felt guilty about it. None of the intimacy issues in our relationship ever struck me as a problem, though. I thought we were the storybook couple. But when my dream dumped me without explanation shortly into college, I had to reconsider my outlook on life. I was convinced that I was a good person, and I couldn't fathom why my girlfriend left me. Her loss, I assumed!

My first sexual encounter in college was a one-night stand with someone whom I was not even attracted to. I then focused on the new-found world of pornography that I had discovered on the internet. With a high-speed connection in my room, I was able to explore thousands of pictures, stories, and pornographic movies. To make the stories more interesting, I downloaded them and used my computer to substitute the names of people that I knew into the stories. I looked for pictures that reminded me of my friends, and my tastes quickly progressed from soft-core to hard-core. Occasionally, I ran across pictures of people who were clearly under legal age, but I could not keep myself from looking. After every session of pornography on my computer, I obsessively deleted every file, hid all evidence, and told myself that I would not degrade myself again.

As college went on, I moved up in student government. I was president of the largest student organization on campus, frequently gave public speeches, and hobnobbed with administrators. I finished two bachelor's degrees and was nominated for an important scholarship. My alma mater named me an outstanding senior and threw a banquet in my honor.

At the same time I was earning another sort of reputation. I had a series of relationships with women who served as vice-presidents under me or on my executive boards. I skated through relationships quickly, always hoping to find true love and never finding anything to satisfy me. With every relationship, I pushed sexual intimacy more quickly and more forcefully. I started having sex with a woman whom I had no real feelings for. It excited me to be with someone who would do anything to please me. We had sex regularly and without protection. I was afraid that that she would become pregnant and I would have to marry her, yet I could not stop myself. Unable to deal with my feelings, I tried to build a relationship with her. Looking back, I think she really loved me. I ignored how she felt, and concentrated on my own acting out.

As with every previous time, my fantasy could not fulfill me in reality. I quickly became disinterested, and I thought regularly of cheating on her. My pornography obsession continued to grow. I had serious problems with depression and anxiety and sought help from a therapist and antianxiety medication. I never discussed sex with my therapist, though. I never even considered it part of the problem.

While still seeing my girlfriend and in therapy, I fell in love with another woman. I felt an emotional connection to her. I decided that this was someone I wanted to marry. This was the time when things started to go horribly wrong. I did not want to hurt, force, or push my new girlfriend into sex. I really loved her, and I really believed that I was behaving gallantly. She was adamant about not having sex before marriage, and every time we talked about it, I agreed wholeheartedly to wait. And yet, I still manipulated and coerced her into having sex with me. I applied steady and firm psychological and emotional pressure to my loved one, breaking down her boundaries and walls with amazing speed. Immediately after agreeing to lay off, I would push forward, and afterwards resolutely agree never to do it again. Before long I had forced her to have sex with me.

I always thought people who had problems with sex were "bad people." There was something psychologically wrong with them. Especially sex criminals—now there was a group of bad people! I always believed that anybody with intelligence and decent circumstances, like me, could avoid such problems. I didn't even have any traffic tickets. Certainly I was not capable of committing a crime. But I still clearly remember the weekend I spent surfing the web for definitions of rape. I could not find a single definition that my act did not fit. I was terrified of being turned in, publicly humiliated, and put in jail. I still had not had STD testing from my previous relationships. By the grace of God, my girlfriend did not turn me in. In fact, she said that she still loved me and that she knew there was hope for me. We agreed to marry, and I promised never again to behave that way.

A short while later, I coerced her into having sex again, followed by more promises and manipulation. It seemed that nothing I did could stop the cycle. I lived a life ruled by sex. In public places, I gawked at every woman I came across. I tried to peep in others' windows, and I spent many hours each day with pornography. In the bedroom, I had coerced and manipulated my girlfriends into doing things they did not want to do. I was never satisfied. I did not know whether I was carrying diseases, and it was possible that I could have passed on HIV to my fiancée. I contemplated suicide. At last, I was ready to admit that I needed help.

About this time, my wife-to-be and I moved across the country to begin our new lives. While planning our wedding, we lived with my wife's parents and I took a good job. While reading the newspaper one morning over breakfast, my fiancée showed me a blurb for Sex Addicts Anonymous. At this point I was willing to try anything, and I decided to attend.

From the moment I walked through the door of my first meeting, my life was changed. I was shaking through most of my first meeting, expecting judgment from a room full of scary people. But almost immediately, hope grew in my heart where I never expected it. Here was a room full of people just like me, who were not only recovering, but were living happy lives! When I left my first meeting, I experienced a sense of peace that must have come from God. I knew it would be a hard road, but somehow it would work.

I attended three meetings before traveling back across the country for my wedding and honeymoon. After returning from the honeymoon, I mysteriously stopped attending meetings. For some reason, I thought that knowledge of the solution was all I needed. About a month later, I nearly acted out, and came back to the program for good, convinced that I was truly powerless. My first order of business in Sex Addicts Anonymous was God. I have always been an arrogant atheist, believing myself too intelligent to accept someone else's reality. I believed that faith was a great thing for those of lesser mind who could accept what someone else told them as absolute truth. I scorned religion as one of the world's greatest problems and God as a myth for the weak. However, my fellow SAA members credited their recoveries to a Higher Power, so I became willing to try letting God run my life.

Within a few months I experienced happy, unexpected sobriety. While I still thought about acting out, my desire to act on those urges did not rule my life any longer. Now convinced that a miracle was relieving my compulsion to act out, I was on fire to learn as much as I could about my Higher Power. The iceberg of my arrogance and contempt began to crack and melt as I came to believe that I was not the center of the universe. Rather, I am a small part of God's glorious creation, here to do God's will and help others.

As I became willing to have more faith, I was rewarded with more blessings. I have found that no amount of time devoted to spiritual growth is wasted. I am actively involved in a church, where I learn from men and women of faith how to involve God in all aspects of my life. As more and more of my life falls into place, I have come to rely on God to guide me. He has never let me down.

The spiritual experience that transformed me has touched every aspect of my being. I feel content with where and who I am. I feel that I actually know myself. Emotions are an important part of my life today. They help me to understand myself and my relationship to the world. When I feel shame, I have probably hurt myself, and I do an inventory. When I feel anger, I need to deal with my resentments. When I feel fear, I pray. When I feel gratitude, I know that I am working my program well.

I find that I can listen and learn from others today, and I seek out contact with recovering people whenever I can. Best of all, I now see my life and experience as a gift. My past, as awful as it was, is a tool that I can use to help others with similar problems. Helping others is the greatest joy in my life, and if I focus on being grateful and helpful, God can use me in wondrous ways.

Today I have over eighteen months of sobriety. My obsession with acting out continues to slowly drain away. My progress through the steps has been sometimes slow, sometimes fast, but always at just the pace that I can handle. Working with a sponsor has helped to curb my arrogance and selfishness. I have made amends for my past, and I lean on God for the present, all the while learning not to fear the future. I have been learning to sing and to laugh, to love and to cry. Step by step, day by day, I am growing up.

24.

A NEW PAST

My addictive sexual behaviors started at a very early age. I was sexually abused by an older cousin most of my childhood, and by other family members, while my mother denied hearing her child's cry. I was forced into male prostitution at an early age by a neighborhood man, and later in my early teens by my boss at a restaurant whom I agreed to have sex with so I could keep my job. I became very confused and untrusting of people in my early adult life, and found myself hating myself as well as the world. Later I found myself battling incestuous thoughts and ultimately acting on those thoughts by victimizing my own children.

The fear of being arrested and facing consequences eventually led me to a counselor, a recovering sex addict himself, who introduced me to SAA. I was reluctant at first, not wanting to reveal my behaviors to a group of people. As I sat and listened to everyone speak, I began to feel as though I were not alone. Members hugged me and thanked me for being there. This helped me to start opening up and talk about my own problems.

For my whole life I never felt like I belonged anywhere, until I walked into SAA. For the first time I felt that I had a home and a family who supported me, understood me, and let me unload all my shame. It was truly a gift from a Higher Power from whom I had hidden for many years, not wanting to be noticed because of my shame. The more I talked, the better I began to feel. Slowly working the steps in a workshop, I began to understand the rewards of taking responsibility for my actions.

Sharing a Fifth Step with another human being was an extremely hard thing for me to do. Yet working that step removed all of the secrets and greatly reduced the power of my sexual compulsions. By the time I had worked through my Ninth Step, I began to feel like a human being, instead of feeling totally worthless. For me there is great power in making amends to someone I have harmed, and I continue to do so with my

Tenth Step work. Eventually I could even look at myself in the mirror without feeling the need to look away in disgust.

As I looked back at my past, I was overwhelmed by grief and pain, thinking of the harm I had endured and the harm I created later in life. Now almost ten years have gone by since I walked into my first SAA meeting. I realize now that I have a new past, and it is a good one.

For many years I was so consumed with sex, insecurities, jealousy and resentments, that I could not manage anything in my life—not my job, my finances, or even my marriage. I always had a fear of dying alone. That fear has left me now, because I know that I'm in the hearts of my brothers and sisters in SAA. I thank all of you for that.

My life is by no means perfect, but the tools that I have received from our program have given me the confidence and courage to achieve goals I had never thought possible. My successes include starting and continuing my own business, allowing myself to have peace of mind through the most trying of times, and being able to reach out and share my experiences with other suffering addicts who are beginning this program for themselves. I learn so much from new members as well as from old-timers and their wisdom. It is a continuous journey in my life. I can never say enough good things about SAA. I thank my Higher Power and the fellowship of SAA for helping to guide me in much healthier directions "one day at a time."

25.

FROM INSANITY TO SERENITY

I grew up in a dysfunctional home. My father was an alcoholic, and my mother was mentally ill. She had multiple personalities, all of which had their own unique problems. I was not allowed to have any feelings or to express them. It appeared to me that my mom was the only one who could have feelings, and most of them were rage. She was physically and emotionally abusive.

I don't ever remember not being sexual. My first memory is sex with my father. That stopped when I was nine, when he quit drinking and went into treatment. During his drinking, he would come to my room when he came home at night and have sex with me. He told me it was my job because my mom wouldn't do it.

Also during this time, I was trying to console my mother, who would cry because my dad was out drinking. She rejected my attempts to comfort her, and when I tried to get physical affection from her, she brushed me off. I learned early on that all I was good for was sex.

I learned how to manipulate, and in turn was abused by neighbor kids, siblings, cousins, baby sitters, uncles, and strangers, male and female. I then abused others.

When I started kindergarten, I developed a crush on much older girls. I would get angry if they wouldn't give me attention or sit next to me. This started the connection in my mind between my self-worth and whether or not people liked me. If they wouldn't give me attention, I would move on to the next obsession.

In first grade, I developed my first crush on a boy. I thought he liked me because he would hit me and pull my hair. The obsession with this boy continued well into my teen years. During those years, I became very jealous of any attention he would give to other girls. I felt like he was my property. I believed that women were useless and not to be trusted.

By the time I was nine, I had experienced my first DTs from drinking with my father. I didn't understand what was happening, and they kept it a secret after taking me to the doctor to find out what was wrong. I was going through withdrawal as a result of his sobriety from alcohol. It didn't take me long to find my own way to get booze, and then I found another fix called pornography. I would sit in my room for hours just poring over the pages, getting lost in another world. I found new ways to be sexual and adventurous with other kids, and felt experienced when having sex with adults.

By the time I was thirteen, I was hooked on drugs, mostly marijuana and speed. I tried everything I came into contact with, whether it was sex or drugs. My mom had also introduced me to diet pills and diuretics, even though I didn't have a weight problem. I became obsessed with how I looked, always thinking about how others would see me during sex. This turned into years of bingeing and purging with food.

I was raped that summer by a stranger and left for dead in a ditch outside of the town that I lived in. This was my first attempt at running away from home. I felt so miserable and just wanted out. I had no real plan. I hardly slept for a month. I kept thinking that he would come back and kill me. This experience took me to some deep dark places. I was afraid of everything and everybody. The only thing that comforted me was booze and drugs. It wasn't long before I was sexual again, and this time I felt very powerful. I felt like I had conquered my demons. I became more isolated from girls and didn't want anything to do with them. I used every boy as a sex object. I would have sex in bathrooms, cars, outside—anywhere I could.

A year of this brought me to another horrific experience at fourteen. I had been seeing this one guy for more than a one-night stand, and really felt a connection. He asked me to be his girlfriend. I was elated. We would go to his house every day after school and have sex and drink and get high. He was sexually experienced and I didn't feel like a freak when I was with him. One day, we went to his house and there was the man who had raped me a year ago. He introduced him as his stepbrother. There were also a few other guys with him. The stepbrother bragged about having me, and my boyfriend went into a jealous rage and left the house, with me still there. His stepbrother offered me a drink and told me to relax and just have a good time. I was freaking out, but felt too paralyzed to leave. I was raped again that night.

I continued on my path of self-destruction, having sex with every guy I came in contact with and using every drug I could find. I had sex with people to get my drugs and alcohol because I decided that stealing money from my dad in the middle of the night was getting too risky. Over the years, the money in his wallet was getting thinner, so I figured that he was on to me. He never said anything.

During this time, my mom was trying to figure out what was wrong with me. I was irritable and sleeping a lot. She decided that reading my diary was an appropriate way to get the answers. After this betrayal, a new rage built up inside of me. She immediately took me to see a therapist. This was the start of therapy for many years to come, and more lying and manipulating to avoid the pain.

When I was sixteen, I found a new boyfriend. He brought me into a world of sex that I never imagined, introducing me to bondage, S&M, bestiality, orgies, and cocaine. It didn't take long before the abuse started, and I was getting battered for anything I did and didn't do. He could be loving and kind one night, and the next night he would beat me for having sex with other people. He fought hard to keep me in line, and I fought hard to stay high and not feel anything. I was living three different lives. I would stay out all night and get drunk and high and have sex. Then I would get home just in time to make it look like I was there all night, and get ready for school. I would pretend with kids at my school that I was like them, and at the same time I was still having sex with guys there. I had to take drugs to stay awake, and drink to go to sleep. But I felt powerful because I was managing all of this.

Around this time I was also falling for a girl at school. She wanted to be my best friend, and I felt on top of the world. I had never had a girl want to be my best friend. I knew she was having sex with girls and boys, but I didn't want to see her that way. We maintained a friendship that was full of obsession for me. I had to see her every day and spend time with her. She wanted me to quit drinking and drugging, and I told her about the sex I was having. She was appalled that I would allow people to do those things to me. I swore her to secrecy, but was afraid she would tell. When she moved, I felt crushed.

Then I started to fall apart. I stopped caring so much if I got caught. I had entered a different reality. Some nights, I wouldn't even go home. My parents started calling the cops, and life felt like hell. Finally, they got sick of it and hauled me to treatment. I was flabbergasted. I wasn't done yet. My mom started confronting me with everything I had ever stolen from her, including her wedding rings. I lied through my teeth. I couldn't tell her that I stole all of those things just so I could get a fix. Treatment was a flop. As much as my mom was sick of me, she couldn't bear to see another family member in treatment. She took me home after the intervention.

Another year went by and it was the same stuff—more booze, more drugs, more sex. I couldn't get enough. I was still seeing a therapist, and he told me that he couldn't see me any more because I was getting high before my sessions and couldn't even talk coherently. He told me that he couldn't watch me kill myself any more, and he challenged me to stop drinking and doing drugs. I told him I would try. I had never tried to do that before.

I couldn't do it. The principal at my school finally pulled me aside one day and said he was sick of suspending me for drinking and drugging, and he knew that I was dealing drugs to other kids. I knew that the end was near and felt hopeless. What was I going to do? I couldn't quit. I had tried that.

About six months later, I decided that enough was enough. My tolerance had started getting low, and I was constantly sick. I believe now that my Higher Power intervened and gave me the strength to do the next thing. I talked with my therapist about going into treatment, since I couldn't stop on my own. He encouraged me, but he said I had to make the call and follow through. I had never had to do such a grown-up thing before.

I made the call and was in the hospital within a couple of days. I went on my last binge the day I graduated from high school, and went into treatment the next day. The withdrawals were excruciating, but I suffered through it and promised to myself that I would remember what it felt like so that I didn't have to repeat it over again.

One of the rules in treatment was that we couldn't have sex in the facility, and that it was grounds for dismissal. I thought that was a stupid rule, so I did it anyway. I had people come to visit me from the outside, and I had sex with them.

I talked with my counselor at one point about possibly having a sex addiction. I felt that I would die without sex and that I would do anything to get it. He told me, "We don't deal with that here." Eventually I got caught for being sexually inappropriate with a mentally ill patient in another ward, and I felt justified and argued with the staff. They told me that it was a warning and that I had better not do it again or I was out. I didn't stop. I felt that if I had to give up booze and drugs, I at least needed sex. How could they expect me to go without sex?

While in treatment, I flew into a rage during a group session. They put me in lockdown and I became suicidal. They then suggested I stay for another six months. I said, "No way!" I didn't want to deal with these feelings that had come up. I felt too vulnerable, and once again I was looking for a way out. I called my mom and told her to pick me up. I didn't want to be there anymore. She wasn't so sure, but she did it anyway. I had lots of excuses: the halfway house didn't come through; I couldn't learn any more; they were just a bunch of idiots. When my mom brought me home, she told me that one of my party friends had just killed himself. I was devastated. I thought I could use this as an excuse to use again, but instead I chose not to pick up that day.

After a few weeks, I came to accept that I needed to go to twelve-step meetings for my drug addiction. The people in the meetings welcomed me, and I could relate to their stories even though I was the youngest one in the rooms. I started to realize that my Higher Power would help me if I just asked.

Of course it didn't take long to find someone to have sex with. I didn't think there was a problem with that. Besides, I was still struggling with not having sex with my ex-boyfriend. He still beat me and wanted me to use with him. I told him that I was done getting high or having sex with him. He was not happy about this, and it tore me up.

I attempted suicide after nine months clean and sober. A couple of my sober friends found me in my apartment with my arms cut up and immediately took me to the hospital. The staff said that I was a danger to myself, and they couldn't let me go. I immediately got a therapist and had a chance to share honestly about myself. No lies, no manipulation. She was very affirming, telling me that I would have gone crazy if I hadn't used my addictions to cope.

It was at this time that I met my first girlfriend. We were just friends, and she was also clean and sober. One day she asked me if I'd had sex with women. I told her yes, but nothing serious. She came out to me and said she was a lesbian. I just said that was cool and felt nothing about it. But after spending some significant time with her, I started to feel a physical attraction. I told her about it and we acted on it. I was very excited about this experience because I actually felt something I had never felt before. I genuinely cared about her. She approached me with the idea of being monogamous, and I hesitated before saying yes. I said that I'd never been monogamous before. She told me that she wouldn't have sex with me ever again if I wouldn't agree to it. Something in me snapped when I heard that. So I agreed.

Within a month, she was cheating on me, and that began a three-year ordeal of pain, lying, manipulation, and verbal abuse. We would break up and I would be devastated. We'd get back together after she would reveal everything, and we'd start over. Sometimes I wanted to kill myself to escape the pain. I couldn't ever get over the feeling of betrayal. Eventually, after we both got sick and tired, we moved on. We had both just finished college, and it was time to start our new lives.

I moved constantly, to different cities, different jobs, and different sex partners. I couldn't keep a job because I was too preoccupied with sex. I would always try to get into relationships with women as a way to stop my behavior. I thought if I could find the right one, I would be happy.

At five years clean and sober, I lost a job working with adolescents because I was having sex with a drug dealer who came to the facility while I was working. This was a real low for me in my sobriety. I had stopped going to meetings, and didn't have any sober friends in the city where I lived. I was having sex with everyone in my neighborhood. I started going to straight bars and hitting on women. They were drunk, and I found it easy to take advantage of them. When they resisted, I raped them. This was such a powerful experience that I couldn't see anything wrong with it, until I came down from my high. Then I was horrified. I thought I had worked through my rage, only to find that I was releasing it in another way.

I was relieved when I found a girlfriend because I thought that would stop my behavior. I moved in within a week and discovered that she had her own addictions, as well as STDs. I found myself masturbating compulsively and decided that I needed to see a therapist again. When I told the counselor about my compulsion, she looked at me like I was from another planet. She told me it was okay to masturbate. She didn't understand that I was doing it to the point of pain. At this time, I tried to call the SAA number that I found in the phone book. The person I talked to said that I needed to go through an interview process before I could go to any meetings. I immediately panicked, because I thought that I would have to tell all the horrible things I had done in my life, or they wouldn't give me help. I didn't make it to SAA that time.

I did find a girlfriend who was codependent enough to be with me, but wouldn't have sex with me if I wasn't going to be present. She had a general knowledge about sex addiction, and she wanted no part of that. I thought I had finally met the person I would spend the rest of my life with. After three years, I asked her to let me go outside of the relationship for sex. I told her that I loved her and wouldn't leave her, but I just needed to have my sexual needs met. She wouldn't agree to that, but after some time, she asked me if I would consider adding a third person to our partnership. At first I refused, knowing that I was too jealous for that to ever work. But it didn't take long for me to talk myself into the idea. She would get some things that I couldn't give her, and I could get some sex from someone else. We had someone in mind; she agreed when asked, and we started what we called a "healthy three-way relationship." It was fun and exciting, and I thought it was everything I wanted, until reality hit.

I became very jealous, and started having feelings for this other woman. We began spending lots of time together, and all I wanted was her. This was very painful for everyone. I told her that if she didn't want me, I was just walking away from it all. She decided that she wanted just me, and so began a whirlwind of craziness. One month of living with her, and I was depressed again. I hadn't found a new way of life. I had just walked into another mess. She was very possessive and verbally abusive. I gave up all my friends and twelve-step meetings because she was so insecure. I thought she would eventually trust me, but because of how we met, she was assuming that I would do the same thing to her.

About three years into the relationship, I found out that I had herpes. I began to be sexually anorexic, and I took out my rage by hitting and kicking her. I had now reached another level of my human condition that I didn't know existed. I was physically abusing her and I felt justified. After five years, she told me she was going to leave if I didn't quit hitting her. A light bulb went off in my head and I broke down crying. I couldn't believe what a monster I had become. Who was I? What was I doing? I told her I needed to get back to twelve-step meetings, or I was going to use. It was another wake-up call from my Higher Power.

I got back in therapy and talked honestly about the rapes I had committed and the verbal and physical abuse I had inflicted on people over the years. The therapist immediately gave me the SAA number, and I called. She also directed me to sex offender treatment. I was not happy about this idea, but I went.

Another thing that my therapist requested was that I go to the doctor and get a full examination and all the STD tests. This is when I found out I had HIV. I did not handle this well and I went into a long period of denial until just recently. The rage continued to build inside of me.

I started going to Sex Addicts Anonymous meetings, and although it seemed like the right place, I found lots of reasons to feel different. Most of the women talked about addiction to love and romantic obsession. I didn't think I could relate to that. I was having sex with prostitutes at the time and taking home strippers from the clubs. I was also frequenting porn shops and picking up strangers there. I had gotten back into the bondage scene and started acting out with asphyxiation. I was also cutting myself as a way to get sexually high with people.

Again, I found myself living all these different lives: going to sex offender treatment, going to meetings, going to bars and clubs, cruising and therapy and work. I acted out with people in the bathrooms at work, and was caught having phone sex and looking at porn. My mind cracked. I had a nervous breakdown and took a leave of absence from work. The shame was swallowing me up. Here I was, clean and sober for thirteen years, and I felt insane.

During my medical leave from work, I decided that I would try to stop some of the behaviors that were obviously killing me. But I wouldn't give up the porn. Yet it was never enough. I would always end up back at the bars, looking for women who were drunk that I could have sex with. This went on for a couple of years. My first SAA sponsor stopped working with me because I wasn't trying hard enough. That felt like the ultimate rejection. And she was a lesbian. The rage roared and gave me an excuse to continue my behaviors. At this same time, my therapist refused to see me any more because I had threatened to sexually assault her.

Then I met another woman. I had just gotten out of the hospital from surgery to have an organ removed as a result of years of bingeing and purging, and she was very supportive while I was there. But it didn't take my anger long to resurface, and in the middle of sex, I became full of rage and hurt her. I wouldn't stop when she said no, and it frightened her. I then told her it wasn't going to work because I obviously wasn't well enough to be in a relationship. She didn't like that answer, so I led her on and just cheated on her like many others before.

I picked up another woman in a bar. This time I said that I just wanted to date, with no sex. Get to know each other. Build a healthy friendship, and then a relationship. That lasted about a month, and then I was back doing what I knew how to do. The rage came up, and I hurt her during sex.

She wanted me to get my sex addiction under control and stop hurting her. She said she loved me and wanted to build a life and family together. Later, I raped her again, and another light bulb went off in my head when I saw the horror on her face. I knew at that moment that I'd reached the end of the line. I did act out for a few more weeks after that, but it was lifeless and painful—pornography, masturbating compulsively, cruising. Nothing was working. I was tired of the consequences: diseases, infections, cops, the legal system, the financial losses, loss of friends, homes, family, therapists. I'd had enough. I was powerless over this thing, and my life was unmanageable. My Higher Power had intervened once more. This time I listened.

I went back into sex offender treatment and took it seriously this time. I started working the Twelve Steps of Sex Addicts Anonymous. I got a sponsor. I started going to more meetings, and I got into service. Something greater than myself was going to save me from this insanity.

It was very difficult in the beginning. My sponsor reminded me that I was in withdrawal. That helped a lot. I knew there would eventually be an end to this feeling of madness. I took two months without any sex, with myself or others. My mind became clear, and I could see the difference in myself. I was no longer looking for sex, anticipating it or manipulating someone to make it happen. No intrigue, no games. I started to feel alive and was attending one to two meetings a day. I wanted to stay sexually sober, no matter what. I had a desire to be alive and free, and that gave me the strength and courage to continue. I had truly turned this thing over to my Higher Power.

When I decided to date, I knew I had to come up with a plan of action. What worked for me then and still works for me is to be sexual only with women that I genuinely care for and respect. I am honest about who I am and what healthy sexuality is for me. If that doesn't fit for the other person, it's not an option. Also, I need to stay present during sex at all times. If not, I need to stop. This has eliminated the feelings of rage that surfaced as a result of being resentful or afraid. I had to take a good hard look at my character defects and how they enabled me to continue this self-destructive path in the past, and I had to want them to be removed.

As a result of doing these healthy sexual behaviors, I feel better about myself and have a deeper compassion for other people. I am still learning more about intimacy, but that will be a long road ahead. I am willing to do this in my Higher Power's time, not mine. If I try to rush the process along, my disease will be triggered. By the grace of my Higher Power, I have been able to stay out of slippery places and away from slippery situations. This has become easier as time passes, since I spend more time doing recovery-oriented things now.

Through the Twelve Steps of Sex Addict Anonymous, I have been given the gift of compassion for myself and others. I've had the opportunity to make amends to people that I'd harmed, something I never thought I would have the courage to do. I've had to write letters to the ones that I can't be in contact with, but I know I am willing to ask my Higher Power for the strength to do what I need to do to rectify any of those situations.

I continue to go to four to eight meetings a week, and this keeps me present to do a daily inventory of my thoughts and behaviors. I have changed the way I interact with people. They are not my next fix or the solution to my problems. I take responsibility for what I do and say. I'm not perfect, nor do I wish to be. Not having to escape my feelings any more is a great blessing.

Without my Higher Power, I would not be here. I truly believe that. I have learned to take time for me, and to talk to my Higher Power every day. This has not been as difficult, because deep down I've known all along that my Higher Power wants me to live. I was the one that wanted to die. That has changed now. By doing a ritual of prayer and meditation, I have lost the desire to self-destruct.

I have come to terms with having AIDS. The doctor thinks that I contracted it back in 1986 when I was 18 years old. Instead of using this as an excuse to act out, I use the steps and tools to get me through each day sober.

I can't do this alone. That's what got me into trouble. The isolation and the belief that I was superior to everyone led me to hit a bottom in this addiction. Service work has been a way for me to channel my energy in a healthy way. By sponsoring, taking on service work in meetings, and being available in every way for the sex addict who still suffers, I stay out of my self-centeredness. I can now do my Higher Power's will, not mine. That is a freedom that I can't explain. I feel like a miracle has happened.

The slogans, the tools, and the daily phone calls and e-mails from other women in the fellowship keep me going. By the grace of my Higher Power, I have been sexually sober from my bottom-line behaviors for thirty months. It has taken me five years of coming into the rooms of Sex Addicts Anonymous to get to this place of serenity and freedom from fear and rage. Without this program, I don't know where I'd be. I don't want to find out, so I will keep coming back, a day at a time.

26.

ABSTINENCE IS THE FOUNDATION

I fell down hard in my active sex addiction. My self-centeredness and lack of boundaries contributed to my molesting a number of mentally impaired persons, making unsolicited sexual contact in crowded public places, and voyeurism. My history also includes using pornography, fondling animals, a deep obsession with objectifying women and their clothing, and being sexual outside of a committed relationship. In addition, I buried my spirit with frequent, compulsive fantasy and masturbation.

I have not acted out in my inner circle since December of 1997, when I did my Three Circles with a sponsor. My sponsor was sober and highly involved in SAA, and had worked through the Twelve Steps. We started immediately to work them together. I trusted my sponsor like I'd never been able to trust anyone before; I guess I had no choice. He had a lot of things in addition to sobriety that I wanted: respect, self-esteem, friends, the courage to be honest with others, and the willingness to help other sex addicts.

He told me from the start to use the resources of the program, particularly to talk with other sex addicts. He advised me to cast a wide net, and somehow I was given the willingness to dial the many phone numbers I wrote down after meetings. I got in the habit of calling people daily, so that if I really needed to make a call to preserve my sanity or sobriety, the skids would already be greased.

My path in SAA has not been crisis-filled, and I believe that's due to the lessons I was taught about putting sobriety ahead of all else and making the program a regular part of every day. SAA taught me to start with just a little openness toward the possibility of a Higher Power, and that openness grew over the weeks and months. For a while I only allowed God into certain parts of my life, but I've learned over time that God's care can apply to every aspect of my life. Today as I make conscious contact in prayer, I seek to open fully to my Higher Power.

I worked through the Twelve Steps, and have begun them again. Step Four was a very important piece of work. Due to my fears, I had become a distrustful, judgmental, and bitter person, always looking at the wrongs of others. Today I am unable to feel that anger without an accompanying reflex to look at myself. My faith in God's care allows me to open myself like that.

I don't know how I am going to make full amends for the sexual harms I've caused. I feel I've made a start by maintaining sobriety, telling my truth to other sex addicts, doing service on a number of levels, and volunteering time both within the program and in the community. My faith is that by staying with the steps and praying for guidance, I am being shown how to best repair the damage from my past behaviors.

Every several months since coming to SAA, I've been beset by a feeling of despair over the boundaries I crossed in my addiction, and have spent a lot of energy trying to figure out how I can possibly see myself as okay. In the early days when I would share about this despair with my sponsor, he would gently respond, "Beware of terminal uniqueness. You did not invent those behaviors, though you are responsible for them. I don't believe you had any other choice at the time, because of your disease. For now the most important thing is to stay sober a day at a time. You'll eventually come to Step Nine, and will be shown how to make the best amends possible."

Today I see that I need to surrender my despair to God. It's too big for me to resolve on my own. I surrender when I'm on my knees, asking to be relieved of this burden for today so that I might better see and do God's will, and thus help others.

The concept and practicality of the middle circle has been very helpful to me. I've been taught that it is not a place to hang out in; rather it is a sort of safety net. I believe that if I am willful about my middle circle, my ability to stay out of my inner circle erodes. Safety nets are for falling into, not jumping into.

My partner and I are in a committed monogamous relationship. She knows all about my past, and knows the importance of my program. Sex is far from the central part of our relationship, but we talk frequently about it, as we are both committed to growth and health. Being able to express my shames, fears, and desires related to sex has been very freeing. No longer is sex hidden in my life. Though there are areas of my sexuality in which I hope to grow—I can disconnect at times, or get focused on orgasm instead of intimacy—the fact that my partner and I practice honest, open communication helps me to be at peace. Also, I have surrendered masturbation and willful fantasy, one day at a time. I caused too much wreckage with them and don't seem to be suffering without them.

Things are really different today. A typical day in my life now doesn't look anything like one from my old life. I feel that I've split off from the person I used to be. I now have a foundation and a path to follow, whereas prior to coming to Sex Addicts Anonymous I was in a survival or at least reactive mode. Today on a daily basis I dedicate time to meditation, prayer, and calls to program friends. I have a sponsor to whom I tell the truth, and on whom I depend for guidance. I can't really think of any accountability like that in my old life.

Today I have faith. My focus is to turn over to God the many things I can't handle on my own. Somehow I've been given the willingness to look at myself and to pay attention when I'm in pain so I can surrender. The Twelve Steps for me are the lessons that I did not learn as a kid, simple things such as: realizing the world doesn't revolve around me; that there is something far more wise and powerful than my will; knowing to give up when I'm licked; taking responsibility for my shortcomings and pulling together the humility to be honest about them; repairing what I've damaged to my best ability; continually working on my own growth; and being of service to others, particularly to others like me.

In my experience, recovery does not work without a sponsor, without deep honesty, or without the willingness to reach out to other recovering sex addicts. My sense of freedom, of self, my hope, my joy—all rest on the foundation of my abstinence from inner-circle behavior. Without my sobriety, I lose all of that. I believe that, one day at a time, I never have to act out again. When I ask God for help, and am willing to do my small part, the help is there. It's a relief to know I don't have to do it alone.

27.

POWERLESS PRIEST

In my story of "acting out" and the shame, guilt, embarrassment, and humiliation that went along with it, I have found comfort in the reality of God's love for me in the depths of my sex addiction.

I began masturbating when I was a sophomore in a Catholic high school. Many fellow students would brag about doing it, and a number of times we would do it together. It was fun and pleasurable. It was also secretive. I began to masturbate more often, and by the time I graduated from high school, I was doing it a minimum of four times a day.

When I discovered that pornographic magazines and vibrators increased the pleasure, I began masturbating at an accelerated rate. I even hung centerfolds on my bedroom wall. My parents laughed at me. It was no big deal to them, but to me anything that would get me to a more intense climax was something I craved.

It was also about this time that I discovered my attraction to men. As a senior in high school, I felt inferior to other male students. But I still denied my sexual orientation. I also began to become infatuated with certain guys. I thought I was in love, but I wasn't. It was more than lust, as my entire being was swallowed up in this obsession with another person. Feelings of intense jealousy and possessiveness dominated my existence. I would wallow in self-pity and exaggerate problems in order to manipulate the object of my infatuation to give me more attention. First it was a next door neighbor, then after that wore off, it was one of his friends, then after that wore off, it was someone else, and so on. It was an addiction to being in love, and it was a seemingly endless cycle.

Throughout my college years I continued to masturbate, using pornography, strip bars, bathhouses, locker rooms, magazines, anything I could use to get enough visual stimuli to pleasure myself. It was during these years that a cousin introduced me to X-rated videotapes, the straight variety. They aroused me intensely. There were times I masturbated to one of these tapes in our family den, when my parents and invited guests were only seven steps away in another room. I was addicted to sex and didn't know it. I took risks of being discovered, and I didn't care. I was late for work, school, and other things because I needed to masturbate first. Nobody knew. I thought I could live two lives and get away with it. But I could not get away from myself and the inner turmoil that I was experiencing.

My habits continued through seminary and my early priesthood years. In the seminary I didn't have videotapes, but I had 130 men to gawk at. I also developed infatuations with two different seminarians. It was miserable. I was suffering, gaining weight. I thought I wanted genital love. I thought I wanted to be touched and held. But I also wanted to be celibate! It was a terrible dilemma.

Four years into my priesthood I was paging through a video catalog and noticed that in the back were advertisements for gay pornographic tapes. I ordered one. When I put the video in the VCR, and watched two guys having sex, I felt a rush unlike anything I had ever felt before. From that day on I ordered more and more of these tapes. I couldn't get enough of them. I even had them shipped to the church I was assigned to. I didn't care about the risk of being discovered. I wanted to achieve the same level and intensity of orgasm as I did that very first time, but it was futile. It never happened, yet I felt driven to keep trying.

At about this time, at age thirty-six, I finally acknowledged to myself that I was gay, and I came out to a few people. These men were priests. I didn't know what it was like to be gay, so I allowed myself to be influenced by them. They introduced me to gay bars and gay strip clubs, where I could touch the strippers for a dollar tip. This also became an obsession for me. The only thing that kept me from going every night was that I lived four hours away. But the memories of those nights spent in the clubs gave me stimuli to masturbate with. I was spiraling downward, leading two lives, trying to keep them separate. I was reaching the limits on my credit cards, and I didn't care.

Then a visiting priest accidentally discovered my gay video collection. Unknown to me, he went to my bishop with the information. The bishop then consulted with mental health professionals. One Sunday afternoon, two bishops and a priest came to my door. They confronted me with knowledge of the tapes and insisted I go to a ten-day psychological evaluation, which I did right away. After the evaluation, I was told that I had an unintegrated sexuality, a mild personality disorder, and that I was a sex addict. If I wanted help, I would need residential treatment in a psychiatric facility for priests.

I agreed, but only to save my priesthood. I didn't believe that I was a sex addict. I wasn't having sex with anyone; I was just masturbating with gay pornographic tapes. Big deal! This is known as denial. (DENIAL = Don't Even Notice I Am Lying).

When I arrived for treatment, I was told that I could not masturbate at all. I thought, "No problem." As the days and weeks went by, I felt my self-control and willpower crumbling. I learned that I was out of control. If I was going to stop, I needed help.

So began my involvement in Sex Addicts Anonymous and other twelve-step fellowships. I went to ninety meetings in ninety days. I learned that I was powerless over my addiction; the desires were too strong. But through the stories and fellowship of SAA, I received strength and hope from others who were struggling just like I was. I also received outside help for my depression and personality disorder.

The SAA meetings have become a source of strength and joy for me. Besides meeting new friends and other recovering addicts, I have gained more serenity than I could ever have imagined. This year, I celebrated eight years of recovery in SAA and fourteen years of priesthood. I have learned to trust in my Higher Power, my sponsor, and SAA, which gives me freedom from my disease one day at a time.

28.

WORKING THE PROGRAM

I have been a member of SAA for over four years, and I currently have three and one-half years of sobriety. My recovery program has evolved; it began with harm reduction. This means I worked first to eliminate the obviously destructive behaviors from my life. I joined SAA because my life had become unmanageable. My acting out caused a condition of acute agoraphobia (essentially profound shame attacks). These attacks forced me to be virtually house-bound for almost fifteen months.

I need to begin by owning the fact that I am an incest survivor. I suffered through protracted sexual abuse and profound neglect, and I believe these two things were the driving forces in my becoming addicted to sex. I was sexually incested by three older stepsisters through exhibitionism and a great deal of sexual contact.

My sexual acting out began at age seventeen when I first realized that I had control over my body. Until that time I assumed only my stepsisters could control my sexuality. My acting-out behaviors became out of control immediately: exposing, one-night anonymous sex, voyeuring, instant relationships, and pornography. I was powerless over all aspects of the addictive cycle in my life. I was in abject despair until I found SAA.

My first year in SAA focused on establishing fundamental sexual sobriety. Since then I have focused on using my personal values as a guide toward healthy sexuality. My heartfelt values have taught me these things: 1.) I can say "No" to myself and others; I no longer involve myself with partners who are disrespectful. I now see the "red flags" which I used to pretend didn't exist. 2.) For sexuality to be healthy for me, it can have no anonymous qualities, either in fantasy or reality. 3.) As a single man in SAA, I can be sexual with myself in appropriate ways. 4.) I need to wait until a relationship is firmly established and safe prior to having intercourse. I have set a limit to wait at least six months. 5.) I really want an intimate relationship. I want innocence, walks, kisses, and movies. I want to be with a person where we actually like each other and share similar values and interests. I want a relationship that is nurturing, non-shaming, and spiritually based.

In recovery I have pursued healthy sexuality by dating. I have met women either at college or through personal ads. In dating I would usually not disclose that I am a recovering sex addict. In one instance I did disclose this information, but only because we became intimate and I wanted to be honest before becoming sexual to the point of intercourse. That relationship lasted for almost one year and the sexuality within the relationship was non-addictive. The split was largely amicable and it was a healthier sexual relationship than others I have had in the past.

As I have continued to date, I have been aware of how my shame and fear levels have diminished. When I dated in the past I was on the hunt. I would push for sex right away. Going on a date always proved to be very tense for me because I felt shameful about my motives. I felt afraid of possible rejection of my forthcoming advances, and I felt shameful that I would get sexual with a stranger. Now I go on dates and don't feel afraid of what I will do to the other person. I know I won't have sex with a person on the first date. I am not as vulnerable as I was in the past. I now look to the experience of dating more favorably. I focus on letting the person know some of who I am. I also interact with the person, trying to gauge if I enjoy being with her. Dating feels safe because I have boundaries.

I work to eliminate potential dangers to my sexual health by consulting with my sponsor prior to making a major decision. Also, I share much of my process with my group members and seek their input. Doing these things keeps me thinking clearly.

In order to become sexually healthy, I need to remember certain things: 1.) I need to be open to my sexuality instead of recoiling from it, because it is much easier for me to recoil from it. 2.) I am a sexual being, and not everything is a slip. 3.) I will not do it perfectly. It is a reasonable expectation that I will make mistakes. 4.) I will back off from a relationship when it doesn't feel good and safe. I have ended, and I am prepared to end in the future, relationships that are not what I am truly looking for. Also, I consciously set limits on behaviors in a relationship when I have gotten more sexual than I feel comfortable with.

Sexuality is part of me, and I am worthy of enjoying it. I literally give myself permission to be sexual in ways that are affirming of me, in ways that do not alienate me from myself or my Higher Power. At times it is a struggle to be sexual because I can get into feeling completely unworthy. Still, sexuality is healthier for me than ever before, which is wholly a tribute to the program.

Healthy sexuality for me includes savoring moments of sexual health from my past. When I was thirteen years old and involved in my first steady relationship, there was one particular night that personifies healthy sexuality for me. I was walking my girlfriend home in the warm rain. She was my friend, and I thought she was very pretty. On the way we stopped in the road under a streetlight; there we kissed and held each other as the rain beat down harder upon us. It was truly beautiful feeling the rain touch me and seeing it shower down from the sky in the misty light. I remember holding her, caressing her face, and feeling the touch of her dampened hair on my face and neck. I remember feeling liked as she held me and kissed me. There was something sweet, majestic, and natural in what happened that night. I felt connected, valued, and physically alive. The thought of that night brings enchanted memories and hope to me. That experience was very sexual, healing, and innocent. I see this experience as a reminder that sex can be very positive in my life. It serves as a touchstone, guiding me toward a loving, nurturing sexuality.

It took a spiritual leap for me to begin enjoying sex again, either alone or within a relationship. I have positive limits around being sexually healthy. By choice, I am not sexual on a daily basis. I am sexual when I feel reasonably happy and centered. Within a committed relationship, I am sexual with my partner by being present, which means I am thinking of only that person and myself. I also do not objectify my partner into just a body.

In discussing masturbation in my program, I need to explain that what I arrived at was the result of much struggle in the search for clarity. I slowly developed a gauge to discern health from addiction. As I recovered, I stopped my primary acting-out behaviors, but in early recovery I allowed myself occasionally to use "euphoric recall"— masturbating to past acting-out experiences. I stopped this shortly, for my heart knew this was not quality sobriety. Still early in recovery, I would masturbate in other ways that I now see as unhealthy. I would see women throughout the day, and sometimes I would allow myself to imagine having sex with them when I masturbated later. I knew this was not right for me because it felt lousy emotionally.

I felt angry because the "old-timers" in my group wouldn't give me all the answers about masturbation. Some of the old-timers seemed to say that masturbation with fantasies that were not about their spouses was a slip. Others seemed to say that fantasy with healthy limits can be enriching. I was left to honestly discern for myself (with the aid of my sponsor) what options worked for me. I explained how I masturbated and how I would feel afterward. My feelings of shame were born of not respecting my natural need for interpersonal limits. In the past I thought there was nothing wrong with random fantasy about strangers or people with whom I was acquainted. I accept that it is natural for me to feel sexual attraction for people I see, but my values show me how unnatural it is for me to think of them to get high sexually as I masturbate.

What also got me out of using fantasies regarding others was the fact that it seemed no different from using a pornographic magazine. I didn't experience this kind of sex as intimate in any way—it felt anonymous. My heart and my Higher Power taught me that sexual expression in my life needed to be loving and intimate. As my awareness grew, so too my program became clearer.

Masturbation in my current program sounds rather technical, but my struggle forced me to achieve such clarity because it took such an effort to peel away my denial and find behaviors that were within my values.

When I choose to be sexual alone I act sexually in two ways that feel healthy for me. For both of these I center myself by reading my written program. I make the conscious choice to be sexual.

Monogamy fantasy: I fantasize about a past partner I cared for and liked. In this way I do not deny my sexuality, nor do I open the door to scanning women, only to later access them in my mind in negative fantasy. With monogamy fantasy I focus on an image of being sexual with a mate in a loving way.

Sensation masturbation: This involves touching myself in a way that feels pleasurable. I continually ask and answer myself, "How does this feel?" I orient myself to my sensation instead of addictive fetishes. When negative "addict babble" enters my mind, I recognize it and let it go, reorienting myself to sensation.

I believe that in the past I escaped personal intimacy by using fantasy—keeping the focus outside myself. Now I orient to myself, knowing that my sexuality is within me. I overcome the initial squeamishness of touching myself by facing my fears, not by orienting to external objects.

After being sexual in a healthy way, I feel connected, proud, self-accepting, satisfied, warm, humble, safe, content, and thankful.

I would be remiss if I didn't mention that my recovery is more full than ever previously. The basis of this improvement is the focus I've put on improving the quality of my recovery. I've taken risks by dating, and they have paid off. I've increased my social interactions. One of the ways I've done this is to play volleyball through a church. Playing volleyball for me is a festive and sensual experience. My soul and spirit get fed by reaching out and living in this way. Health for me is a holistic experience, which means I need to attend to the differing areas of life.

29.

A NEW JOURNEY

I believe that in my natural state I am a sexual creature—that our sexuality is a gift and that it is a part of what makes us whole. I feel good when my body moves—dancing, exercising, all physical movement feels good to me. I believe that part of honoring myself is acknowledging my sexual nature as part of my whole self, and that it has the potential to bring joy to my life. My journey is to reconnect my spirituality with my sexuality.

I learned very early that behaving seductively was a good way to get the attention I craved and that it made me feel powerful. By the age of eighteen, I was confident of my ability to manipulate the opposite sex, and it felt like a game to me. I thought of myself as being very independent and not "needing" any particular man in the way I clearly "need" my family and friends. I think now that this was a defense mechanism against not feeling protected.

As a child I remember instances of sexual abuse by one family member, and sexualized encounters with other men. I also suspect that there may be other "blocked" instances, or it could just be that there was a lot of sexually charged energy in the adults around me. I started masturbating before I can remember, and I was punished by my parents for this and teased by my brother and sister. I remember thinking, "When I'm ten, I won't even remember doing this," only to have age ten come and go with the same shameful secret in place.

When I was old enough to baby-sit, I found myself looking through drawers for lingerie and sexual literature. Sometimes I would pretend to be sick so that I could stay home alone to masturbate. I started using different objects to masturbate with and began to expose myself in the windows of our home.

In my teenage years I started acting out with sex, drugs, and alcohol. One night when I was about fifteen I prayed to God and told him that

I was "signing off," as I consciously chose to live "the wild life." My relationship with God was too incongruent with my reckless life at that time to continue to have both.

The "relationship" that made me most excited was one in which I was blatantly used by a boy a couple of years older than I. Being used emotionally and sexually was a clear turn-on for me. I acted in a seemingly contradictory fashion—needing respect and protection, yet acting very bold and independent. I see now that this blocked true intimacy in my relationships.

In college I found some other "wild" girls, and together we set out to get the maximum rush. I always seemed to be looking for some kind of better, higher, alternate sexual thrill. There were nights when I would lie in bed filled with shame and remorse, but I had healthy, happy experiences during those years too. I would go back and forth between my "good" and "evil" twin to meet the needs of both sides of my personality.

During my early twenties I began to work as a stripper on weekends. Talk about a double life! I had a job in my field during the week, and on the weekends I had found what was the most heady experience yet—exposing myself to a roomful of men absolutely worked in a way that nothing else had. I danced for over a year, but eventually it was just too draining to keep up, and I was depressed by all the drinking and drugging. I needed a healthier lifestyle.

When I look back now, I can clearly see how I had set up a double life. I was an overachiever. I worked hard and I played hard. I needed success in other areas of my life to balance my "dark side." While I learned how to balance my two lives, I wondered why I was so different from my girlfriends, especially in how they related to men. I rarely had an exclusive sexual relationship, and when I did I was unable to remain faithful to one partner. I felt bad about being dishonest, so I usually avoided any implication of a committed relationship. By staying aloof, I was able to guard my independence and protect my "boyfriends" from my infidelities.

I thought that I could never be faithful to one person. I didn't even think about marriage much, but when I was twenty-nine I met my future husband and everything seemed right. For the first few years, while I was having children, I was almost without addictive behaviors, and I certainly didn't have any feelings of wanting to act out sexually. My body was going through many changes, and my time and emotions were wrapped up with my children. I was as happy as I have ever been, but my husband

and I weren't close. I was less and less able to feel sexual with him, and I used alcohol when we were together to help ease my discomfort. I accepted my disinterest as a part of married life until I met someone who triggered my sexual addiction.

My world began to crumble in every way. When my sex addiction kicked in again, I also returned to abusing alcohol. Soon my husband found out that I was involved with someone else sexually, and I discovered that he had a cocaine problem. I eventually began using cocaine with my husband, hoping that using drugs would satisfy my need for an intense high while keeping me from getting into trouble with infidelity.

Eventually I realized that my biggest problem was not acting out, but continuously fantasizing about acting out, to the point that I was completely distracted from my job, my children, and my marriage. I could not sleep well and lost my appetite. I had the classic symptoms of a drug addict. I soon became involved with another man and found myself addicted to our e-mail communications. I could be sitting in front of my computer completely high, without anyone being aware of what was going on. This way of acting out fed into my life-long preoccupation with secrecy.

My life was becoming more unmanageable with the increased use of alcohol and drugs. Using drugs while being a mother was completely unacceptable to me, but I couldn't stop. I finally realized that there was no way I would be able to get control of any part of my life without giving up alcohol and drugs, and I started to go to twelve-step meetings for my drinking and drugging. At the time, though, I had no interest in giving up my addictive sexual behaviors. In fact, I didn't know they were an addiction. I thought that getting alcohol and drugs out of my life would solve my other problems, but it only proved to be the necessary step for me to be able to see that I had an addiction to sexual fantasy.

Six months into my sobriety my husband went into treatment for alcohol and cocaine abuse. It was during his treatment and my involvement with his recovery that I first became fully aware of how powerful my sexual addiction was. I began to see that all of the things cocaine did for him were what happened to me when I "used" sexual fantasy. When I had critical thoughts about his addiction, I asked myself, "Is there some way I do the same thing with my preoccupation with sexual fantasy?" The answer was usually yes. I had to have private time away from my family just so that I could fantasize in peace. I became irritated when my fantasies were "interrupted" by my children. I was finally able to see how completely obsessed I was with getting high through sexual fantasy. It was as if I carried a supply of cocaine in my body that I could activate immediately, and silently.

I couldn't find a Sex Addicts Anonymous meeting for women during the day in my area, so I started one. This meeting has proved to be the most important tool in my recovery. In this small meeting I receive the support and encouragement I need to face my addiction issues. Another tool that helped me make sense of my addiction was keeping a private journal. I think it was important to list the "pros" and "cons" of some of my acting-out behaviors. I was able to acknowledge why my addiction was so "cunning, baffling, and powerful."

I was finally able to recognize that my acting out was a way of trying to be seen. I used to call that part of myself "my evil twin," but now I see her more as a hungry child. I had to realize that I needed to feed the hungry child, not deny her existence. The only way she knew to feel seen was through being sexual.

With my newly formed relationship with God and the tools of the program, I was able to acknowledge the pain and loss of what happened and what didn't happen in my childhood. During this period of grief it seemed like I cried every time I was alone. But this crying was good; it was the turning point. It was accepting the pain, feeling it, and letting go of it that allowed me to experience the serenity and peace the program offers.

It is very liberating not to have relationships in my life that need to be controlled or hidden. I don't have to worry about covering anything up, and this leaves me free to be "in the moment." I am able to be alive in my primary relationships again—I feel like a real "mommy" to my children.

I know now that having affairs or even having relationships that feel like affairs is dangerous and harmful to me. They aren't worth sacrificing my sobriety or making my partner feel insecure. I still struggle with how to be intimate in my marriage. I also try to find safe and healthy ways to be open with others, to feel seen. I try to find ways of being known that support my whole self, including my spirituality.

30.

A TIME TO GROW

Sex to me was, and can still be, an opiate. Addictive sexual arousal produced chemicals inside my brain so strong that alcohol and drugs pale in comparison. What an amazing effect was the "rush" of a new sexual experience!

For most of my life, I welcomed the excitement and morphine-like effect of these chemicals. Until, that is, a combination of alcohol, drugs, and sexual addiction tore my life apart.

As a young man, I started reading and looking at pornography, and constantly rerunning it in my mind. As time went by, I had affairs and built a porn library. My experience is that sexual addiction is a progressive disease, always requiring me to up the excitement ante.

I sought danger and excitement, seeking prostitutes in dangerous locations, and once I had an irate husband visit me with a weapon in his pocket. I date-raped a young woman—actually a relative from my family of origin. That is still very hard for me to realize and admit.

As my feeling of shame and the consequences of my behavior increased, I decided to leave it all behind and move to another state. I abandoned my wife, children, work, friends, and everything else that I valued and loved. There was no restoring these losses in this new life. I couldn't even make new friends. I couldn't succeed at a new job. Alcohol, drugs, and even sexual addiction would no longer work. Visiting strip bars and going to porn movies left me feeling desperately lonely and weird. Sex became a constant preoccupation. At times, I couldn't get it out of my head even when important things were demanding my attention. I developed a strong homophobia—a fear that I was homosexual—which frightened me and was ever-present in my consciousness. Life became pure pain.

I know now that growing up in my family was a confusing and disorienting experience. There is sufficient direct testimony for me to believe that both my father and his father were sex addicts. How much farther back it goes is anyone's guess. Some hope for recovery started when my wife called late one evening while I was still on my "geographic escape" to tell me of counseling that we could take as a family. I returned home to find us enrolled in a family-oriented chemical dependency program. While the program, together with twelve-step meetings for my alcoholism, helped somewhat, sexual addiction never relaxed its tight grip on me.

I constantly confused sex with love, and imagined myself a person that simply loved people in a noble and selfless way. I was not accepting the reality of my exploitation of others and my truly selfish actions. It was a matter of ignoring the spiritual dimension of love. I remember thinking once during treatment: "They might get me to give up alcohol and drugs, but they'll never get me to give up sex." My wife and I divorced soon after leaving the treatment program.

I spent the next five years recovering from my addiction to alcohol and drugs, but slipping frequently into a "nasty little world." By that I mean that my brain contains a model of the world. All of us have such a model, but a part of that model for me is highly unrealistic. In this model, women's intentions toward me, even in the most innocent of situations, are sexual. Images from the past haunt or arouse me. I imagine that past sexual encounters still might have some meaning, or I experience shame from recalling them. Sexually arousing images on TV, for example, develop all of the power of a lifetime of addiction. All of this can occur completely automatically, and faster than I can hit "enter" on my computer. Access to this world in my life can be a habitual/compulsive response to stress, happiness, fear, disappointment, travel, car trouble, or the common cold.

I spiraled increasingly into a separation from reality. Fantasies were acted out secretly as sexual partners and I tried dangerous escapades. But as the song says, "I can't get no satisfaction."

Redemption for me came during a camping trip. A remarkably brave friend confronted me. Opposition, as William Blake said, is true friendship. While I resisted, as most sex addicts would to what she said, in the end I saw the truth. She told me that I needed to deal with my sexual addiction. This, of course, like everything else in life, was easier said than done.

The memory of my first SAA meeting is still clear in my head. I felt so good at the end of the meeting, that upon leaving, I raised both arms over my head in that universal recognition of victory. Slowly I began to recognize the "nasty little world." I won't tell you that I worked a perfect program, or that the demons of my brain don't affect me still. As they say, addiction is cunning, baffling, and powerful. This is a one-day-at-a-time program.

Before joining SAA I had decided to find out if I was indeed gay, in spite of my compulsive sex with women. So, after meeting a gay man, and talking to two counselors, we were sexual. I was still confused. Over the years, I have come to realize that I am truly a bisexual man, that I can love both men and women physically and spiritually. The fact is, however, that I can only be in one full-time, committed relationship. I choose to make that relationship with a woman.

This isn't to say that my bisexuality doesn't get expressed in other ways. I am able to be physically connected to other men, and women, through hugs and sports, and I make sure I am. And I love these people spiritually as well.

While in SAA, I developed some adaptations to allow me to stay connected to my addiction while not acting addictively. This allowed me to tell myself that I was recovering while still getting some of the benefits, or so I supposed, of addiction. So even though I looked and sounded pretty good, the nasty little world in my head was very much intact. I could, as we say, take the lion out for a walk, imagining sexual situations, and rationalize it away as something normal people do. I started to ponder what exact reason I have for working toward sexual sobriety. After all, is sexual addiction so bad? With care, perhaps it can be controlled. Perhaps it can be held entirely secret, for most of it is in my brain, beyond outside observation.

What a delusion! My experience is that there is no controlling this disease. Things simply go from bad to worse. Furthermore, scientists today believe that the most complex thing so far discovered in the universe is the human brain. It seems to me that it follows that this powerful information system will, given some time, discover the secrets held in other brains. I now assume that people who know me, know the truth about me, whether they acknowledge it or not.

I had forgotten one of the famous twelve-step slogans: Honest, Open, and Willing (HOW). I needed to become entirely willing and honest if I wanted lasting recovery. Beyond a desire to stop hurting and using people, it seems somehow subhuman for me to turn my will and my life over to the care of addiction, to act compulsively, to not be capable of choice, and to remain locked in some fantastic past.

For me, just letting God take care of my addiction is simply not enough, because I can have sexual obsession in my head, and I don't have to plan anything, go to a bookstore, arrange to meet someone, or anything else. I can just jump to that place in my brain.

The God of my understanding requires that I take action. Just showing up was no longer sufficient. It was time to grow, to put my feet on the ground and not be a victim any longer. Again, easier said than done. But this is a program of progress, not perfection, and things, quite amazingly, have a way of turning out all right.

One of the most healing moments of my recovery came when I told a woman whom I was seeing that I was a sex addict. To my utter amazement, she wept. I have never felt such compassion, acceptance, and love. We are now married and have a wonderful daughter. I owe a lot today to friends, to actively working the Twelve Steps, having an SAA sponsor, and talking with him and other SAA members.

Just as in my addiction the quality of my life went down from being an idealistic kid to a person I could not be proud of, so it has gradually moved up in recovery. Today I can give and receive love, be challenged, have friends I can trust, have ideals, and, best of all, feel integrated and whole.

31.

BREAKING THE SILENCE

I began acting out sexually at age five. I was self-sexual in a hurtful, addictive way, and my acting-out behaviors were bizarre and beyond what most people would consider normal childlike sexual play. I was terrified of being found out in my secret, so I was very careful not to hurt myself in any ways that would be discernible or require medical attention. Though I wouldn't come to understand or acknowledge it for many years, my acting-out behavior bore three telltale components that placed it in the realm of deep addiction. It had a fetish quality about it. It was accompanied by violent and hurtful fantasy. And later in my life, even when I tried to stop it, I could not.

I made and broke many promises to God about ending these behaviors, because something inside hungered for recovery. In my heart I always knew something was very wrong with what I was doing, but I felt hopelessly trapped in a child's mentality, accompanied by an immeasurable degree of shame. Though I felt fearful that I had somehow acquired what I sensed to be the family's sexual perversion, I comforted myself with thinking that I was somehow different. After all, my behavior was very private and singular, while theirs was overt and involved acting out with multiple sexual partners. Still, in my heart I knew that what I was doing was not right.

I think it was my intense shame that fed my need to find God and some kind of spirituality at age seven or eight. As I grew in my understanding of the Bible, I was deeply affected by the realization that I would have to give up my sexually sick behaviors if I wanted to live by Biblical principles and have a relationship with God as I came to understand him. I developed a very self-destructive and punishing outer symptom that became a reflection of the self-hate and continual inner spirals of guilt and shame that enveloped me. I would chew my fingernails and cuticles until I was in so much pain that I could hardly use my hands. Clearly, I was addicted to hurting myself.

As a teenager, I became chronically depressed and even suicidal, and felt hopelessly trapped in an almost unbearable shroud of isolation and silence. My parents somehow sensed the gravity of my depression. They took me to a doctor and friend who seemed to be a psychologist ahead of his time. He tried to loosen my death-grip on my secret with some very insightful questions. Was I unhappy at home? Did I feel unnecessary guilt, as many young people did, about the practice of masturbation? He had been a friend of my parents for years. The family's silence prevailed and prevented me from telling the truth about my private or family life, as this would have been an unforgivable treason. So though a part of me wanted to trust him, I lied about our family circumstances and denied that I had any sexual problems.

Since then I have been caught in a horrible struggle between my addiction and my relationship with God. I was married at seventeen and finally felt some relief from this struggle. So I rationalized that I was simply a person with high sexual needs who could find solace in the safety of a committed relationship. I believed that my struggle had finally ended, and I fantasized that it would never become a problem again. And though I stayed away from compulsive sexual behavior for most of that time, I was painfully reminded of its baffling presence once when my husband and I agreed to be celibate. Two years into my marriage, he suggested that we avoid sex during my pregnancy. The constant obsession I experienced during this imposed deprivation rudely reminded me that my addiction hadn't gone away.

My husband had initially been attracted to my seeming extroversion and independence. But my addictive practices and the family system that fostered them left an incredible void where parenting should have been. I continued to feel suicidal and exceedingly depressed. These festering poisons battered our relationship and deprived me of bringing a whole self to my marriage. I idealized my husband, making him too big and myself too small. Of course I was blind to his addictions and dysfunction. I had no idea that selflessly trying to be everything he wanted and allowing him to be unaccountable would eventually cost me my home and family.

After seventeen years of tending to his every need and wish, I was horrified to learn that he was involved with another woman. A three-year separation marked by his repeated pleas for more time, and promises to return home, ended when I finally summoned the strength to give him the ultimatum that led to our divorce. Needless to say, my addiction returned in all its fury. I was horrified at my inability to control my behavior despite my religious values, my fear of jeopardizing my relationship with God, or the intense pain my persisting climate of self-hate produced.

One way in which this insanity has rendered my life unmanageable has been in my inability to believe that God would ever love or reward me for anything. Even though I believe very deeply in his Biblical promises of loving kindness and forgiveness, I found it impossible to let God's love in. And even now, I cry and beg him to teach me to understand that he could be there for me too. My dysfunction and shame and lifelong belief that I am bad somehow superseded and negated my faith.

My acting-out behaviors escalated, and I was out of control. I was committed to keeping my secret forever. Nonetheless, my profound sense of shame and its impact on my relationships brought me into therapy in 1978. It was my misfortune to encounter a novice therapist who didn't enforce professional boundaries or understand sexual addiction. So I ended up feeling more alone and hopeless than ever. Focused on what she thought to be the evils of religious injunctions, she tried to validate and encourage masturbatory practices, completely missing my compulsiveness and the violation of my values. The path to healing was obscured for another ten years. I put it all away, deciding that I would have to fight the battle on my spiritual ground. I felt too much shame to trust anyone with such vulnerable realities. I promised God over and over again that I would make myself talk to someone about this behavior if I could not stop on my own, and when I finally realized that I couldn't stop, I began to think about who I could talk to about all of this.

Perhaps my first introduction to grace around this issue came in my finding an insightful therapist who had herself been in twelve-step programs. She gently, lovingly, and patiently took me on a journey into my inner life and brought me to the core of my shame. Though I had promised myself I was never going to trust my secrets to another therapist, I soon realized that this insightful woman would never give me permission to transgress my values and could be trusted with this kind of vulnerability. In the process of speaking with her about my fear that my daughter might be getting trapped in her own addictions, she explained that when a parent has a secret compulsion or addiction, certain things can align in their outside lives that invite and even create the necessity for their children's addictions. And then she said something that brought me to my knees and the doorstep of SAA. She said, "If you want to help your daughter with her addictions, the best thing I know is to begin working on your own." This really hit me where I live, because I would do anything to help my daughter to live a better, happier, and less lonely life. And although I resisted, pleaded, and swore that I could never come to SAA, that I didn't belong here, that my life wasn't unmanageable or out of control, I agreed that I would think about her strong recommendation that I attend just one meeting.

So while she went on vacation, I decided that I would try to appear open-minded by going to one meeting and proving once and for all that I didn't belong. However, when I came to the group, I was deeply impressed with the quality and kindness of people I met and the depth of their commitment to the recovery process. I felt impelled to come back to learn more about what sexual addiction looked like. And soon thereafter, the sexual addiction assessment questions helped me to realize that I was in trouble. All my outside barriers crumbled as I decided to break the silence and talk specifically in therapy about these behaviors. I was crushed by the painful fallout and aftermath of guilt and shame those admissions precipitated. I don't know how I could have imagined that it would be painless to break a forty-year silence! But I soon began to understand that my secret addiction had taken a terrible toll on my self-respect, sense of peace, and spirituality.

In my early days of group attendance, I had a highly questioning attitude. I felt I had worked the steps in my religion and didn't really need them. Still, I had to admit that I hadn't made a smashing success of sobriety or sanity on my own. So I begrudgingly decided to begin experimenting with them, including those which I felt I had done in my religion. It's been two and a half years that I have been in the group now, and it would be an understatement to say that I have learned immeasurable lessons as a result. I have learned that I am not alone and that others have felt the same as I do. I have never felt that I belonged anywhere, and I have had to fight that feeling of isolation every time I attend the meeting. But in the kind faces of the friends I have made here, I have found glimmers of grace and small servings of serenity. I have found understanding and patience. I found a sponsor who has given me much support and kindness and yet helps me to keep reaching for new program challenges. And with all of these resources, I have begun to break through the nearly impenetrable walls of shame, isolation, and silence. I am beginning to have a sense of belonging and value.

I have been sober from those hurtful behaviors for almost two years. But I want and work for sobriety of a much stricter kind now. In therapy, I have begun to trace the causes of my addiction, and I've realized to my horror that I was raised in an incestuous family where almost everyone was acting out. How I didn't add it up or see it, I don't know. Almost every child in my family manifested serious acting-out behaviors and abnormal childhood disturbances. I never understood the profile of an incestuous family or the compulsion to repeat until I came into therapy to deal with my own woundedness.

While my desire to please my therapist pushed me past my shame to attend my first SAA meeting, my hunger for recovery, loving support, and healing has motivated me to stay. Until my divorce, my outer life passed for presentable, and even today very few people in my outside world would ever know or dream of the struggles I have had. Still, I realize that my inner life has been totally unmanageable and that I have been confronted with the ultimate choice all addicts must face—the choice between recovery or death. With all my heart, I want recovery. I want to be able to feel God's love and to learn to love myself. I have to understand that I can't do it perfectly—that it's progress, not perfection, and it's a formidable struggle. But there's one thing that's really different now. I know I don't have to pretend anymore and that I don't have to try to do this alone. Thank God for SAA and this wonderful group that has helped me to break the silence and the wall of isolation that I have lived behind for most of my life.

32.

THE PEACE OF RECOVERY

When I saw the list of suggested topics for personal stories, I thought I could, maybe should, write about all of them. My narcissism told me I was qualified not only to write my story, but to cover all the subjects within the scope of any recovery process. I began my SAA journey in the fall of 1989, so I had to admit I could not write about the earlier days of SAA. What a blow to my ego!

I was diagnosed a "narcissistic pedophile" with probable "chemical dependency" before my recovery began. I was incensed that I would be labeled a pedophile. I was angered at those five professionals who had placed their brand upon me, notwithstanding I was an admitted incest perpetrator, having abused all three female children in my nuclear family, two by marriage, one by blood. But, I thought, that had been nearly twenty years before, certainly nothing to mark me with at this time. And so what if I drank a bit of alcohol from time to time—didn't everyone? Hadn't this been a normal part of my life with many of the persons I grew up with, and did it not still prevail in my circle of friends?

I was in a torrid extramarital affair at this time, only one of several throughout my then sixty years. I was not interested in giving in to the suggestions of counselors, friends, or family, despite my wife's threat to leave the marriage. Nor was I concerned for the welfare of the family of the woman with whom I was having the affair. I was not interested in doing anything any way but my own. Was I being unreasonable? Of course not—I wanted what I wanted, and wanted it now! And I felt I had a right to it.

There was another exhibition of aberrant sexual behavior about this time that I totally denied I had a problem with, saying it was only because I was "tipsy" at the time. I was uninhibited because of alcohol, an excuse I had used for years to cover any inappropriate behavior I ever had. I was playing a musical instrument in my home, in the presence of three couples, singing songs of my own writing—naked. I really didn't want to think about that aspect of my behavior.

My first contact with the recovery world was with the female director of a nearby crisis abuse center who was in her own recovery from alcohol and sexual addiction. She seemed to care and understand. I was ready, but scared, as she referred me to another professional.

They spoke plainly. It was suggested I go to a treatment center that dealt with "sex addiction." It was also suggested that I meet with a man known only as "Ray," from a nearby recovery group. He was my first contact with SAA. Since my insurance would not pay for the treatment center, I was asked to participate in a chemical dependency program in which the director would modify the program to include my sexual problems along with the drinking part (which I believed was not a problem anyway). And so I began.

I refused to quit my work 150 miles from home, which meant I would continue to be in the same town, in the same environment as before, with the woman of my affair. Her husband, who was himself beginning a program of sobriety, took a dim view of our behavior. So did my wife, and she left me.

My lover didn't move out, but began a graduate program in a town near to where I attended weekly SAA meetings, a round trip of two hundred miles. We both refused to give up our behaviors together, and saw each other at least weekly, despite warnings from counselors and friends, even while we participated in individual programs of recovery. I say "participated" since there was very little "working the program" as defined by SAA.

After I was "twelfth-stepped," I practiced in my head how I would respond in my first SAA meeting. It was almost a recitation, intellectually perfected like most of my lies, and without a lot of feeling. I left out the part about the "exhibiting." I dealt with the incest issue as if it were a long ago, long forgotten, already solved problem. I also had a "religious addiction" that kept me from treating the seriousness of my life's current and past issues—there was an easier way, and I'd already found it.

My counselor also ran a church-supported recovery program, complete with books, tapes, and videos. Since I drove four hundred miles a week to treatment, SAA, and other meetings, there was ample time to use these audio resources. The books helped with my feeling of aloneness. I was understanding recovery in my head, my behavior changing to the extent that I was avoiding my inner circle, except for the affair. And that relationship was having problems as well. We continued joint therapy, not having any definite destination, for the therapy or our future, together or separate.

I finished my Fifth Step in the first five months. I was still in the chemical dependency program as well. I see now the shallowness with which I worked these first steps. There was a lot in my journal but precious little in my gut.

I was "co-sponsoring" with another SAA member, the most senior in the group. He had been in the program about seven months longer than I. We clashed in service meetings—over "group conscience" issues, over recovery in general at times. In retrospect, we both had something to offer; both of us suffered issues of control. In all my days of recovery, I never made a success of being a sponsor. It took a long time to uncover the unrelenting control issues and the underlying fears from which they were born.

My new partner and I were divorced from our respective spouses in 1991. I still had not, even after a heart attack later that year, touched real recovery. I avoided inner-circle behaviors. Of course, the best way to avoid violating inner-circle behaviors is not to put certain behaviors in the inner circle. This yet uncommitted relationship was not in my inner circle. Whether it should have been is now only conjecture.

To some degree I did practice service within my home group, and was elected by that group to be delegate at the 1992 SAA convention. There I was elected to a trusted servant position as "National Service Organization Board Member." There were some problems already in place concerning the management of the NSO office and other important matters. Being a control freak and without many boundaries, I proceeded to solve problems in the same way I had in the corporate world. My behavior was less than admirable. These actions later required me to make amends to those I had harmed during this period. I had little healing, much bitterness, much shame, anger, frustration, and sadness. Thankfully the efforts of my fellow trusted servants would transcend my behaviors and meet the issues of the day.

While in another city, I was invited to an SAA group where the sharing was the deepest, most honest, and most profound that I'd ever seen or participated in. I saw, and felt, some of the most moving, gut-level intensity of my life. I knew I had never been this way before. My ivory tower recovery processes would not, could not, survive this kind of participation. Where had I been for the last four years? Thanks to my Higher Power I was aware of the limitations of my program. But I had done some recovery work; I had given some service; I did acknowledge the need for lifetime commitment to the recovery process. It was not as if I couldn't learn from my experiences. The next move would place me 375 miles from any SAA groups.

I attended the meetings of a different "S" program when we first arrived at our new home. Occasionally an SAA member from another community would come by for a personal visit, but there was no one waiting in line to become a member of a local group. With some renewed courage, I decided to start an SAA meeting. I did an anonymous interview with a reporter from the daily paper. I installed a special telephone line to answer inquiries. I got a P.O. box. A new group would be added to the fellowship. We grew.

Sometimes we seem to lose as many as we gain. The core who remain, however, seem to recognize all that encompasses the twelve-step process and are diligent about keeping the group going. We lost our meeting places and had to find new ones. Referrals from the counseling community are few and far between. We keep reaching out to attract, not promote. Patience? A commodity that is hard to come by, yet in great demand. All these things are good lessons for those of us, like me, with control issues.

During all this period, my personal life, as it was known in past years, was changing. In some respects, it was ending. Each of my children had borne their own pain, living lives that had little appropriate direction from their addicted father. They had innumerable reasons for contempt, anger, sadness, and frustration. Not only did I lose them all for a time, but my grandchildren and great-grandchildren as well. I found that all the recovery I thought I had did nothing to enhance these relationships. It merely renewed the concept of interference with their lives that was the norm for me during their childhood and adult years. In reality, I was not well enough to even think that I could introduce myself back into their lives. The same was true for my family of origin, including my half-brothers and sisters, and their families. The annual family picnics, with the young people present, were no longer a part of my life. I was seen as the cause of the separation, and as the issues of my life became known, no one was anxious to have me near any progeny, particularly the female children.

I am not yet a patient person. Although I am a man aging fast, time never keeps up with my demands. Denial is denial is denial, whether from knowing obstinacy or willing blindness. The character defects that still beset me are those of self first. My addiction, whose faces are many, and whose behaviors are intricately linked, are borne up by anger turned to rage, disagreement to hatred, hurt to resentment, self-acceptance to entitlement, and true self to abject failure. In my grandiosity was a modicum of worldly success, blinding me, not to who I was as a human being, but to what I had become, from infancy to adulthood. Now my narcissism seems as destructive to my recovery as my pedophilia. I didn't have a clue as to what I would be dealing with in the first six to seven years of my recovery. Nor did I discern the real trauma to those who had been part of my life, most of all to my victims, my children.

I worked the Steps of SAA a few times over. But I never saw myself so vividly until I had to deal with the "self" that had taken my place as a human. How little is my success until I can make changes in my belief system, and the behaviors that result from it. Empathy may be only a word, but until I live the meaning of the term I cannot uphold the rights of all mankind as being just as important as my own. I still grapple with lustful thoughts, but for less time and less often. I have boundary problems and inappropriately enter the lives of others, and allow them the same privilege. I still argue over inconsequential matters. I have trouble taking constructive criticism, especially when I am plainly in the wrong. But I did make it past Step Nine, and I know that I didn't stop long enough the first time to give it enough meaning for progressive recovery. By doing it again and again, and placing an honest Step Ten beside it, I have found new hope by being able to make amends for these transgressions and promptly admitting it when I continue to err.

There are so many forces that have given me experience, strength, and hope. Time itself, hard as it is to cope with, is necessary for transformation. And as time passed, I was helped by persons in recovery, in SAA and other twelve-step fellowships, who were willing to put up with me through my hard times.

The separation from my family becomes lessened somewhat by the return of a few. I have had nothing to do with that, though I tried to force all issues and all persons, as I had in the past. It was this separation, thanks to my Higher Power, that finally convinced me I was not in charge. I am grateful for what I have and for what I do not have. I can handle only so much, and I am not too good a judge of how much. In addition to what I have learned from my peers in SAA and other recovery groups, I have found wisdom in the lives of people outside the recovery community. I could not see it from where I was when I began this recovery process. I could not subordinate myself to believe that others had the same rights as I did. There is support all around me. I have finally had the slight awakening to realize this.

My conception of a Higher Power for my life has changed greatly. My fears are minimal, life is not scary, and death even less. The light years that separate the universe are no less complicated than are the components of life itself, and there are some things about me I cannot know. Is this the peace of recovery that passes human understanding?

33.

A LIFE CALLING

Age 11: My dad gives me a book that explains what's about to happen to my body as I hit puberty. The book explains it well and doesn't use shame or fear like some books do. My parents aren't into shame and fear. They love each other and they love me, and they want me to grow up to be a healthy adult.

The book teaches me a new word: masturbation. I decide to try it. Before long I'm spending hours each day doing it. I start to get scared about that. It's not that I think it's so wrong to do it, but I can't stop doing it or even limit how often I do it. Sometimes I do it so much that I injure myself, and I still can't stop.

Age 13: I spend two or more hours in the bathroom at a time, making the rest of my family upset. My mom finally tells me I have to find some other place to masturbate. She even uses the word. I'm so embarrassed. I am obliged to move my masturbation routines to my bedroom. I fantasize about doing sexual things with other kids and sometimes write dirty stories about them.

Age 14: I'm writing even longer stories now. I have a whole file of them hidden in my room, and I also keep a list of all the names of people I like to fantasize about, so when I feel like masturbating, I can pick one from the list. I also figure out a way to spy on people in the upstairs bathroom of our house. I can watch them and masturbate while they're getting out of the shower and they don't know I'm there. It's more exciting than just masturbating.

I'm scared about the fact that almost all of my fantasies are about boys. I used to think it was just a phase, but now I can tell it's not. I pray to God to help me stop thinking about other boys this way. That doesn't work. So I strike a bargain with God: for every fantasy I have about a boy, I'll balance it out by having one about a girl.

Age 15: My bargain with God doesn't work out. I finally quit fighting the fact that I am gay. I don't like it, but in my heart I know it's something I can't change. I wish I could talk to someone about it, but I'm scared. I'm sure that my friends would reject me and I'd get beat up at school. My family would still love me, but I know they would be disappointed. I decide to just keep it a secret forever.

Age 16: I still spend a lot of my time making up fantasies. Sometimes I change my route between classes so I can follow a boy in the halls and take mental pictures of his body. Sometimes I go out with my camera and take real pictures of boys in public places, and I keep that collection separate from my other pictures.

I start having conversations about sex with a female friend. She has the same beliefs about sexual freedom that I do. Eventually she propositions me and we have sex. I'm not attracted to her, but I'm curious about it all, and I want to lose my virginity as soon as possible. Later she starts complaining that I'm not paying enough attention to her. She was hurt by the experience.

Once, in a public bathroom, I see a younger boy enter a stall. I go into the next stall, climb up on the toilet, and look down over the wall at him. He looks up and sees me, freaks out and runs out to tell his father, who confronts me angrily. I invent an excuse and act apologetic, and he lets me go. I'm terrified by what I have done.

A couple weeks later I go into a restroom in a shopping mall and there's a middle-aged man in there who says "Hi" to me. Somehow I can tell he's looking at me the same way I look at cute boys. We end up having sex right there in the restroom. Now I'm even more afraid. Sex has a power over me that is more threatening all the time. I try to comfort my fears by retreating into my fantasy world. I'm reclusive, moody, and irritable.

Age 17: I now see that my sexual feelings are connected to emotional needs that are more important to me. I want to be close to someone. I'm not as interested in pursuing sex now. I just want to find someone I can fall in love with. I make friends with a lot of boys, but no matter how close I get to someone, it's never enough.

Age 18: I'm obsessed with this one boy whom I've known for a few years. I dream about him every night and day. I put pictures of him on my wall, and I write poetry about him. One night he invites me to sleep over. I share some beers with him, we stay up late talking, and we end up having a sexual encounter. Even though I wanted it more than anything else I didn't really want it to happen because I knew it would freak him out and probably end our friendship. Now he's pretending it never happened and acting like he doesn't want to see me at all. I plunge into depression.

Age 19: I finally admit to myself that I have a problem, though I don't know what to call it. It always seems to center around getting so obsessed with somebody that I can't function. Since the guys I fantasize about are usually younger, that means a lot of my fantasies are illegal. I don't want to think of myself as a freak or a monster, but I don't know what else to call myself.

Age 21: I meet a boy who sweeps me off my feet. I feel euphoric whenever we're together. I ignore the warning signs I should have learned when I was in high school. No matter how close we get, I always seem to want more. That scares me.

I crash into depression again. I drop out of one of my major programs and come close to quitting school altogether. This time I seek counseling. I tell the counselor everything and end up being recommended for a comprehensive psychosexual evaluation. The evaluation labels me as a "severely disturbed individual" and recommends I begin both therapy and psychiatric care. Those feel like harsh words to someone who most people think is just an innocent church boy. In a way, though, I'm relieved at the diagnosis, because it means someone is taking me seriously, and maybe I can finally change whatever is wrong with me.

I see the psychiatrist every week. She talks about issues of growth and control, and recommends antidepressants, which I refuse. Meanwhile, I'm also seeing a sex therapist who is very strict with me. He mostly works with people who have committed major crimes, and he seems to think I have done that too and am just afraid to admit it. He keeps trying to get me to admit to things I've never done. I tell him the truth, but he doesn't believe me. I feel violated. I do my best to work his program anyway for a while, but eventually I walk away, feeling a weird mix of guilt and relief.

Age 23: I'm burned out on fantasy and isolation. More and more, I medicate my loneliness and frustration by having anonymous sexual encounters with men. I did this when I was in college too, but not nearly as much as I do now. I act out with men in all kinds of places. I know all the public restrooms in town. I spend hours in parks, even late at night when they are closed. I drive long distances to rest areas and spend hours there.

Sometimes I feel the urge coming on for days; sometimes it hits me out of the blue while I'm on the way to the supermarket. From that point on, there's a typical pattern to my madness. I used to try to resist it, but I don't even bother anymore. I spend hours on the hunt, sizing up and being sized up by strangers, sizing up the place, always on the watch for police. I finally decide on someone to act out with. The sex itself is never enjoyable, but I guess that's not really why I'm there. I love the hunt. I can't get enough of it.

And then it's over, and I'm never satisfied. I'm groggy, I feel like I just woke up from a trance, and often I have only a vague memory of how I even got there. I remember that I left the house at four to go on an errand, and now suddenly it's eleven at night, it's dark and cold, and I'm at a rest area in another town. I have a bizarre craving for chocolate, and I binge on it at the nearest convenience store. And then I go home and crash from exhaustion, both physical and mental, vowing never to do it again.

Age 24: I meet someone I'm actually attracted to while I'm cruising the bathrooms at the local mall. He likes me too. We trade numbers and start seeing each other. He's twenty years old and very insecure, and he looks up to me as a sort of father figure. For some reason I don't understand, I resent this. I finally can't take it any more, so I break up with him.

My lifestyle rages on. I discover phone sex. I start running up huge bills, and I can't stop doing it. Sometimes when I get the urge for phone sex I go act out in the nearest park instead to save money. I'm a regular at various adult bookstores and peep shows. I pick up men on the street, at the swimming pool, on city buses. I go to strangers' apartments and get in their cars. I go to the airport and cruise the bathrooms there even when I'm not traveling. I have a couple of close calls with the police, but I never actually get caught and I don't really care anyway. I don't have much to lose.

Age 25: Something plants a seed of hope in me. A friend from out of town comes to visit, and we spend a wonderful week together. I fall hopelessly in love with him, even though I know he's straight and there is no chance of anything romantic happening. But after he goes back home and I get over my grief, I start thinking that maybe I could meet someone like that who is gay, and we could have a loving relationship. After all, I had more fun just spending time with this friend than I ever had in any of my numerous sexual encounters. I decide that what I need is a relationship with someone I love—someone I love so much that I won't even be tempted to screw it all up by cheating on him.

Age 27: I get a computer and am introduced to the world of chat rooms and message boards. I realize that many people are using the internet to meet sexual partners, but to me this seems like too much work to find something that's as close as the nearest park. I post a message to see if there are other gay men in my area who are interested in pursuing an "old-fashioned" long-term relationship: being friends first, causal dating, etc. I get a flood of responses. I start a healthy correspondence with other gay men. I start meeting guys for lunch instead of for sex. I'm amazed that this is all happening, and considering my history of only craving dysfunctional or impossible relationships, I'm surprised at how excited I am by this. I feel like fortune has finally smiled on me. Soon I will meet the man of my dreams and be delivered from the bondage of my obsessions and compulsive behavior.

By the end of the summer I have my first serious boyfriend.

Age 29: We've been together for two years. I haven't cruised a park or rest area or gone to a peep show or adult bookstore or had phone sex in that time. I spend a lot of time downloading porn from the internet, but I figure I'm doing pretty well.

Age 30: We live together now. Our relationship is loving, but our sex life is dead, and I think I know why. I was having too much of the wrong kind of sex before, and I saw this relationship as a way of avoiding sex.

I'm getting more and more daring with the porn I download. I'm sure a lot of it is illegal. I don't like that, but I tell myself that at least I'm not paying for any of it, so I'm not supporting it. I store it on a disk. Sometimes I get so freaked out by the stuff on this disk that I erase the whole thing. Then I start collecting it again.

Age 31: I get hooked on cybersex, spending hours online and creating elaborate characters and fantasies. I forget to eat. I get resentful whenever my partner is home on one of my days off, because it's harder for me to act out. If he's gone all day, I never leave the house. I ignore phone calls and commitments. Sometimes I get up in the middle of the night to act out while he's asleep. Sometimes I get up early in the morning to do it before work. I set time limits for myself but then never follow them. This goes on for months.

Before long, this starts taking a toll on my health. In a moment of clarity, I realize I need to quit cybersex altogether. I delete all the related programs from my computer and spend a day writing an elaborate "obituary" for the characters and fantasy world I had created. I make a deliberate effort to pursue hobbies I had been neglecting. I go on vacation with my partner and start feeling like I can breathe again.

About two weeks later, I fall off the wagon. I'm right back to where I was before.

Age 32: I keep trying to quit cybersex. I make it for a week if I'm lucky, and then I fail again. I'm frightened because I'm taking more risks. I start doing it without the anonymity software. I start having phone sex with people I meet online, which means giving them my phone number.

I'm feeling a deeper shame than I've ever felt before. And now I actually have something to lose: a new career that I love. I think my partner would stay with me even if I were arrested and got my name dragged through the mud, but my new career would be history. I feel like it's my life's calling, and I don't want to do anything else. Every time I engage in risky behavior, I wonder if this is the time I will get caught, and if everything I worked so hard for will go up in smoke. I'm under great stress, and the worst thing is that the only way I know how to deal with stress is to escape into my sexual fantasy world, which leads me back to the behaviors that are causing the stress.

Age 33: I am desperate to stop, and yet I don't know what else to do. Sometimes I almost wish I would get caught so the whole thing would be out in the open, and I could finally get help. But that would have such a high price for me that I'm not sure I would even want help anymore.

I start seeing a counselor and manage to go three weeks without acting out—a new record for me. But I'm afraid to tell the counselor much about what's really going on with me. Ironically, the obvious "safe" place to look for help is the internet. In a short time I discover the web site of Sex Addicts Anonymous.

I've always assumed that twelve-step groups were for people with problems more severe than mine, and I was afraid I wouldn't be taken seriously if I attended a meeting. So I go to an online meeting and chat with someone about my concerns. He encourages me to get involved, explaining that the only requirement for membership is the desire to stop addictive sexual behavior—a person did not need to have committed any specific behaviors or suffered any specific consequences in order to qualify! I also answer the twelve questions from the "Are you a sex addict?" section on the SAA website and find, to my surprise, that eleven of the twelve factors are true for me.

Soon after that, I attend my first SAA meeting. I can tell from the minute I walk in the door that this is where I need to be. I go to another. I begin attending regularly and socializing with people from the group. I ask someone to be my sponsor. With his help, I define "sexual sobriety" for myself and begin work on my First Step.

Two months later I complete my First Step and I read it to the group. The whole experience is amazing. I feel a powerful connection to the others in the room. I've never had that kind of support. Best of all, I don't feel like I have to hide who I am. I used to define "safety" in terms of not getting caught or not having my secrets revealed. Now I'm hanging out with people who know my secrets, and it's the safest place I've ever been.

Age 34: I've been a member of SAA for seven months now, and I have been sexually sober since my first meeting. I have never known such sanity in my life. I attend meetings regularly and socialize with group members. I attend the local SAA retreat and serve as secretary for one of the local meetings.

I "hit the ground running" when I join SAA, because this is generally my approach when I start something new. But in doing so, I am forced to confront the source of many of my problems: I try to be in control, to play God. I've gotten away with this in many aspects of my life over the years, and I'm sure that to many people, my life seems very balanced and controlled. My recovery does not depend on my ability to convince them otherwise. It does depend on my ability to follow the slogan "To thine own self be true," and to take the First Step seriously. No matter how well I clean my house or balance my checkbook or perform at my job, I am not ultimately in control. Working the Twelve Steps is not a project, like getting a college degree, remodeling a house, or even writing this story. Working the steps is a lifestyle and a life calling. It may have a definite beginning, but it never ends. When I try to rush it, I am missing the point altogether.

"One day at a time" has never been my approach to life, and I have never wanted to admit powerlessness over anything. My inclination has always been to put my trust in myself, and yet that never did any good. In fact, it made things worse. I was always able to project an illusion of control to myself and others, and I justified every action by saying, "Sure, what I did was bad, but at least I had the good sense not to do such-and-such!" Even at the end, when I was looking online for help, I defined my problem as a computer addiction, rather than seeing my online activities as the latest in a long series of behaviors that were all symptoms of the same sex addiction.

I never had much of a belief in a Higher Power before. But as I work the Second Step, I finally begin to believe that the only thing that can help me be sane is God. My challenge now is not to work the steps as fast as possible or to try to fatten up some sort of imaginary "SAA resumé" with good deeds and service. My challenge is to work the program, one day at a time, and seek a relationship with my Higher Power.

I know now that I need God in my life more than anything else. But that's about all I know. I am still fearful of religion. I don't yet have any kind of spiritual rituals or practices established in my life. But little by little, I'm becoming capable of doing today's work today and leaving the rest in God's hands. I feel God's presence in my life when I attend SAA meetings. I have a lifetime to put the steps into practice in my life, and the only way to do that is one day at a time.

There are times when I am very tempted to return to my earlier behaviors of acting out. I still find myself tempted to have phone sex or computer sex, or to have an easy anonymous encounter somewhere with another stranger. I am still prone to love addiction as well, obsessing with getting someone to like me and thinking that will solve my problems and make my life complete. Even though my acting-out behaviors always caused more problems than they solved, they were often the only coping mechanisms I had for all of my stress, loneliness, fear, and anger. The patterns of behavior that developed over more than two decades will not just magically disappear. But each time I attend a meeting, the stories shared remind me of why I need to be here and why I need—and want—to keep working the program.

I still don't know what a healthy sex life is, but I am blessed with a partner who loves me and is very supportive of me in my recovery process, and I trust that with God's help we will be able to navigate these waters together and reach a better place. The hope I feel now is real. I am only beginning to know God, but I feel God's presence in the group, and I see the miracles God has done for me and for the recovering addicts around me. I am amazed.

34.

NOW SHE HAS HOPE

About five years ago, I started on my path to recovery and healing. I had a weekend fling and was feeling hopeless and despairing. I thought that if I just lost excess weight, men would be attracted to me. A co-worker introduced me to a twelve-step program where I could deal with food and weight issues. I slowly started being honest with myself—I was terrified of men, sex, and intimacy. I went to a therapist to get into an eating disorder program. When she heard about the incest and sexual abuse in my past, she referred me to a therapist who specialized in incest.

The reason I am telling this part of my story is that my eating disorder, incest/sexual abuse, and my sexual addiction are very intertwined. I kept going to meetings and healing from the sexual abuse, but I didn't have very much physical recovery (losing weight) in my program and kept feeling frustrated about this. I knew that part of the problem was that I had fears about what it meant to lose weight. In my head, losing weight meant that I would no longer have my wall and protection from men anymore. It would also mean that I would need to be sexual, and I was very afraid of that.

I was also in a lot of pain around certain behaviors and elements in my life. I was once again obsessed with a co-worker who wasn't available. I was constantly sexualizing people. I was reading several romance novels a week and compulsively masturbating. Finally, two years ago I was "twelfth-stepped" into SAA. Even though it was extremely painful, I started defining my bottom-line behaviors and made contracts to abstain from these behaviors.

I got a promotion at work and no longer had to face my co-worker on a daily basis. Sure enough, my subsequent attraction and obsession with a co-worker in my new department was even stronger. Four months later, this co-worker left for a new company, and I breathed a sigh of relief. A couple of months later, this same person called from his new company and asked me to work for him at a huge increase in salary. The offer was so enticing—not only for the money, but also for the part of me that was obsessed with this man. It also appeared to be a way to be free of my resentments about salary that I had with my current employers. After a lot of agony, my gut kept telling me to try to negotiate with my employers. I asked for several things and gave them a specific amount of time to respond to my request. This was truly an example of turning it over to my Higher Power, since I didn't think they would respond. I had to trust that my Higher Power was taking care of my life.

And it was successful! This was a turning point in my recovery. I could have chosen to go work in an addictive place. Or I could stay where I was, ask for what I wanted, and release the resentments. I still thank my Higher Power for this miracle. Recently, I continued to struggle with some mental obsession about these same co-workers, so I cleaned my home and office of any objects I had received from them. This mental and emotional housecleaning really helped me.

I continued to bargain with myself that masturbation was okay and could be part of my program. But I started to see how masturbation was tied to self-hate for me, so I set up a contract to be abstinent from masturbation for a while. Instead of masturbating, I read spiritual/inspirational books, and this felt very nurturing.

The longer I abstained from the novels and masturbation, the more I realized how both my acting out and "acting in" behaviors kept me from connecting with myself, my Higher Power, and other people. It was easy to see how acting out behaviors hurt me, but I have struggled with the "acting in" behaviors, since they have really been a long-standing wall and protection. To me, "acting in" is about behaviors where I don't express my sexuality at all. This includes not seeing or valuing myself as an attractive woman, not taking risks to date, and not challenging the old belief systems that keep me afraid of expressing my sexuality in healthy ways.

It took a long time to start to feel okay about myself as a woman. As a little kid, I remember wanting to be a boy, since I saw my brothers having power and not being sexually abused as much. I'm not sure when the "acting in" behaviors started, but they were certainly with me while I was a teenager. I always felt isolated and alone, especially growing up on a farm. I found that working, whether on the farm or at a bar and restaurant, was safer than having a social life. I rarely went to dances, which were the usual events where people socialized. Dances were the place to drink, get drunk, and be sexual. I felt that if I didn't get someone's interest by the end of the night, I was a failure. These feelings of shame damaged my already almost nonexistent self-esteem.

Another part of the "acting in" is the fact that I haven't really dated anyone. I still have some shame about this, but I know that I wasn't ready to date until recently. In the meantime, I have learned a lot of information about how traumatic my childhood was. I also know that had I gone out there and just found someone, it probably wouldn't have been a healthy relationship.

Although I'm still not comfortable in many social situations, I've come a long way. I have learned how to socialize, have fun, and take risks in social settings. Sometimes it still feels safer to work than to be in social settings. I'm still not comfortable at dances and in bars, since there is a lot of murky sexual stuff there for me. I trust this will change as I continue my recovery.

Things that I've been doing to express and nurture my sexuality in healthy ways include: receiving massages, attending yoga classes on a regular basis, being around recovering women, wearing clothes that feel wonderful, exercising, and doing fun things on a regular basis.

My goal is to treat myself as I would a lover. I recently have been experimenting with masturbation. I need to be honest with myself about whether I'm feeling compulsive or hateful toward myself. It isn't always clear, but I'm feeling a lot cleaner about it.

I'm in the process of making a change that feels like another turning point in my recovery. I'm moving to my own apartment. I learned how to live with a roommate and have a close relationship, and now it's time to learn to live alone.

One thing I really want to emphasize is that the level of shame I carry around has dropped dramatically. I didn't realize before that I could feel any differently. Now there are times when I am actually joyful. I am starting to pursue dreams that I had when I was a kid. I am realizing that I deserve the good things life has to offer. Now I have hope. I have the tools to change. And I am learning that it's okay to express my sexuality in appropriate ways.

35.

THE ROAD TO RECONCILIATION

Most of my life, I have had trouble in my relationships with women, beginning with my mother. Her least endearing quality was an explosive temper, a quality I came to share. Though I now know she always loved me, as a child it was hard for me to tell that in the midst of some of her diatribes. My self-esteem as I was growing up was fragile.

As I look back, my first addiction that I can identify is thumb sucking. I sucked my thumb until I was thirteen years old. This demonstrated a typical addictive pattern. When my mother would catch me sucking my thumb, she would often get furious and scream, "Get that thumb out of your mouth!" and occasionally add, "You make me so mad!" I would skulk away to be alone someplace where I would eventually find comfort in my thumb again. I was seeking comfort in an object, and acting out anger at my mother, a cycle that was also evident in my later sex addiction.

One of the reasons I married as young as I did was that I felt that if I did not marry my fiancée, no other woman would ever have any interest in me. The idea of being unfaithful to my wife was not a consideration. But most marriages have a tendency to develop problems, and ours was no exception. With my feelings of rejection intensified by the pain of my childhood experiences, I now realize what a setup I was for infidelity. Besides, some women did seem to find me fun and attractive, and I began to stray. I continued doing so, off and on, for twenty years. In my mind, I minimized the importance of my behavior. After all, I didn't approach women more than two or three times a year. Over twenty years, however, that was forty to sixty women. And, as time went on, I became less discriminating and less careful about how I approached women.

In my relationship with God, which I held at a distance anyway, I could often find a way of rationalizing the appropriateness of my actions.

As time went on, my spiritual life began to grow. I became more involved in church. I served on the governing board and became involved in a lay-based renewal movement. I became a lay reader, gave talks, taught adult Sunday school classes, and tried to serve God and share a message of love with others. But my disease interfered with the authenticity of my spiritual journey. How I related to women persisted as a battle for me. I truly wanted to stop my philandering, but found that I was unable to do so. I couldn't stop on my own. I needed to surrender to God in order to get help. When dealing with tough subjects, God sometimes will hit us over the head with a two-by-four. That is exactly what happened to me.

I practiced as a physician, primarily in a hospital setting. All of my affairs involved office or hospital personnel who, though not under my direct supervision, were subordinate in position. One year, I made a pass at a hospital employee and she filed a complaint. I had been warned by the hospital administration on two previous occasions, once after making "playful" advances to two employees, and another time after calling a woman at her home and asking to see her. This time, I was disciplined with a four-week leave of absence. I felt as though God had pulled the rug from under me to get my attention.

For the first time, I revealed my infidelity to my wife. I had to tell her, or live an even bigger lie. I was already worn down by the inability to change the deceit of my ways. It was time to be honest. She began questioning me about whether other indiscretions had taken place in the past. While I answered all her questions with nearly complete honesty, I have to admit I held back on some of the whole truth because I could not stand the pain of it.

My relationship with my wife has grown considerably since then. But despite that, I faltered, and my addiction continued to raise its ugly head. Several years later, I resumed a previous affair, and eventually I made an impulsive pass at yet another hospital employee, who reported me to the administration. This time I was advised to go into a treatment program for my compulsive sexual behavior.

A few years prior to this, I had learned from my sister that my father had abused her as a child. At first I had a very hard time believing her, just I guess as I had a hard time believing I really had any sexual addictive problems. With time, it has become more obvious to me that her recovered memories fit right in with our family and with my own propensity to act out.

When I went into treatment, my denial was initially very well intact. I did all the work that was required of me, and I thought I was doing well. But later I wound up acting out with another sex addict in treatment. I was found out, and as a result my wife understandably wanted a divorce. I felt both sad and relieved, and never tried to question her decision. I did sink into a deep depression as I began to experience the consequences of my actions. Fortunately I transferred to another treatment center, where I was supported in experiencing feelings I had never allowed in my life. I went on to identify another addictive behavior: rage. I also came to admit that fear had controlled my life, even while I was doing all I could to deny that I was afraid. The dynamics of fear and anger had dominated me for most of my life. By raging, I "controlled" the miserable feeling I experienced when someone else's anger surfaced. What a paradox that I have "controlled" what I perceived as the onset of another's rage by raging myself! Like most addictive behavior, this expression of rage would give me relief for a few seconds. After that, shame and regretful feelings would overwhelm me, and my depression would deepen. By realizing and owning up to my fear of anger and my dysfunctional response to it, my behavior has gradually improved.

As a child, there was only one circumstance in which either of my parents verbally expressed love for me. When I had a temper tantrum and did something in my anger, such as tearing a towel rack off the bathroom wall, I would be sent to my room. About twenty minutes later, my father would come talk to me in a very calm tone and tell me that he loved me. I think I learned some unconscious secondary gain with my tantrums. Understanding this has begun to help me to better accept myself and my anger.

Today, whenever my anger heads out of control or seems extreme for the situation, I sit down, meditate, and write down what I am afraid of. I ask myself, "What are the possible fears I have that are underlying my current state?" "How best might I address those fears (e.g., prayer, counseling, talking to a friend or sponsor, discussing my fears at a meeting, or discussing them at some point with the person with whom I am angry)?"

When I realize my fears, I often become sad. I have learned that it is important for me to acknowledge the sorrow I feel and not attempt to avoid it. I have found that when anger turns to sorrow, it helps put an end to the vicious cycle of rage and depression.

I finally embraced the Twelve Steps. Working my Fourth and Fifth Steps turned into one of the most spiritual things I have ever done, and my life began to turn around. I really believe that acting out in treatment was what I needed to get through to me how sick I was. I needed to hit bottom in order to accept my powerlessness. When I finally accepted my need for the program, I became open to a moving spiritual experience, one for which I feel blessed.

When I came back from treatment, the hospital I worked for disappointed me by not allowing me to resume practicing there. I hired a lawyer and appealed, but to no avail. After two years and with great reluctance, I gave up fighting to reestablish my practice. I really think that God was telling me to do something new in my life.

When my wife saw the changes in me as my recovery progressed, she decided to reconsider taking me back. She and I continue to work on our relationship, most times joyfully, sometimes with difficulty. We are each working our own twelve-step recovery programs. I see the Steps as following what my Higher Power, Jesus, taught us—turn ourselves over to God, own up to our shortcomings, repent, make amends to those we feel we have harmed, and share our spiritual awakening with others. At the same time, we are to love and respect ourselves as we do others. My upbringing had taught me to honor others, but not myself.

I have three grown daughters who have been understandably angry with me. The effects of my past rage and infidelities have given them much to dislike. From my perspective, though much anger remains, I sense a slow healing process is occurring with them. At times, I wish this healing would proceed more quickly. Most of the time, I am thankful for the patience that God is teaching me.

Over several years, I have come to share my experience with good friends and in meetings. With time, I have also shared it more openly. Although this was difficult at first, it has gradually become easier. Sharing has become therapeutic for me and has helped tremendously in my healing. By baring my soul, I have felt liberated and have become more intimate with the love of God. I have been able to better realize that God accepts me as I am. One way in which God's love has been evident is the support I have received from friends with whom I have been honest. People in my church family have ardently supported me. After refraining from activities within my church for nearly three years, I began again to serve as a lay reader and teach an adult Sunday school class (one based on the Twelve Steps).

Becoming open to my weaknesses and sharing them with others has proven to be one of the largest leadership roles I have played in my life. Taking this "road less traveled," though difficult, not only has resulted in my personal betterment, but it has led people to share with me things about themselves they'd previously not told anyone. One friend whose leadership qualities I admire told me how meaningful my wife's and my handling of our crisis had been for him. He added how this had helped him to share with his wife about a sexual matter that he had been struggling with, and how this had resulted in a closer relationship for them.

My road to reconciliation has not been easy. I have found that most things of great value in life are not easy. Pains still exist for my wife, my daughters, and me. Still, my wife and I have never been closer, and I have never felt closer to God or to other people than I have following this difficult part of my journey.

I still have to be aware of my pride. I often want to run my own show, and that can get me into trouble. Too often, I want to make my own plans for God, and some of these may seem good. I need to remember that He wants me a lot more than He wants my plans. There is a saying, "If you want to make God laugh, tell Him your plans." If God has me rather than my plans, then God's plans can work through me. In living a more authentic life, I feel God has more of me.

36.

BEING "NORMAL"

I am a 41-year-old man, and have been a member of Sex Addicts Anonymous for eleven years. I have not acted out since I came to SAA and became willing to go to any lengths to recover. Eleven years ago, I remember talking on the phone with a friend I greatly trusted and respected, the closest thing I had to a mentor. In the past I'd told him about the sexual behaviours I was doing and couldn't seem to stop. He said to me, firmly like a true friend would, that I should either go to a counsellor or look into a twelve-step group for sex problems. Paranoid about people finding out about my sexual behaviours, I avoided therapy and found SAA on the internet. I ordered lots of SAA literature and tapes from the ISO. We had no Green Book back then, so I read the first few chapters of another twelve-step fellowship's book dealing with addiction to alcohol, translating it into terms of sex addiction in my head. I had a very rude awakening!

Soon after this, I was jogging around a park with my friend and said I was willing to go to any lengths to stop my behaviour. I realised it didn't matter if everyone in my home town thought I was a disgusting pervert to be shunned, I simply had to recover. The progressive nature of sex addiction was something I did not want to experience. My friend helped me do my three circles, after I showed him the leaflet, and it turned out he actually knew someone else who had a problem with acting out, very different than mine. So the two of us formed an SAA group at my house (there were no meetings in our town then). We didn't really know what we were doing. Then we found a venue and rented it weekly. Soon another person came along. We began to listen to the ISO tapes as a form of speaker meeting. We talked about our circles and our acting-out behaviour. I had a sponsor and thought I was practicing the principles of all the Twelve Steps.

I remained sexually sober in the fellowship. The group slowly grew and so did I. But as is often the case with growth, sometimes it can feel like moving backwards. After three years or so, I thought that the best way to put my behaviours behind me was to decide I wasn't a sex addict and to leave SAA! My thinking at the time was that I hadn't acted out for years and that SAA was just keeping me obsessed about my old behaviours. "Out of sight, out of mind," I thought. Also I didn't like the idea of explaining to potential partners where I was going every meeting night.

At first all seemed fine. My friend from years before whom I'd gone jogging with did not seem to disagree with me, though he said I should keep an eye on my thinking and not get too complacent. But then a funny thing started to happen. I realised that deep down I was still deeply attracted to my acting-out inspirations. When I would walk around the town, watch TV, go to the beach, etc., I would be uncomfortably aware of how I felt, and that I was not "cured." I was not a changed man. All I wanted was to be normal—and to feel normal! One day I fell to my knees in my front room while watching TV, begging God to remove this thinking. It didn't go.

Soon I returned to SAA, to see what could be done. I didn't realise it, but something had changed. I now had a sneaking suspicion I really needed SAA, and that I was not capable of living happily without something like it. This sense has grown over the years, and I now realise it has a name: Step One. So I had not been practicing all the Twelve Steps after all. And because I didn't have Step One, how could I have done Step Twelve—helping other sex addicts? How could I have taken them through the Twelve Steps of SAA? But now, with a better grasp of Step One (and practicing the principles of all the other steps), people started to ask me to help them, to sponsor them. I then took two people through the Twelve Steps and they are still sexually sober, years later! The word "miracle" definitely springs to mind.

As I practiced the steps, the spiritual experience of SAA really started to happen. Now my feelings about SAA, and myself, have changed drastically. I am no longer the insecure person who felt so abnormal. I am now filled with a confidence in the power that SAA and the Twelve Steps give me, a day at a time. I am not tempted to act out. I am no longer obsessed with thoughts of my acting out when walking around the town, or watching TV and so forth. If it does come up, it does not bother me so much. I know I am trying, with as much honesty as possible, to be the best man I can be, given the disease I have. What used to be a shameful dark secret, has now—through sponsoring people—become a tool that I can use to help people recover. I have seen sponsees' families return to them; I have seen them get married and start families. What a gift to have contributed to that!

By admitting, after a long struggle and many excuses, that I really needed SAA, and that I belonged there, I have been given the opportunity to feel more *normal*. It was only by admitting that I did not fit in with my definition of "normal" that I was able to feel so much more normal, to feel a part of the mainstream of life. For my first few years, SAA meetings sometimes seemed like rooms full of sick people, which I was demeaning myself by taking part in. Now they seem like places where I can truly belong and be myself, but more importantly, give of myself. What I bring to a meeting and to SAA gives me much more than what I hope to take. There is a power and vision in SAA so much greater than I could ever be—it is my hope for the future. I pray, meditate, take inventory, do service and outreach. I am sponsored and I am a sponsor. I am part of a home group, and I speak at meetings. And I do all this not because I should, but because I want the life these actions give me, because of the person they make me.

37.

SELF-ACCEPTANCE

I grew up in a hostile, abusive environment and was taught harmful things about sexuality. I had a mother who was newly divorced and overwhelmed with the responsibility of raising children and trying to work and complete a degree. Starting at about age four, I was severely punished for wetting the bed. I did not stop until I was ten, and the six years in between were filled with beatings, threats, and humiliation. None of it helped me to stop, and it taught me my first lesson in shame—that bodily functions were especially dirty and bad.

I also learned several things about men and women that were harmful to me. I was told that any sexual abuse or assault was always the woman's or female child's fault. I was confused when my fifteen-year-old brother was allowed to sleep over at his girlfriend's house, but I wasn't allowed to spend nights with boys—not even my gay male friends. I was told that most men were dangerous people, that I should not "tempt" them by wearing revealing clothing or acting seductively, and that even "non-dangerous" men would become dangerous if they saw a woman in provocative clothing.

The first time I remember feeling sexual arousal was when I was six years old and found some pornographic magazines. I locked myself in the bathroom to look at the magazines and decided that when I grew up, I was going to be in magazines too. For years I would masturbate until I developed serious medical problems, which I never sought help for because I knew I would be in trouble. I was also sexually abused by various people, mostly strangers.

When I was twelve, I decided that I wanted to be a prostitute, although I had not had sex with anyone. I thought that I had found a way to live up to my mother's expectations and seriously disappoint her at the same time.

For several years I alternated between living with my father and sisters and with my mother and brother. When I was still in junior high and living with my mother, she received a catalogue full of phone sex ads in the mail. She threw it away, but I dug through the garbage and found it. I would look forward to going to bed every night because I knew that was when I would be free to look at the catalogue. Sometimes I would call the numbers and listen to the ads. Later I stole a credit card and actually talked to one of the women, pretending to be a man. I tore the card out of the back of the catalogue, checked off the box marked "Keep sending me exciting offers," and dropped it in the mail. I would try to be home as early as possible so I could get the mail and keep the catalogues. I would also take them to school, show them to friends (who were not interested), read them in the bathroom, and leave them there. Then one day my mother managed to get the mail first. She didn't figure out that I had requested more catalogues, but she checked off the box marked "Take me off your mailing list."

Later I started taking nude photos of children. Sometimes their parents would find out and be disgusted, but they never saw my behavior as something to be concerned about. I also started to be sexual with younger children in ways that could easily be explained away if I were caught. I would play "Truth or Dare" with my younger sister and her friends, and dare them to be sexual with each other. I would also expose myself to them, knowing that if I were caught by someone I could always say it was just "part of the game." This continued until I was fourteen, when I began abusing children I baby-sat for. That was also the age I began having sex with adult men. I was scared, but I didn't think that I had a choice. I felt a lot of shame about it and was certain that I had done something wrong. It has taken me years to learn that it was actually the men who were wrong.

As a teenager I would also expose myself in ways that looked accidental. I would go to school or go shopping with my skirt unbuttoned, and most of the time people would look but not say anything to me because they would be too embarrassed. Occasionally, a woman who thought she was being helpful would point out my exposure, and I would feign embarrassment, fix the clothing, and then unbutton it and hope I wouldn't run into her again.

I sought out pornography whenever I could and became obsessed with ways to obtain it. I thought I could get my own post office box and order magazines that way, but that attempt failed, as did my other attempts at receiving "free samples" of adult material in the mail. I think the companies could tell by my handwriting that I was not of legal age.

Several times girls at school would threaten to beat me up for having sex with their boyfriends, and I kept telling myself that if I could just stop having sex, everything would be okay. I think I would have joined SAA then if I had known about it. I didn't understand why I continued to be sexual with other people when I clearly didn't enjoy it, but I somehow felt like I was doing what I was supposed to do.

Later I moved back in with my mother and tried as hard as I could to be normal. When I was sixteen I was working as a cadet at the city police department, but I continued to use pornography and looked forward to the day when I would be old enough to buy my own. I had friends sending me some in the mail, and I had recently discovered the internet, but I was caught at school the first time I accessed a pornographic site. I pretended it was an accident.

I continued to be sexual with adult men, strangers, and occasionally with boys my own age. I managed never to become involved with any of the other cadets at the police department. Years later I would use that as an excuse for "not really having a problem." Later I joined a group of "Satanists," because I thought it would be a good place to meet sexual partners. I also started using various drugs, and quickly became addicted. I really felt like I was living a double life then, and for a while I pulled it off well. I continued to work at the police department and was always told how well I was doing and how my hard work was appreciated. Eventually my drug use caught up with me, and I was confronted by the department. They were willing to give me another chance, and I remember the horrible guilt feelings I felt when they told me I would make a great officer, and they didn't want me to quit. However, I just couldn't stop the lifestyle I was living.

A few months later I was living in a small apartment with twelve other people, most of whom regularly had sex with each other. Sexually transmitted diseases were passed back and forth between us. Sometimes the chemical fog would part just enough, and I would realize that this was not what I wanted, and that in fact I was really scared. But I didn't think I had a choice. I told myself that this kind of sex would be better than none at all, and that it would be easier to pretend it wasn't happening than to try stopping it.

By the time I was eighteen I was in a destructive, addictive relationship with one of the housemates. We were homeless, after having been kicked out because of my drug use and his violent behavior, which was frequently taken out on me. This later became another addictive behavior—the incorporation of asphyxiation, drawing blood, hitting, and humiliation into our sex life. I thought at the time that we were simply trying new things and being sexually liberated, and I continued this behavior for years with other partners. I thought that being sore and having marks the next day meant that I was having really good sex, and that surely everyone else was jealous. I never sought medical attention for any injuries because I thought that someone would try to convince me to stop what I was doing. I decided I didn't want to see this man anymore because the physical abuse outside of sexual activity got to be too much for me. Eventually I went back to him because I was still homeless, and he could always find places for us to stay. As long as I was willing to have sex, I was welcome to stay there too. Finally I was able to leave for good.

I got a job at a large factory and found plenty of sex partners there. I was also working as a nude model for someone who had advertised for one in the paper. At first the pictures were tasteful and artistic, but later they became more degrading and pornographic. I didn't like doing the things this man told me to do, but I felt compelled to do it anyway. I simply pretended it wasn't happening, and I was pretty good at it by now. When this man started buying me underwear and asking for hugs, I got scared and stopped returning his calls. A few months later, former partners told me they had seen me in magazines. I was outraged—but only because I thought I should have been paid more. However, I was happy about fulfilling the dream I had for myself when I first looked at pornography.

When I was nineteen I joined a twelve-step fellowship for my drug addiction. After a few months of not really trying to stay clean, I got a sponsor and began working the steps. I noticed an immediate improvement, in that I stopped using drugs, but I hadn't even begun to deal with my sexual behavior, and wouldn't for a few more years. I was caught having sex in a public restroom with a stranger and the police were called, but I didn't concern myself with that because they let me off with a warning. I thought it was really neat that I had gotten away with it, and I bragged about it to my friends. They looked at me like I was crazy. I continued to be sexual in public places. One time I convinced a man to follow me to the top of a parking garage where a large crowd of people had gathered to watch a fireworks display. He looked scared when he realized I wanted to have sex there. We somehow weren't caught, but all it would have taken was one person turning around.

I got into a relationship with a newcomer to the program. We were together for about eighteen months, and amazingly we both stayed clean the whole time. Our relationship was troubled from the start, since we were both learning how to do life, and I was a sex addict. I was staying faithful to him, so I figured I didn't really have any problems. But things kept happening that made me think otherwise. If we went without sex for more than two days in a row, I would hint that I thought he was gay or accuse him of being unfaithful. He was really hurt by this and did not understand, but I thought "it was the only way to get him to learn." I continued to be obsessed with another man in the program and would make excuses to see him. I even mentioned this to my sponsor and hinted about some of my other sexual concerns, but she told me that I was normal and that she knew I would do the right thing. I believe she simply did not understand sex addiction. I still looked at pornography whenever I could, and I even agreed to have some more nude photos taken from a different photographer, this time for free. My partner was really upset about this and didn't know what to do. We fought about it a lot. I accused him of being sexually inhibited and a "woman hater." Eventually I agreed not to do any more photos.

Towards the end of our relationship, I started thinking I really might be a sex addict, and by that time I had heard of Sex Addicts Anonymous. I thought that joining that group would be the worst thing I could possibly do. I talked to my sponsor about my sexual behavior, but later I realized I was leaving out just enough so that she wouldn't tell me I had a problem. I read several self-help books and thought I could find the answer to my problem that way. The whole time, I kept telling myself that I was really okay because I was faithful to my partner, but soon I couldn't even use that excuse anymore. I had a brief fling with the man from my fellowship that I had been obsessed with, and for a while I continued to see both men. I told myself that nothing was wrong, because my relationship was obviously about to end, but later both guys found out what was going on, and it caused a lot of pain for all of us. I also started seeing my boss, and had a brief sexual encounter with a co-worker. Finally the relationship ended, and I thought it was for the best, but I still felt terrible about hurting my partner.

I thought that perhaps I could develop a positive relationship with my boss. He had a longtime girlfriend (another co-worker) that I really liked and who was friendly to me, but I thought that somehow the whole situation wasn't that bad. I would stay at his place most nights, he would leave and go to his girlfriend's house, and I would be up half the night looking at pornography on his computer. I actually preferred that to any sexual contact with him. I felt that the internet was perfect and that

it was what I had really needed the whole time—it couldn't leave me or get jealous; it was free if I used someone else's computer; and it had stuff that the magazines didn't. Most of the images I looked at depicted rape scenes, dead people, animals, and children. Eventually my boss saw everything I had been looking at and told me how sick he thought I was. But he never told me my job was in jeopardy, so I saw no reason to stop. I would look at the images until I felt sick to my stomach, and complain to my sponsor that I couldn't stop looking at pornography and couldn't get the violent images out of my head. I tried to control myself in different ways, limiting my computer time to only an hour, looking at only legal, non-violent images, and switching back to magazines—none of it worked. Eventually the relationship stopped working, and I was no longer allowed at my boss's home. I was limited to the computer at work, but I continued to do the same things. My boss had told the other employees what I had been doing, and they all started treating me differently. Later I found another job.

At this time, I had about two years clean, had worked through all the Twelve Steps, sponsored people, and had several service positions. I was well liked by most people, and I tried hard to practice spiritual principles in my life and to carry the message of recovery to the still suffering addict. I was living a double life again—no one in my fellowship knew of my addiction to pornography. To them my life looked great, but I started seeing how my current sex life was similar to my drug addiction. I continued to look for sex partners in the twelve-step meetings, thinking that somehow one of them would fix me. Every encounter I had left me full of shame and despair. A few months later I was seeing a man I had no respect for. In fact, I hated him. A friend pointed out to me, "You're only seeing him because you finally found someone you hate more than yourself." Later I realized that he was right.

Our relationship was off to a bad start right away because I felt that all our sexual activity was forced on me. Sometimes I would verbally say no, sometimes I would fight physically, but in the end nothing worked, and once again I found that the easiest thing to do was to pretend it wasn't happening. I believe he was also a sex addict. He told me he had been to SAA, and I eagerly asked him what the meetings were like. I sensed that someday I would end up there too. No one understood why I was seeing this man. My friends urged me to leave him. I sometimes thought that I deserved everything I got from him, but I thought more about joining SAA.

Finally I called SAA and asked for information about the program.

A member called back and put me in touch with another woman in my area, and we made plans to attend a meeting together. A few days before making the call, I had nearly been raped by an acquaintance. I was scared to go to the SAA meeting because I thought it would be full of men I had already acted out with, or who had seen me in magazines. I thought surely everyone would judge me, and that SAA was all about self-deprivation and denial of natural sexuality. At that point I was so beaten down that I didn't care, but I was relieved to find out otherwise.

One thing I noticed right away was that the men in the fellowship were very mature and respected my personal boundaries. Members of the program talked to me about the difference between healthy and addictive sexual behaviors, and I learned a lot from reading the literature.

I have had several behaviors in my inner circle, but today it consists of any use of pornography, including participating in it; any sexual violence, including watching it in movies; and any illegal sexual acts that victimize others. I have abstained from these activities since I came to my first meeting in July of 2000.

What I especially liked about the program is that I could choose my own inner-circle boundaries and not have to limit myself to sexual behaviors that other people find acceptable. Finally, my opinions and choices are being respected. Some people seem to have the idea that addicts aren't capable of making positive choices for themselves, but this program allows me to do just that. Today I maintain my sexual sobriety by remembering the First Step. I know that, no matter what, I will always be powerless over addictive sexual behavior, and when I act out, my life will become unmanageable. Experience has shown me that there is nothing I can do to control or lessen the impact of my addictive behavior once I choose to engage in it. I also maintain conscious contact with a loving, nonjudgmental Higher Power who gives me new insights every day.

Another thing that has been helpful to me is choosing to live my life today in a way that is different from the way I lived in my addiction. In my addiction, I worked hard to do what others wanted, to cover up feelings that other people didn't like, and to be sure I always had a low opinion of myself. In my recovery it is necessary to practice self-acceptance, even if others don't accept me; to allow myself to feel any emotion that may come up, even the so-called "negative" ones like fear, anger, worry, and resentment; and to take pride in all of my accomplishments and positive choices, realizing that I had a lot to do with their occurrence, as well as my Higher Power.

SELF-ACCEPTANCE

When I take inventory of my life and my actions, I like to keep it as balanced as possible—that means the assets list will be as long as the lists of resentments and ways I have harmed others. I can use this inventory to look for my "character defects," although that is not what I call them. I don't believe anything about my "character" is "defective"; I simply believe that like all people, I have room for improvement. I don't believe that I'm somehow "worse" than anyone else just because I happen to be a sex addict. I know that my Higher Power accepts me just the way I am, and would accept me even if I never improved, and it's important for me to reach that same level of self-acceptance.

Another thing that has been essential in maintaining my sexual sobriety is to know that I am not responsible for any time I have ever been victimized. I know it wasn't because "I set myself up," "I wasn't working my program," or "It was a message from my Higher Power." This program has allowed me to see that I am never responsible for the sexual behavior of anyone else. I also know that it's okay to acknowledge the fact that I was, in fact, victimized, that I'm not just "thinking and acting like a victim," and that any feelings I have around any particular incident are okay too. I can have positive, healthy feelings of anger for as long as I need to, and I can choose when and whether to forgive someone. I believe anyone who has been a victim of any crime has this right.

One of the greatest things about recovery today is that I can refuse physical contact from anyone without having to give an apology or an explanation. This includes hugs from people at meetings. In the past I would feel like I didn't have the right to turn down a hug from someone, or if I did turn it down, I would feel the need to make excuses. It's great to be able to say no to someone and know that it doesn't matter why. I've also been able to heal from the harmful things I learned about sexuality as a child, and I'm becoming more and more comfortable with myself and my sexuality.

At first, the concept of a healthy sexual relationship where no one gets hurt was too much for me to comprehend. I really believed that I enjoyed violent sexual acts because that was all I had ever gotten from anyone. Now I know I never really liked anything I did while I was acting out. Today I don't enjoy things that are self-destructive or that hurt others. I know that if I'm enjoying something, sexual or otherwise, it means I should keep doing it! I have found that SAA is not any of the horrible things I thought it would be. I can't imagine what things will be like for me in the future, but I know that as long as I stay in the program, I can have healthy sexual relationships and I never have to act out again.

38.

BY GOD'S GRACE

I was born into a broken home. At age four, my mother deserted my sister and me. We then moved to another state and lived with my father and grandparents. Within a few months of moving there, I was molested by my uncle. This went on until I was ten. While molesting me, he would show me pornography to arouse me.

I ran away from home several times. My dad thought I was rebellious. Actually it was from fear that I would be blamed if anyone ever found out about my being molested. I was told that I would be put in an orphanage if I ever said anything.

My mom returned when I was ten and carried my sister and me back to live with her. We lived in a run-down project, filled with prostitutes and drunks. When my mom was broke, she would drink with whoever had money. I was used for bartering purposes. Men and women had their way with me if they kept Mama drunk.

I began stealing and doing drugs about that time. Mama would go into rages and shoot up the house. She set my stepfather on fire one night for beating me, then tried to shoot me. The police put her in a mental hospital, and I disappeared into the ghetto. I began running with gangs, stealing, and robbing people. I'd pass a gay bar and play pretty boy, coaxing gay men to come around the corner so my associates could rob them. Other times I would go alone, hoping to steal their money for drugs.

By the time I was nineteen, my mother had been in and out of a dozen mental institutions. She died in 1977, and I went to prison, receiving a seven-year sentence for two burglaries. I did four years on that sentence. The whole time I was in prison, I masturbated to pornography. It hit chronic stages of two or three times a day. Within six months of my release, I was married to a woman who had the same addictions I did:

alcohol, drugs, and sex. We began renting pornographic videos and buying several magazines a week to enhance our sex life. We could have sex twice a day, and I'd still masturbate to pornography.

Our marriage was rocky the whole time. She needed a son she had left in her first marriage. I needed a "mama." Everything finally came to a head when I started having violent blackouts. I'd come to the next morning with blood all over me and not know where it came from. I needed help, and I went into treatment.

I stayed dry for two years while attending twelve-step meetings for my alcoholism. I never stopped my compulsive sexual behavior, though. Then I caught my wife cheating, and ran her off. We kept moving back in together, though, until it fell completely apart. I ended up in a mental institution with a nervous breakdown. Then I tried several suicide attempts. The only reason they failed was that I really didn't want to die. So I started drinking again while taking psychotropic medication. I'd go into blackout rages—I made death threats against my ex-wife and four other people at that time. I was deadly serious. I confronted my ex-wife on a Friday night and told her I'd kill her and her friends the following Wednesday. That Tuesday I started drinking and taking medicine. I blacked out about ten that morning. I came to at 10:30 that night in a woman's house whom I'd been doing yard work for. I committed rape that night.

Every time I'd stop, I'd see her for an innocent person who never did anyone any harm. Then I'd flash, see my ex-wife, and start all over again. I wrote my name, address, and phone number on a piece of paper and gave it to her before leaving. I knew I was going to prison for the rest of my life.

I received ninety-nine years for first-degree rape and had several other charges pending that were later dropped. I tried two more suicide attempts, by hanging myself and setting myself on fire. Today I still have these scars.

I walked around in prison for four years, not even admitting to myself that I had committed this terrible crime. I kept using drugs, alcohol, and pornography on a regular basis. I finally burned out to the point that I started attending meetings in prison.

Step Three was a problem for me. I didn't know God. Every time I tried to picture God, I just couldn't do it. I finally bottomed out so bad, I cried out to the God I never knew, and the steps became clearer to me. I knew the God of my understanding for the first time.

I enrolled in a sex offender program at prison, five years after my arrest. I knew that just because I believed in God, it didn't mean I still didn't have problems. I had a serious sex problem. And it had to be dealt with. I also had a lot of skeletons in my closet that needed to be faced. For the first time in my life I saw just how sick I had become. I became responsible for my actions.

It's been a long row to hoe over these last four years. I've dealt with a lot of problems. I haven't looked at pornography in four years, and I haven't masturbated in eight months. I'm alcohol and drug free. I married again, and my second wife knows everything about me. She's my best help.

I still have to work daily on my program. I can recognize the difference between fleeting thoughts and willful lust. I know my triggers, and I know what must be done to avoid creating another victim. My crime was among the worst a man could commit. I take full responsibility for that. And by the grace of God, and working the steps, I hope to never harm another human being again!

I may not be able to change the past circumstances of my life, but I can do something about today. By God's grace I don't have to fall into my old pattern of thinking. The Twelve Steps do work, but you have to want them to work.

39.

ONE OF THE CHOSEN PEOPLE

My family was a family of secrets. No one ever said anything about sex, and no one ever told me about masturbation, but I discovered it on my own somewhere around the age of five, and until I was twelve, I thought I was the only one in the world that did this bad thing. At ten my cousin, who was a year older, grabbed me and tried to play with me. I became so aroused that I got ashamed and ran out of his house. This began my relationship with sexual play and fantasy, which has plagued me my whole life.

Most of my fantasies were about people I had been with or wanted to be with. Later this became an addiction to pornography, but not visual—I preferred stories, and they were most exciting to me if I was being humiliated in some way. I was using this type of pornography on a daily basis for over twenty years, whether I was in a relationship or not.

When I was nine I started longing for attention from boys and men, and I realized that I was homosexual. At twelve I told my father what I had discovered—he told me that it was just a phase and not to worry about it. I fell in love with my best friend when I was fifteen. He was heterosexual, and at some point our relationship ended because he was more interested in girls. Thus began my first withdrawal from a love relationship. I was constantly in pain, constantly depressed, and it seemed as if nothing could fill the gap that he left. Eventually I fell in love with someone else. We became sexual, but the level of shame that he felt was so overwhelming that he ended our friendship. I was once again left feeling the pain of a lost love. Sex and love were already merged for me; it was the way I could justify feeling the way I did, but when it was reduced to just sex, I would feel ashamed.

Two weeks before I graduated from high school, I had my first anonymous sexual experience. It was if I had been doing it all my life. I could no longer rationalize my feelings. I was homosexual—everything that I did not want to be. Later that summer I had sex for the first time with someone in a public place, on the ground in a parking lot. It was very exciting, but I was immediately consumed with shame when it was over.

College was very difficult. I continued to masturbate every day, sometimes several times a day, including in public restrooms. I would fantasize while reading sexual ads in one of the weekly papers. It seemed like acting out was the only way that I could escape from pain. It was during this period that I began to act out regularly in a public park.

I was so desperate and lonely that I dropped out of school, feeling unable to take care of myself. I wanted help, and I even entered a drug rehab, although I was not on drugs. They told me that my problem was that I was gay and that being gay was like being a heroin addict. They said I could change and be straight, and for three years I was back in the closet. When that ended, inevitably, I started cruising adult bookstores.

When I was twenty-three, I met my first lover, with whom I had a long-distance relationship for three years. My acting out continued, however. I would spend hours at a time in a public restroom waiting for some sexual contact. In 1980, while cruising a park late at night, I was jumped by seven guys and viciously beat up. They broke my collarbone, and my face was unrecognizable. I think they would have killed me if a car had not driven by and honked. This was the start of a bout with post-traumatic stress disorder and night terrors that did not begin to be resolved for another thirteen years. I was scared to go to that park at night, but it didn't deter me completely. I just switched to another one that was better lit.

In the 1980s I got into a long-term relationship. We were extremely codependent; we were together for a sense of safety, and though our sex life was not good and full of addictive behaviors, we truly tried to build a life together. My addiction led me to believe that we should include other people, so I was constantly on the hunt for possible sex partners. I continued to masturbate to pornography daily and cruise every moment I could get away with it. The biggest shock of my life was when I found out that my partner was HIV-positive. This was the closest I had ever been to another human being. He pretended that my acting out didn't bother him, and that it relieved him of being pressured by me for sex. After we broke up he let me know that he often knew when I had just acted out because I would bring him a gift.

My next relationship was the most addictive of my life. I tried to control the relationship, but I thought that if my partner didn't have sex with me every night, it meant that he didn't really love me. I would cry and manipulate and get angry and do everything I could to convince him to have sex with me. He got tired of this and became less and less available, and I kept trying to convince him that if he really loved me, he would act the way I wanted him to. This relationship caused me to hit my first bottom, and in September of 1989, I started attending meetings in an "S" fellowship and began working the steps. After two years we split up.

I struggled with my addiction for a while in the program and then started acting out regularly again. In 1992 I met another man with whom I repeated the same pattern. Once again I attempted to control our sex life, cried and manipulated, and picked fights. He finally got fed up and ended the insanity. Without a program, I got lonelier; I spent most of my weekends acting out and most of my nights watching television. I became suicidal. The pain and the depression were so great that I felt death was the best option. Then I realized the best way out of isolation was to start attending meetings again. On New Year's Eve in 1997 I attended a retreat, and I heard a woman speak who had thirteen months of abstinence from her inner circle. It was at that moment that I knew the jig was up. I had to get sober.

By the time I entered the rooms of Sex Addicts Anonymous, my life was in shambles. Many of my friends, including two of my lovers, had died of AIDS. I was living with a roommate who was stealing from me, having drug parties in my home, and abusing the premises, and I was powerless to do anything about it. I had never learned the basics of taking care of myself, like making my bed every day, or doing the dishes more than once a week. I had not been to a dentist in three years. I lacked the skills to maintain relationships. I would become so volatile when faced with hurt or conflict that I would scare people away. I was hopeless about ever having a relationship.

In January a friend took me to my first SAA meeting. In many ways that day was the beginning of my life. I saw people there that I had known from years before, and they were sober, not just a day or a month, but years. For the first time in my life, I actually felt hopeful about stopping my active addiction. They had a tradition that a person was a newcomer until he or she had thirty days of sobriety. I was determined to make it through that first thirty days. I started counting days. I attended meetings every day, and I averaged nine meetings a week for my first three years. I defined my inner circle as anonymous sex of any kind, masturbation to any form of pornography, phone sex, cybersex, and sex (including masturbation) in my office.

I figured that my way had not worked, so anything that I had tried before, I considered doing the opposite. Where I was exclusively attending morning meetings, I started attending noon and night meetings also. I cut my television watching way down. I made calls to friends every night. That was the beginning!

I got myself a sponsor and started writing my First Step. Doing my First Step publicly was an experience that I will never forget. To have a room full of people show up to be there just for me was a gift of generosity that I had never experienced before. I broke down halfway through as I was talking about my first lover who had died, and the group told me I could come back the following week and complete it. Taking the First Step in this fashion felt like a rite of passage, and from that moment I felt a part of this fellowship. I also began to experience the true meaning of "From Shame to Grace."

Early in my recovery I realized that as long as acting out was an option, I would eventually go out again. In order to stay sober, I needed to make sure that, one day at a time, acting out was not an option. If I woke up in the morning and my "acting out meter" read "option," I knew I had to do everything it took to move that lever back. That included going to a meeting, calling my sponsor, calling other program friends, writing, and praying. Sometimes it meant sitting in my favorite house of worship until the desire passed. My program had to come first. It had to come before my job, relationships, or anything else. I tell my sponsees that even though they are married and have children, if their program doesn't come first, the rest of their life is at risk. If they are not actively working a step, they are endangering their sobriety. That has been the truth for me.

At this writing, with God's grace, I have a little over four years away from my inner-circle behaviors. One of the things I have found is that recovery started the moment I walked into the rooms, and paradoxically, recovery started the day I got sober. Both are true for me. The process of recovery started for me twelve years ago when I first admitted that I was powerless and that my life was unmanageable. From that day on, I became more present and more truthful about my life. I began showing up for the pain that I had been running from. I truly began the quest for understanding my life, and I discovered how my addiction had robbed me of happiness, and that it was the main cause of my depression. I was able to begin taking responsibility for my actions and seeing my part in things. I was able to be present for the deaths of my friends and lovers, and grieve the losses. And through all my slipping and sliding, my acting out never had the same appeal or intensity as before I walked through the door. I even began to feel some acceptance of my imperfections.

I have found that I need to be willing to share about all areas of my life, at the meeting level as well as individually, to stay sober. If I was having a hard day, it was important for me to tell the truth, no matter how tempting the desire to look good was. If there wasn't a meeting that addressed my individual issues, I found other people with the same issues to help me start a meeting. We started a meeting called "Feelings in Sobriety" because there were some of us that felt we needed to talk about our deepest feelings in order to stay sober. We started a meeting that focused on survivors of abuse. But I never lost sight that without sobriety, I could not concentrate on any of the issues, and I would never grow up. For me it has been important to acknowledge my sobriety every month on my anniversary and to remember that if I were to go out again, I can't be sure when or if I would come back.

All of us have different paths. I knew that if I was going to have any hope of staying sober, I had to replace acting out with something better. What I found was a community of people that could hold me and help me heal. I have learned how to make and keep friendships alive. It's a normal thing for people to desire connection and love. The only way I knew how to do this was in addictive relationships or anonymous sex. In SAA I became aware of the responsibilities of being a member of a community. We are a community that takes care of each other. If people slip, we are not there to shame them, we are there to hold them up and support their return to sobriety. If someone is ill, we take meetings to his home. If someone needs help moving, people show up to do this. I used to be afraid of being a lonely old gay man. Now I know that, however old I get, I will never be alone. I will always have a meeting to go to and a group of sober sex addicts to share my life with.

And then there is the gift of God. I had always believed in some power greater than myself. I thought God was somewhere way outside of me and would only make an occasional intervention. In recovery I have learned that God makes interventions in my life every day. I only have to be awake enough to notice, or smart enough to remember to turn to God when I need help, or even to express gratitude. When I am feeling a lot of pain and have nowhere else to turn, I am not alone, because I can communicate with my Higher Power. For me the best communication has come in writing to God. I keep an HP journal and check in with God almost every day. Somehow if I pour out all my feelings, my fears, and my resentments to God in written form, it frees up the energy to meditate and wait for an answer from him. When I was recently redoing my Second Step, I realized that my core belief had changed. I no longer feel that life without a partner is not worth living, I believe that life without God would not be worth living.

Many times I am overwhelmed with a sense of gratitude. I am Jewish by birth and was raised with the concept of the chosen people. I do feel chosen, one of the few sex addicts that are sober. There are thousands of suffering people out there who don't know that there is an answer.

My life is very different today. I live a simple life in a small clean apartment, alone but not lonely. I take care of the mundane things in my life on a daily basis, and they no longer feel mundane. I am almost fifty, and for the first time I have the sense that I can take care of myself, and that my life is worth living, whether partnered or single. When I am afraid, I turn to my God, I turn to my friends, and I turn to my program.

40.

MORE WILL BE REVEALED

I have been in Sex Addicts Anonymous for nearly four years and in another fellowship for eighteen years recovering from alcoholism. In all of these years of not drinking and drugging, there seemed to be something missing in my recovery. I would increase my efforts at recovery but couldn't shake that feeling. They said "fake it 'til you make it" and I felt like a phony. Now I know why. At the end of my second marriage, and with a miracle from God, I now feel like I am finally at peace. I go to SAA.

Even as a four-year-old I was interested in sex. I have the feeling that I must have seen something sexual in my grandfather's house, because once I took my younger cousin out to a building and tried to have sex with her. To my shock, I found that I couldn't, and I felt embarrassed. She looked puzzled. Later I found myself playing with my female cousins' private parts and was caught when they told their mother and my mom. I felt great shame, and denied everything.

I have a vivid memory from school of trying to get attention from a blonde girl. She became weary of my aggressiveness, turned to me, and slapped me on the cheek. I felt hurt, shocked, and embarrassed because I was shamed publicly. I think from that day on I was afraid of women, while still craving their attention.

As I grew, so did the compulsion for sex. My dad had pornography that he kept in a drawer in his bedroom. My younger brother and I would sneak into the bedroom and look at all the dirty pictures. As an adolescent I was really shy with girls, fantasizing at night about saving them from burning cars and being the hero. In my thoughts at night I would acquire great favor from the girls for my heroics, but during the day, when I was face to face with them, I was so shy that I could barely say Hi. During this time I began to make my younger sister masturbate me, and I forced myself on her. This caused me great shame and a fear of getting caught.

After high school I had my first experience with intercourse. It lasted maybe two minutes. I had an orgasm and figured it was finished. She protested, I became embarrassed, and I dropped her off at work and left. I felt "less than." I knew that I hadn't performed sex well and felt degraded.

Later I met a girl in a college near the vocational school I was attending. She fell in love with me and I fell in lust with her. She was a virgin. I was slowly becoming a drunk and a pothead to cover my bad feelings about myself. I took her virginity and felt obligated to marry her because of that. We had children. As I went out to the clubs looking for women, I drank my frustrations away. This became a pattern for me. In 1983, I ended up in a program to recover from my drinking. My marriage dissolved, mainly because of my abusive behavior. With five years sober, I met and married another woman. She loved sex and would do everything I wanted with me. I was in sex heaven.

I was in the military by then, still in recovery from alcoholism, and sponsoring a guy who had a definite sex problem. He was having an affair with a married woman. I knew that he needed help, so I volunteered to go to a large town sixty miles away, go to some sex recovery meetings there, and scout one out for him. This was about 1987. I went to several different "S" programs. I thought a meeting would help my sponsee, but I discounted any problem that I might have had.

As the years rolled by in my volatile second marriage, I found myself flirting with my wife's girlfriends. I didn't actually cheat on my wife, thinking, "I'm free of drugs and alcohol, and a man in recovery should never go out on his wife." Later on in SAA I found out that I had been "rain checking" my wife's friends. Without being conscious of what I was doing, I was making sexual contacts for a rainy day—if my present wife happened to leave me I would have other sources for sexual contact readily available to me. My wife and I did split up later. She was an incest victim in the past and was feeling shame about the sexual games I wanted to play. She was in recovery from alcohol for five years, and when she let her recovering friends know of the sexual acts that I wanted her to perform, they told her that I was sick. I resented this label, and I resented them for telling her. But she would no longer cooperate in my sexual illness.

I separated from my wife in January 1997. I had started having sexual thoughts about my fourteen-year-old stepdaughter, and I was afraid that if I stayed in the marriage I might make a sexual move toward her. I didn't want to cause the devastation in her life that I had witnessed my wife going through from being an incest victim. I felt crazy and out of control. I had gotten into internet porn and at times felt a compulsion to look out the windows with binoculars into other homes nearby. I waited hours to get a glimpse of someone walking across in front of an open window nude or in skimpy bedroom attire. I'd asked a sponsor several years before about my behavior, and he said, "I do those things too, don't worry about it."

Here is the miracle that God performed. I had read in other recovery literature that "more will be revealed" by God if I stay in recovery. I had been praying to God about helping me—that my life was crazy, and would he intervene. On Christmas of 1996 I was invited to go to the house of a friend whom I had met while working at a treatment center. In the past I had turned this Christmas Day offer down, but somehow this year I knew that there was something there for me and that God was involved. I sat at my friend's house, listening to people talk, and I was bored. Then I noticed a woman who was wearing a see-through skirt, and I began staring. A man sat down beside me and we began talking. It seemed as if I had known him all my life. I figured he must be a recovering alcoholic, and I asked him. He said yes, and that he was also attending "S" meetings because of his sexual addiction. He gave me his number, and a meeting time and place. I blew this off after I left the party, but a few weeks later in a twelve-step meeting a member pushed a pamphlet across the table to me and said that he was attending meetings for sex addiction and that he was going that Sunday. I asked if I could go, and he took me to my first meeting that I attended for myself. Later that year, I moved to another state and started attending Sex Addicts Anonymous.

This program is a godsend. I feel more alive than ever. I am remarried, presently working on a Fourth Step inventory, and have already made arrangements to do my Fifth Step. I found that my experience in alcohol recovery wouldn't carry me in this addiction: I needed to be in the right place to recover from compulsive sexual thoughts and behavior. I use the tools of the program: a Higher Power, meetings, help from others, the Three Circles, and the three-second rule (look for three seconds and then turn back to my business at hand). I am discovering many more tools to help me stay sober. The Three Circles have given me great perspective on defining this addiction and the recovery process for me. Thank you, God, for revealing this to me, and as always—"More will be revealed."

41

IT WORKS IF WE WORK IT

Sexual acting out began at a very young age for me. I remember trying to hide my compulsive masturbation from my parents and from my sister, with whom I shared a room. As I grew older, I added fantasies and obsessions about boys I knew or imaginary situations and partners. My senior year in high school, I began going out with my future husband, and we became sexual almost immediately. Our relationship took on a frenzied quality, as we tried desperately to find places to be alone so we could touch each other. I remained physically faithful to him through most of my college years, although I was obsessing about other men.

However, in my senior year of college I began a relationship with the boyfriend of one of my closest friends. Although my life had always been filled with obsession and addictive masturbation, this was the first time I had consciously done something I believed was wrong. I was terrified she would find out, and totally relieved when we all graduated and went our separate ways. My husband and I were married and moved away that summer. I was very unhappy and lonely for my friends and my family (even though we had never had a good relationship). I gradually began drinking more and more heavily. About two years after we moved, I had my first post-wedding affair. It didn't last long and ended painfully, but the second one lasted eighteen months. I became very dependent upon other men to convince me I had value, and I didn't spend much time between affairs.

After the second man left town, I gradually became more promiscuous, using the excuse that these relationships were totally unrelated to my marriage and I could handle them. My acting out was always related to alcohol or marijuana; I never could seem to manage sex with someone else if I wasn't at least well on the way to being drunk or high. During the last year before we moved again, I taught at a major university as a temporary faculty replacement, and became very socially involved with my students. We spent a lot of time drinking together, and I began an affair with one of them. By the end of the year I had tried to come on to three other male students, and I woke up one morning in bed with a woman student of mine after an alcohol-induced blackout. I didn't feel good about these times, but I always managed to put them out of my mind before the next opportunity to act out.

My husband got a good job in another state, so we moved. I realized that it was probably time to have children and that my behavior would have to change in order to be a good parent. I tried very hard on my own to clean up both my drinking and sexual acting out. I did get pregnant and we had our first child. I became more and more depressed. I felt desperate for help and began counseling. Although some parts of my life changed for the better, I again began to drink more. My therapist sent me to a twelve-step fellowship, where I was able to stop drinking. I assumed that all thoughts of other men would leave me along with the alcohol. Over the next year, however, my obsession with other men increased, until it became totally unmanageable and out of control. I spent whole days lost in obsessive sexual thoughts, while my work and children were neglected. Giving up drinking left obsession as my drug of choice, my primary painkiller. I wasn't overtly sexual with anyone, but other men were constantly in my mind, and I did a lot of flirting and veiled come-ons that were potentially dangerous for me.

When my therapist gave me the phone number of the local SAA intergroup, I called and was twelfth-stepped into my current meeting. I tried to work the steps, to attend meetings regularly, and to be honest as I had learned in other twelve-step meetings. Although my obsessing had increased, I had not actually been sexual with anyone besides my husband for several years, and I thought I was "safe" from that behavior. The next spring, I learned how cunning and baffling this disease really is.

I took a trip as the faculty advisor to a group of college students. On the way home, my car broke down in a small town. All the students took the bus home except one, a very attractive and (I thought) mature young man. Neither of us had much money left, so we agreed to stay together and checked into a motel room. From that point on I felt as if I was aboard a train to somewhere that I had no control over. It was an old and familiar feeling. As we walked back to the motel after dinner, I remember thinking, "Here we go," with a feeling of total helplessness. I took him to the local liquor store and bought him whatever he wanted, since he was underage, although I had no alcohol myself. I tried to seduce him that night, and I count my blessings that he laughed and said that was the most ridiculous thing he'd ever heard. Feeling totally ashamed and defeated, I made amends to him the next morning, but I was haunted by this episode for years. It was a total shock to me that I could "come on" to someone while abstaining from alcohol or drugs. I had not realized in my core that sex addiction was its own problem, even though I'd been going to meetings for nine months. This incident more than any other convinced me that I am truly powerless over my sex addiction, and that if I do not use the tools of the program and take care of myself in very practical ways (like getting a separate motel room, and calling my sponsor), I am very likely to act out.

When I came back to my meeting the next week, I began working the SAA program very seriously, trying to recover from my slip. I concentrated especially hard on the obsession problem, because it seemed to lead to my come-on behavior. During the next year, I discovered that when I seriously turned over a problem to my Higher Power, it would be removed if I was willing to do the footwork. When obsessive thoughts came into my mind, I learned to say the Serenity Prayer or the first three steps over and over, like a mantra. Those thoughts always eventually disappeared; and after a period of months, the problem of obsession in general eased and has not been a big factor in my life since then. It is such a gift to have tools available to deal with these addictive behaviors and problems.

My husband changed jobs and our family moved to another state for a year. I had been doing therapy for childhood sexual abuse and realized that it was vitally connected to my sex addiction. I perceived my sexual acting out as repeated reenactment of my sexual abuse. I found a twelve-step group for incest survivors and worked that program, but there was no SAA group nearly. I spent the year investigating other groups and trying to work the SAA program as I remembered it. I didn't keep in touch with my sponsor or other SAA members, and I began to think I had some control over my sex addiction. I now view that as major denial of the problem. In my life, therapy and work on sexual abuse has been helpful for healing, but I needed the SAA program to address my acting-out behaviors. Therapy was not enough.

When we returned home, I was slow to come back to my SAA meeting. Many old issues had surfaced between my husband and me during our time away, and our marriage began to disintegrate. He went away again for a six-month work commitment the following

February, leaving me at home alone with our two little boys. I was angry, discouraged, and finally began attending SAA meetings again, because I knew that I was in a dangerous spot. By the next April the marriage issues appeared intractable to me. I felt full of rage and empty inside, and I decided it was time for divorce. A close friend appeared more and more attractive, and soon we became sexual. When my husband came home for a visit, I told him about my decision for divorce and my new partner, and he decided to cut short his professional commitment to see if our marriage could be saved. Through that summer I continued to see my friend occasionally, and my husband and I began intense marriage counseling.

Since returning to SAA, I had been meeting with my co-sponsor regularly, and over a period of months she helped me sort out reality from the mirage of denial I was living in. My husband and I made a commitment to work on our relationship for six months, then reevaluate our progress and decide what to do. My friend moved away, eliminating many distractions for me. I began to see exactly how addictive I had been. I was unable to take the pain of all the issues in our marriage that moving and separation brought up. I had chosen to find another sex partner with whom I thought it might be possible to build a relationship, rather than to face working on our marriage. That friendship had many positive aspects, yet it was a slip for me because I was not yet divorced. My sobriety involves being monogamous, and that line had clearly been crossed.

For those first six months my husband and I lived in a state of ambiguity. We "decided not to decide" anything, but to turn over the future of our marriage to a Higher Power and see what happened. Putting aside my characteristic impatience and need to know the future, and living in the present, was the hardest thing I've ever done. We also agreed to an open-ended period of celibacy, since we both realized our sexual relationship reflected the dysfunction of our total relationship. We made another six-month commitment, and eventually began working toward a healthy sexual relationship. This happened very slowly and gradually, by changing one boundary or behavior at a time, stopping if it felt too scary, and always trying to stay in touch with our spiritual selves and emotions when we were being physical.

As we began reestablishing what marriage and commitment meant to us, I continued to attend SAA meetings and meet with my co-sponsor. I also began working the steps intensely, because I finally realized that length of time in the program didn't guarantee sobriety. Sexual sobriety was only available through trust in my Higher Power and hard work. It became more and more important to admit the extent of my powerlessness over my addictive sexual behavior and to turn my will and life over to the care of my Higher Power. I began to explore different concepts of a Higher Power and to meditate regularly. Eventually I became much more active in service, both within my home group and at the national level. All of these things have been critical to my recovery. Through working the steps, going to meetings, and participating in service I have been blessed to find a strengthened marriage, a relatively stable family, and a sexuality moving toward health.

The spirituality of this program began for me when I was serious enough to take the steps home, read about them, and try to do them. When I couldn't do it by myself, I got a sponsor to help me. Slowly I began to open up to the women in my meeting and let them help me grow, through their feedback and their understanding of the steps. As our group has changed and grown through use of the group conscience and the traditions, I have changed and grown too. Doing service work has given me a deeper understanding of this program and of other sex addicts, and the opportunity to reach out with my own experience, strength, and hope. I now feel a very deep commitment to sobriety, to the SAA program, and to my own spiritual growth and recovery. I know in my heart that if it were not for SAA, I would not be married or living with my family right now. I am grateful to call myself a recovering sex addict.

42.

THE GIFT OF SOBRIETY

I got involved with Sex Addicts Anonymous seven years ago. For a long time I had been thinking and worrying about my sexual compulsions. I had joined self-help groups, read books on the subject, and gone to a psychotherapist. I was still acting out sexually. Nothing was working. I thought that I could never enjoy anything as much as the sex. Seeking out and finding the kind of sex I liked was the great adventure. Everything else seemed to pale in comparison. Periodically, when I got so physically worn out or so deeply depressed that I couldn't bear it anymore, I would stop doing it. Then, sooner or later, it would all start up again. This is really the essence of my situation as a sex addict: I can't leave it alone. I always go back for more. What is truly miraculous about the SAA program is that it taught me how to stop, and stay stopped.

I grew up in a small town in the South, in a large extended family. I don't know anything about my family's sexual history, but there was alcoholism and mental illness, with all the pain and suffering that go along with them. There was also love and concern for my well-being. Like many families, it was a mix of good and bad.

Some cousins of mine lived on a farm outside of town. They were younger than I, but seemed to know more about sex. Their father had pornography, and we used to sneak and look at it, sometimes masturbating to the images. I also had sexual contact with my cousins. I remember feeling self-conscious. Although I was older, I was more reserved and timid. I worried about getting in trouble, getting caught.

There were other places I found pornography. I liked to look through my parents' things when they weren't at home. A soft-core magazine was usually on my father's bedside table. He never seemed to buy a new one. Some of my parents' friends also had adult magazines, and I would look at them when we visited. My relationship with pornography was one of secrecy, fear, and excitement. It was a potent mix for me from an early age.

As a teenager, I got into drugs and alcohol, and I think they further separated me from the reality of what I was doing. At age thirteen or so, I discovered a Super-8 movie projector in the attic and some adult films that my father had hidden away. It required a good deal of planning to watch these films and then get all the paraphernalia back in place without being found out.

Gradually, I began taking more risks, wanting more excitement. At some point after I got my driver's license, I found myself stuck for the night in an unfamiliar city. Unable to find pornography, I tried to seduce strangers by lying on my motel bed, partially dressed, with the drapes open. The hotel security knocked on the door, took me to their office, and made threats to call the police. They told me never to come back to that motel.

During high school, I visited a gay strip club for the first time. I was living more and more of a double life. At school, I looked like a regular guy, dating women and sometimes having sex with them. And then I had my secret life. In college, I told my friends I was gay, but I kept many secrets. I was often sneaking away, visiting the local bars and adult bookstores for anonymous sex.

My excesses with drugs and alcohol came to a head, and I was introduced to a twelve-step fellowship. During the early years of my sobriety from drugs and alcohol, my sex life cooled off. It was limited to a small stash of pornography. I didn't recognize my powerlessness in this area.

During the next ten years, my sexual acting out gradually increased in intensity and frequency. I moved to a big city, and I found many new venues for sex in public toilets, parks, and gay gyms. I discovered that I could get a massage and then a little masturbation at the end of it. I began paying for sex. When that became problematic, I would search for new ways to act out on the telephone lines or the computer. I began to masturbate compulsively with fantasies of incest and children, particularly while I was on the phone lines. This could go on for hours at a time. There were periods when I was completely drained of energy. My knees and my back often ached. Ultimately, having sex on the phone or the computer became just as destructive and dangerous as acting out with strangers or prostitutes.

One day, a friend invited me to a group that discussed relationship and sex problems. I went mostly for a lark and did not take it seriously.

The idea of a true addiction to sex did not seem credible to me. To my mind I was liberated, free to engage in behaviors other people were too uptight to pursue. Even so, I was clearly having problems, and I went to this group off and on for a few years. The discussions often focused on recovering from incest or codependency. I could identify with some of it, but I was confused about what it might mean to be sober around sex and whether that was really my problem.

One solution I came up with was total celibacy. I tried it for two months, in part because my boyfriend was fed up with my acting out. He eventually moved out, and I went back to having sex the way I wanted. Between the jolts of sexual excitement, I felt hopeless and desperate for something new. I wondered if I would spend the rest of my life acting out. I was starting to pray about my sex life. Despite the intensity of my urges to pursue sex, I began to have some willingness to try a different way.

The turning point for me came when I came in contact with someone in Sex Addicts Anonymous who had learned how to stay sober. An acquaintance visiting from another city told me that there were people in SAA who had long-term sobriety there. This information had a powerful effect on me, and I called their local intergroup, looking for help. Eventually, I spoke with someone who had been sober for many years, and he agreed to sponsor me over the phone. At this time there were no SAA meetings in my city.

I knew a few other guys with problems similar to mine, and we decided to start meeting once a week at my house. Most of us had been in and out of various groups, with no success. We were all sex addicts in relapse. We were desperate, and for the first time, we realized that our sole purpose was to stay sober and help other sex addicts do the same. Our other problems were secondary. Out of years of bitter experience, we knew that without sobriety, there would be no recovery.

I wrote out my Three Circles and started putting together longer periods of sobriety from my inner circle, which for me includes going into adult bookstores, paying for sex, having anonymous sex, buying or renting pornography, having sex over the phone or computer, masturbating more than once a day, or masturbating to fantasies of incest or children. It has been a messy process. I got angry. I went through awful periods of withdrawal from the addiction. Often I was staying sober when I couldn't see a reason to. There were moments when it seemed like I was dying inside. Luckily, I had a sponsor who had gone through withdrawal and had made his way to long-term sobriety.

At first I stayed sober for four months, and then once for fourteen months. The relapses lasted for months at a time. When I would go back into acting out, it was not just a brief fling. I always felt like, as long as I was in relapse, I might as well do what I really like. I can see now that I was just not finished. I had reservations about being sober. I still thought I was missing something by not acting out.

Today I have been away from all those inner-circle behaviors for more than four years. It is a miracle. I have made some wonderful friends in the process. While sobriety is not free of problems, it is a much happier way of life. Being connected to SAA and a Higher Power who knows all about my sex addiction, I am more a part of the world, more engaged with other people.

An important part of my recovery is to share my experience with other sex addicts who are trying to find a way out of the insanity. I feel strongly that we have an obligation to carry the message of sobriety for those who want to hear it. The message is that there is an answer to all the craziness of sex addiction.

I will never forget a conversation I had with someone during one of my relapses. I was feeling hopeless; the solution I thought I had found in SAA was not working. I was baffled. He listened and then shared with me that he had relapsed and that he had now been sober for years. It made such a difference to hear that. I often feel that my sobriety was transmitted to me by people like this man.

It has been a wonderful experience to watch the SAA fellowship grow. The group that once met at my apartment has long since moved to a public space, where it is easier to welcome people who are new. I have been lucky to have sober sex addicts around me. I am accountable today for my sobriety. I check things out with my sponsor and other members on a regular basis. I have the kind of Higher Power who works through other people.

43.

THE KEY TO HEALING

Loneliness follows me like a shadow. There is some empty space, some child's hurt uncomforted, that still haunts in quiet moments. As a child I was not fully conscious of how I was different until others excluded me. Why was it not okay to feel something that came so naturally to me—an attraction to people of my own gender? I was not able to name this until, at seventeen, while walking hand in hand with my girlfriend, some young men shouted out of a car window, "Goddamn f--- lesbians!" They were trying to be mean, but this was a gift to me. I came to know that I was not totally alone, because there are enough people like to me to warrant a name: lesbian.

Society had taught me the value of honesty. It had demonstrated that good relationships are committed, married relationships. Yet gay and lesbian relationships are "unnatural," "sinful." How could I be both honest and an accepted member of my community?

I chose to enter a committed relationship with another woman when I was twenty-two, nearly twenty years ago. We exchanged rings and vows in a ceremony in our home with friends present. My brother and sister sent gifts. In our work lives we remained "in the closet," but we had a circle of friends. Soon after our ceremony, however, my partner got involved with another woman. So both the relationship and I split apart, with most people not noticing that anything had happened. My mother not only refused to support me, she angrily told my sister not to call me, denying that anything of meaning had happened.

The day my partner moved out was the first time I went out and found someone to be sexual with out of that lonely, empty space. Over the next seven years there was hardly a day when I was not involved in a romantic or sexual relationship of some kind, most lasting a few months.

While I usually lived alone or with friends, I desperately needed to have someone "on the line" at all times.

I had perfect radar. When a relationship ended, I knew who was looking, so that I could arrange another within twenty-four hours. I never picked people up in bars, and I rarely slept with people I hadn't known for a while. I was not involved with drugs—sex was the drug. It masked the pain I felt when I was alone. It masked the pain I did not know how to deal with when my partner left. It masked the emptiness of the child within me. It muffled the echo of my mother shouting that I was immoral and unnatural because of feelings of love that seemed to me the most natural thing in the world.

By the time I was twenty-nine, I knew that something was very wrong. I could not keep commitments in relationships. I had seen the pattern of stringing one relationship after another with not a day in between, and it didn't feel healthy to me. I set rules for myself about who I wouldn't be sexual with and promptly broke them. I knew I was in trouble and didn't know how to get help.

From the first time I heard the words "sex addiction," I knew that my problem had a name. For two years I did not know how to find help for my disease. When a friend who is a social worker gave me the phone number for SAA, my healing process began.

After starting in SAA, I stayed monogamous in a partnership for several years. When I realized that it wasn't healthy for me to stay with a woman who was emotionally distant and who refused to be monogamous herself, I left. Then, for the first time in years, I was alone. And I was okay. I kept going to my group and was very, very grateful.

Seven years have passed since then. During that time I was involved for five years in the most deeply loving partnership I have ever known. Now, when I feel that overwhelming emptiness, I cry or write in my journal. When I'm lonely I call a friend or meditate or take a walk.

I went through a serious depression after my father died and my most significant relationship ended, within a few months of each other. I started obsessing about another woman, and I ran back to SAA. My group accepted me, nurtured me through my depression, told me their own stories, and gave me the warmth, love, and acceptance that neither my mother nor society would offer. This unqualified acceptance and love encouraged me to attend to my own spiritual journey.

My group helped me to recognize that I was in a state of obsession rather than in an ideal relationship. I changed jobs, in part to maintain my sobriety, and eventually came through without the kind of acting out that I had been stuck in for so many years. When I felt tormented, by being out of control with this obsession, I consciously turned this problem over to God, again and again and again, until it no longer plagued me.

All those years I tried to fill emptiness and loneliness with sex. But the kind of emptiness I feel cannot be filled by a physical act or even by an emotional bond between people. This emptiness is spiritual in nature and can only be filled by spiritual practice and awareness. For me, this includes such things as meetings with my religious community, twelve-step meetings, quiet meditation, walks in nature, outdoor physical exercise, calls with group members, listening to music, and writing in my journal.

I am a top manager and attorney in a company with several thousand employees. I'm single and share a house with a friend. I'm very active in a religious community. I feel more deeply and less fearfully than before. While I still fear being hurt, I've become better at allowing myself to feel the hurt. I'm thankful that I'm becoming more able to laugh and reach out to others as well. These last two years, I've felt more hurt than at any previous time in my life. But I do not feel the guilt and shame and lack of control of actively living out my addiction.

The greatest lesson from all this is compassion. Before I learned the lessons of SAA, I masked the experience of feeling: my addiction would not let me feel either deep pain or deep joy. In the periods when I am not acting out of compulsion, I know my own sadness and have learned to live through grief. So now I am able to recognize when another human being is feeling grief and pain. And some part of me knows how to reach out to that other being in pain. This is the essence of the Twelfth Step, and the key to healing in a broken world.

44

TOUGH LOVE

I never wanted to become an addict. When I started peeking at my brothers' wives through a slit in the door, when I began buying magazines and masturbating as a teenager, the whole experience was exciting and fun. Like any teenager, I was curious. Feelings were aroused that I had never experienced before. The feelings were pleasurable not only in themselves but also in their ability to change my mood—blotting out those negative feelings I had when things were hard at school, at home, or with friends. More importantly, they started to compensate for the overall feeling I had that there was something fundamentally missing in my life—a lack of security, a sense of not being worth anything, a feeling of inner emptiness. Life felt at root intolerable, bleak, boring—I just didn't feel right. I needed a way out, a way to fill the emptiness, and sex seemed to promise to provide both those things—at least temporarily.

It seemed logical that the more often I indulged in sex, the more often I would experience that temporary comfort, so that it would begin to feel like a permanent comfort. It didn't occur to me that I was developing compulsive behavior and was beginning to act like a slave. So sex slowly started to become a necessity, an experience that had to be fulfilled on a daily basis and eventually at more frequent intervals. Yet at the same time the messages I was receiving about sex from those around me, especially my parents, who mentioned next to nothing about it, was that at best sex was something that you didn't talk about, and at worst it was something that caused pain. Unless I brought it up, it was not referred to—the implication being that it was either silly and of no importance at all, or it was of such immense importance that it was something that had to be kept secret, meaning that there was something bad about it.

It was certainly of immense importance to me. The fact that it was a growing necessity in my life proved that, and so I concluded that there must be something bad about it and that I should keep its importance to myself. With the lack of information about it, sex also became confused with activities related to going to the toilet (another taboo subject), which gave an underlying feeling of disgust to my fascination with it. Added to this was the fact that I was constantly finding my father's pornography—the only readily available source of sexual information I had—hidden away in boxes and drawers where supposedly I couldn't find it, confirming to me that sex was something I should not even know about, let alone be actively involved in. This appealed to my growing teenage sense of rebellion and independence and made sex even more attractive to me (and consequently more compulsive). It also meant that the feelings of illicit excitement that pornography added to my sexual acting out only paved the way for increased feelings of guilt and shame that always followed.

Gradually my sexual acting out became instrumental in creating the very feelings I was trying to numb and pacify. In trying to avoid pain, I was now creating it. As time and the addiction progressed, this dynamic became more and more entrenched. I became trapped in an unending and degrading cycle of self-defeating behavior, with shame and guilt eventually joined by despair. With the pain and pleasure inextricably linked, the negative feelings were as necessary to me as the euphoria that preceded them. I was dependent not only on sex but on pain—sex with pain, sex that degrades.

Though I didn't want to admit it to myself, it soon became apparent that I was different from other people around me. When my teenage friends suddenly stopped coming to see sex films every weekend while I continued to do so; when I was spending all my pocket money every Saturday morning in the secondhand magazine shop and trading old porn magazines for new, six or seven at a time; when I was spending a whole day masturbating in front of the television whether there was sex on it or not, it was clear that something was wrong. Though I sensed that what I was doing was not normal, there was nothing else I would rather be doing—unless of course it was to have real sex with a real woman, a fantasy my mind was constantly preoccupied with. But real women scared me to death. I idealized women and put them on a pedestal, where they sometimes appeared as angels and sometimes as whores, but seldom as real people with an identity and sexuality of their own. Real women had the capacity to say no and could hurt you, something my fantasies had no capacity to do.

To disguise my uneasiness around my preoccupation and compulsion,

I rationalized that everyone was as preoccupied with sex as I was, and like me, wished for a life of continual sexual excitement. They were only too hung up or stupid to allow themselves to get it. I also argued that I was just oversexed and that using masturbation was better than using women to satisfy my urges, the implication being that somehow I was being responsible and virtuous. But as my addiction progressed, this attitude soon became something I was eager to break. I changed my thinking, believing that I wanted to have sex with lots of women and that masturbation was purely compensation for my cowardice. The needs of my addiction were such that no boundary, moral or physical, was too precious or sacred to hold me back in my efforts to try and achieve another greater and better sexual fix.

In fact, even when I finally became sexually active, I could not directly ask for sex, not only out of fear but also out of denial. I had to convince myself that my motives were pure before I could approach a woman. I needed to believe that I really wanted to get to know her "as a person" and sex was only a secondary factor. I could not accept that I was the type of man to just want to sleep with a woman and leave her, though I secretly envied and admired men who could. I would befriend a woman—showing great interest in her, making intimations about wanting a relationship, and showing all the external signals of someone primarily interested in intimate communication rather than casual sex— and yet at the same time turn on the charm required to seduce her into becoming my next sexual fix. As my disease progressed, my instinct to target women who would respond to this line of behavior became keener. Though few of these encounters ended up being purely one-night stands (even after the event I was unable to admit to the secret sexual motivation behind my actions), most of them were sexually abusive in nature.

In the meantime, my voyeuristic acting out had not decreased. I visited "adult" cinemas, bought just as much pornography as ever, and began trying to involve my partners in acting out my pornographic fantasies. If anything, my "hunger" for voyeuristic sex increased. Even when no sexual activity was going on, the urge for some kind of sexual fix was always below the surface—an underlying motor driving me from one situation to another. Like the urge to survive, the urge to act out became an involuntary reflex. More and more, it overtook the urge to survive, creating life-threatening situations. "Rubbernecking" and constant preoccupation ended in incidents where I found myself driving up onto the curb or even crashing my car. Always there was this preoccupation—before a person was touched, a video picked up, a magazine bought, there was a preoccupation with sexual thoughts and fantasy. Always absent in the fantasies, however, were the inevitable consequences of acting out—the pain, despair, guilt, and shame.

Even though I recognized the compulsiveness of my behavior, I thought that ultimately I could control it. It was only in the aftermath, when all the attendant problems (which for a moment had disappeared in the sexual euphoria) suddenly returned, that the recognition came that this was just another sorry event in a seemingly unending story of a life out of control. My powerlessness stretched even to moments when I was feeling quite content and happy with myself. There was always the thought that I could somehow enhance these feelings through sex and make them even better; but inevitably the acting out that followed only served to sabotage them. My need to act out overrode any sense of values I had. I began to think I was mad, and in some strange way hoped that I was.

However, I was obviously not mad, or not yet. In every other walk of life I was quite together. I was capable of finding and holding down a job. I was praised for my abilities, was considered reliable, and was trusted and given responsibilities that I fulfilled as well as any other person. I was involved in spiritual growth, self-development, and the healing arts. I was concerned for the environment and for the rights of people and animals. I was somebody whose opinion was valued and often sought. People admired my rationality, level-headedness, and intelligence. I was good at sports and had passed several levels of school in one sitting. All of this seemed to indicate a positive, wholesome individual. And yet despite my gifts, I still acted out.

Far from being a source of pride, these other aspects of myself actually added to the pain—my public persona and my private persona simply did not fit together. As an addict I felt inadequate, self-obsessed, anxious, and out of control. The split between the two selves, and the progressive increase in the need to act out, was such that I began to think the addictive side of myself was in fact the "real" me. Everything else was a fraud, simply a device to ensnare people into liking me, keeping me company, and taking care of me, while I conducted my "real" life in private.

I entered therapy, believing that if only I could discover what it was in my childhood that had made me so sexually compulsive, I would be able to finally bring my behavior under control. I believed that if I dug deep enough, I would discover the event that had given rise to my behavior, the compulsion would be lifted from me, and I would be normal. But with each new discovery about the imperfect circumstances and events of my upbringing, and the attendant excitement I felt each time I believed that I'd finally discovered the reason why I was the way that I was, came the disappointment and pain when no magical transformation took place and my acting out continued unabated. I also believed it was my circumstances that made me the way that I was, and that if I could only control the influences around me, then I would change. I thought, surrounded by so many advertisements, so much sexual imagery on posters, television, magazines and newspapers, that "no wonder I was out of control." I thought that if I could get away from my urban environment and return to nature, my compulsiveness would end. But when I went into nature, I found myself still preoccupied with sexual thoughts. I longed to be back in the city, in front of my television or in a sex shop.

Changes in other areas of my lifestyle made no difference either. I thought, "If only I had a job...," "If only I had a job I liked...," "If only I were unemployed...," "If only I had money...,"' If only I lived with people...," "If only I could be completely alone...," "If only I had a different flat...," "If only there were no women...." No changes in my external circumstances seemed to make anything other than a temporary difference. Sometimes I blamed my partners. One partner was not attractive enough, another was not emotional enough, another was not intellectual enough, another was not sexy enough, and another I didn't love enough. If I could find the perfect partner, then once again I believed my sexual behavior would be brought into line. But one relationship after another, with every different kind of woman I could dream of, made no difference.

I also believed that if I could avoid those things or people through which I acted out, I could stem the problem. So I got rid of my TV—only to find myself creating excuses to use other people's TVs when they were out of their houses. I closed the curtains to stop me from spying on windows across the road, only to find myself walking the streets targeting windows with curtains not fully drawn through which I anticipated seeing people undressing or having sex. I was able to convince myself that this was an improvement in my behavior. But in fact it was simply a fresh excitement for an addict who was hungry for new and more risky and exciting ways of getting a fix. Similarly I got rid of my store of pornographic magazines (a number of times) only to find myself buying contact magazines where people advertise themselves as available for sex. Again I deemed this an improvement, since I was at least letting go of the fantasy of anonymous sex and going for the real thing.

I started to make bargains with myself. I thought if I could not cut out my addictive behavior altogether, then at least I could control or manage it. I set limited boundaries on my behaviors with women, but unable to resist each next step, I widened them, until finally setting any boundary seemed ridiculous. My original boundary had been forgotten, and yet afterwards the memory of it would return, and the self-hatred around having lost control again would also return. The same process would occur renting videos or buying magazines. I agreed to limit myself to one video or magazine. When I walked into the shop I believed I could keep to it, but in the end it proved useless. Even when I got the videos or magazines home, the bargaining would continue. I would use them in moderation, I thought. But inevitably I would be there for hours. And that wouldn't be the end of it—on some future date I would find myself back in the same shop going through the whole process again, and believing again that this time would be the last.

Despite my attempts to control it, my addiction didn't slow down, and gradually the boundaries began to dissolve. Things that I vowed I would never do started to become commonplace. I began using my position of trust as a teacher to target possible sex partners. I had always prided myself on how I managed to keep my secret sexual life from affecting anybody other than my sexual partners, who were adults and knew the score. But then one day I found myself putting my girlfriend's ten-year-old child at risk, masturbating in front of the television in the same room where she lay (seemingly) asleep. On another occasion, I was shocked when my partner confronted me with a pornographic video she had found left in the VCR where her child could have turned it on unknowingly. I was stunned with horror, certain that I had taken it out and replaced it with her child's video. But I had obviously gotten them mixed up and put mine back in. Fortunately, for some reason, her child chose not to turn on the video that day, as she usually did first thing when she came in from school. It was through incidents like these, where I realized that the secret life I believed I had so well under control was in fact beginning to bleed into and endanger the lives of people I thought I cared for, that I finally came to admit defeat and accept that, like an alcoholic, I was out of control.

Finally accepting powerlessness was a frightening realization, but a necessary one, if insanity, suicide, or imprisonment were not to occur. It was frightening because if I were to admit my powerlessness over my behavior, where was the power to come from? When sex that degrades had been my god for so long—to the point where I had separated myself from the belief in any other spiritual force, and separated myself from people beyond their ability to help me maintain my addictive lifestyle— the only prospect that seemed left to me was the void. Who or what could help me? Was I capable of being helped? I had no idea that there were others like me. I began to call myself a sex addict before I knew that there were other sex addicts or that there was a twelve-step program where I could meet people who had gone down the same path as I had. But it was only when I had admitted my powerlessness and called myself a sex addict that these things were revealed to me. Like a prayer being answered—not too soon, not too late.

By admitting my powerlessness, I became open to help, and help was then offered to me. Accepting powerlessness was the beginning of freedom: freedom from the insanity of all the lies, manipulation, guilty secrets, wasted energy, and abusive relationships. As I started and continued to go to meetings, and went through treatment, I met others like myself who were able to offer me a way out. I was finally able to begin talking about the double life that I had been leading, and instead of finding rejection and judgment as I had expected, I found acceptance and understanding. I found identification, recovery, and hope. I did not find sympathy, though. Sympathy could only paper over the cracks, and in the end become an aid to my acting out again. Within the acceptance and understanding was a tough love and an honesty that had no space in it for continued abuse of myself and others. That tough love put me in touch with a much needed and almost submerged tough love of my own—something that could cut through the addictive drive and override the self-centered thinking and justifications—and with a deeper self that flowed with love, respect, and compassion for myself and the other humans around me.

I could begin caring again. I could gather the strength to take on an abstinence program, with the support of others to help me during the difficult time of withdrawal. With the clarity that this brought, I could begin to distinguish between healthy and degrading sexual thoughts and behavior; I could begin to accept the possibility that I too could have what I had always really wanted: a healthy, exciting, satisfying, and loving sexual life, with myself and, if I chose to, with another person. With the admission of powerlessness, suddenly I found myself returning from a world I had peopled with objects into a world with both people and objects, and a recognizable ability to distinguish between the two.

With sex no longer my higher power, I could begin to wonder what I really did consider to be my Higher Power. And miraculously, in place of despair, my life was beginning to have some hope in it, perhaps for the first time.

45.

DREAMS RESTORED

The Native American beads were amazing. It was difficult to imagine that those colors existed 150 years ago and that we were unearthing them after all of that time. My sisters and I were out in the desert with an elderly man who liked to take us to remote places. My oldest sister was six, and my younger, two.

That first trip seemed harmless. The next, however, seemed entirely wrong. Even at the age of four, I knew that what we were doing was not right.

When we got home and were ready for bed, my mother made me kiss him good night. It made me sick. There was one more excursion before his wife warned my mother that he shouldn't be alone with us. It was two trips too many.

There were a couple of other such incidents later in my youth. One was with another friend of my family. The other was with an uncle. My mind has blocked the details out.

My father was a very angry man with his own dark secrets. I was scared of him and never once thought of telling him the bad things that I was doing.

Shortly after the above encounters I remembered playing "peek and see" with the neighbor boy. We were both five years old. My mother told me, "Nice girls keep their underclothes on." The message I heard was that I definitely was not a nice girl.

When I was sixteen, a friend of mine told me that people who masturbated were perverted. Well, I masturbated and fantasized, so I thought I must be perverted.

My sexuality became more hidden, secretive, and separated from the rest of me. My more visible image was of a sincere, innocent seeming, faith-seeking young woman who had been raised in a deeply religious Christian home.

The part that people did not see was obsessively hungry for sexuality and would spend hours and hours fantasizing about sex and encounters. The more this occurred, the deeper my shame and guilt went, and the more separated these two parts of my personality became.

Discovering erotic magazines at other people's homes further drove my obsession. I would read and masturbate, and I felt so deep a toxic shame that I would completely block out the existence of this part of me.

The few boyfriends I had were troubled men with deep emotional wounds. They were seldom people one would consider bringing home to meet the family. Actually, I never wanted anyone to know I was involved with them.

At the age of twenty-two, I partnered with a non-recovered alcoholic. In the beginning, I was deeply uneasy, but I ignored this feeling. We had two daughters together. After a five-year relationship, I ended it by acting out with another man.

Over eight years my acting-out world included a high level of promiscuity, six abortions, some deeply traumatic sexual experiences, and sexually transmitted diseases. I turned to women as lovers for a while and viewed myself as sexually liberated. This lie allowed me to continue to debase myself.

People tell me that in spite of all of this I was still a good mother. I guess I was, as long as I wasn't obsessed with a romance. Unfortunately, I was acting out frequently and intensely. I am still deeply pained about what I put my children through.

It's a miracle that I'm alive. During the height of my acting out, I slept with a man who had full-blown AIDS. What this means to me today is that I'm here on borrowed time, and whatever God asks of me is a blessing.

Nearly twenty-one years ago, I met and married a really good man. We had a son together, and he adopted my daughters when they were eight and ten. In the first year of marriage I embraced twelve-step recovery. I wish I could say we lived happily ever after. In the ten years we were married, I acted out with other men when I felt he wasn't meeting my needs. Becoming tired of the deceit, I asked for a separation and then a divorce. At that time, the pain of pursuing unavailable men and throwing myself at them became unbearable.

I joined SAA, and recovery became my number one priority. I got a sponsor, desperately worked the Twelve Steps, and began going to a meeting a day. Doing an extensive and thorough sex inventory became part of my work. With the grace of my Higher Power, I was able to have a year of sexual sobriety before I found the door to the rooms of Sex Addicts Anonymous. I was beginning to mature, but I noticed that many people squirmed when I talked about my sexual history, and I knew it wasn't normal. I also could tell that I wouldn't be able to hold onto my sexual sobriety unless I found people who understood me.

It was then that a friend gave me a booklet from SAA. It contained stories just like mine. I went to my first SAA meeting one year after my abstinence from unhealthy sexual practices began. I have never looked back.

What a gift it was to listen to other people tell stories like mine! There was so much I was willing to face about myself from hearing other stories. I asked someone who had what I wanted to be my sponsor. Because he is gay, I feel safe having a male sponsor. I worked the steps again in SAA. I did whatever was asked of me, which was to go to a lot of meetings, maintain a close relationship with my sponsor, work the Twelve Steps and Twelve Traditions, and be willing to do service work, including being a sponsor myself.

My recovery has definitely been one of progress but not perfection. By the grace of God, I have not needed to act out again. I am grateful that my sponsor respects me enough to let me make my own mistakes. Some of them have been "doozies," but they have cemented my recovery and deeply rooted my commitment to my spiritual journey.

In making my Ninth Step amends, some true miracles happened. I was reunited with my mother and sisters, and some very painful but necessary family secrets were revealed. My ex-husband and I have been remarried for over three years. We have made recovery a high priority, and he attends a fellowship for co-sex addicts. We also go to meetings for couples and are working the steps together in that program.

Last April, I celebrated six years of sobriety in SAA. My daughters tell me that I have really changed. When asked how, they say I hold myself accountable for my behavior. I wish that I always had, but I am deeply grateful that I do today.

What has recovery given me? Everything. Recovery has graced every aspect of my life. It has integrated parts of my personality that used to be walled off from one another. This has happened by bringing all of my secrets out of the darkness and into the sunlight of the spirit. It has reunited not only my family of origin, but also my husband and my children. It has given me back my self-respect and a renewed confidence in my ability to have healthy relationships. I am willing to deepen those relationships in meaningful ways.

My professional career has flourished because my time is freed up for productive endeavors. My creativity continues to expand.

When I was a young girl, I certainly did not aspire to become a sex addict. I had dreams of love, freedom, and happiness. A lot of my acting out was the misguided pursuit of those dreams, which, unfortunately, were pushed further away from me because of my disease.

When I became willing to accept the painful truth about myself and my actions, God set me free, and my dreams have been given back to me...with so much more.

46.

STEPS TO FREEDOM

It's hard to say exactly when my sex addiction started. I know that in elementary school I seemed to think about sex more than most people my age. I had sexual fantasies about my third grade teacher, and I was absolutely fascinated by nudity. My brother and I discovered my father's pornography, and I learned from him and male cousins of mine to sexualize and objectify women, first in pictures and then in person. This probably isn't that unusual for young boys, but I know it had a powerful effect on me in the formation of sexist attitudes that I am still working to overcome.

I don't have any memories of sexual abuse, and I can't point to any "reason" for my becoming a sex addict. Fortunately for my recovery from sex addiction in SAA, it doesn't matter how I became addicted. What matters is that I accept that I am a sex addict and focus on what I can do today to stay sober.

The earliest "acting out" I can clearly identify was in the sixth grade. I can remember masturbating under my desk. I knew it would be horribly embarrassing if anybody caught me, but I felt driven to do it. Now, masturbation is certainly normal at that age, but the public location and the risk of getting caught intensified the experience enormously. It got me high.

Another instance was when my brother and I crawled into the attic, while my dad was having a party, to watch women in the bathroom through a fan in the ceiling—my first voyeurism. This, again, might be chalked up to adolescent curiosity, but it really took off in me, and I started seeking every opportunity I could to secretly view women nude.

As I grew older, I not only masturbated daily, but also experimented with animals. I told myself I was just a red-blooded American boy who wasn't getting enough sex—that's why I was doing all this weird stuff.

"Our society is sexually repressed," I reasoned. But even years later, when I was living with a woman and having a very active sex life, I was still acting out—in fact, more than ever. I would leave for work in the morning an hour early so I could prowl our neighborhood and peek in windows. I would "accidentally" expose myself by wearing very short shorts while riding my bike, or by undressing and masturbating in front of an open window or door.

We moved to a major city, and my addiction really took off. The city offered a degree of anonymity that I could never have had in my hometown. I started exposing myself by the side of the freeway, as commuter trains full of people rushed by. Randomly exposing myself to hundreds of women, children, and men, I still told myself that this wasn't hurting anybody. "If they weren't so sexually hung-up, it wouldn't bother them" was a rationalization I used over and over again.

In the city I also discovered pornography arcades and strip clubs. I found these immediately addictive. These were activities that my fiancée objected to, so I kept them secret. I started making excuses to get time by myself and setting aside money that wouldn't be accounted for. My hidden sex life became a daily routine. I would go to the grocery store and stop to act out on the way there or back. My wife would ask what took so long, and I would make some lame excuse or just shrug it off. I would slip into women's restrooms on the campus of a local university and sit in a stall, wait for a woman to use the stall next to me, and then masturbate with her on the other side of the partition.

My search for voyeuristic thrills went as far as sneaking into a shower room in a co-ed dormitory early in the morning, to peek at a woman getting out of the shower. The woman saw me, and I ran for it. She yelled for help, and I thought a bunch of guys would chase me down and beat me up, so I ran until I was out of breath and I couldn't run any more. I didn't get caught, and I told myself, "This is crazy! What are you doing?" I swore that would be the last time, but a week later, I tried again to enter that same dorm, only to find the door locked. (Thank God!)

I continued to act out, regardless of the consequences. I knew that if I were caught, it could mean humiliation, arrest, a beating, or the end of my marriage, but I didn't stop. Often, immediately after acting out, I would feel terrible, even sick to my stomach, and I would tell myself, "I'm never going to do this again!" Then, the next day, I'd do it again.

Troubles in my marriage, many of them alcohol-related, resulted in several separations, the last of them in 1995. This final break-up was precipitated by the fact that I could not stop drinking. Now that I was single, it was "anything goes." I didn't even try to hide it anymore. I started drinking nonstop and acting out more than ever. There were things I had told myself I would never do that I found myself doing. I had lost all respect for myself. I had said I would never pay someone for sex, but on two occasions, after hours-long binges in strip clubs, it just wasn't enough anymore. I had often exposed myself to men in pornography arcades, but I had never let them touch me. Now I was having anonymous sex with people I wasn't even remotely attracted to.

This went on for another ten months, until I hit bottom in my alcoholism and started going to twelve-step meetings. When I stopped drinking and started working a spiritual program of recovery, my acting out diminished considerably. It disappeared almost completely for a time, but it kept cropping up, and I still hadn't really dealt with it. I tried addressing it as corollary to my program or as a "character defect." I had some limited success when I sincerely asked a Higher Power for help, but I wasn't working any kind of consistent program. I was still acting out occasionally and trying to control it.

In 1997 I was confronted by my ex-wife about some acting out I had done ten years before. When my stepdaughters were very young, I used to go into their bedrooms when they were asleep and masturbate, in order to intensify the high. However, there were times when they weren't actually asleep, and they had seen me. They hadn't told anyone at the time, but now they had started talking about it. My ex-wife was furious and called the police, then called me.

When I hung up the phone, I said to myself, "I've got to do something. I can't just keep going on like this, trying to control it." I had always told myself that my acting out wasn't hurting anybody, but I had to face the fact that it had hurt some people very close to me. The fact is that, when I was active in my addiction, it really didn't matter who got hurt. That's hard for me to admit, but that realization was the beginning of my journey into recovery from sex addiction. I picked up the phone, dialed information, and asked for the number of Sex Addicts Anonymous.

At my first meeting, I heard people sharing honestly and openly about behaviors that most people never talk about. This helped me let go of a lot of shame and embarrassment and gave me permission to be equally honest. I heard people share that they used to act out the way I did, but that they hadn't acted out in years. This showed me that the program worked.

That program is the Twelve Steps of Sex Addicts Anonymous, and the story of my recovery from sex addiction is the story of the Twelve Steps.

The steps are a simple, practical method for putting spiritual principles to work in my life. Anyone can work them. I don't have to be a genius or a saint to make this program work. All it takes is the willingness to follow some simple suggestions, and any sex addict can stop acting out, lose the desire to act out, and have a happy and useful life.

I worked the Twelve Steps with a sponsor, someone who had experience with working the steps himself. It was important for me to get help from someone who had recovered through the steps, instead of trying to do it all by myself. My addiction was all about isolation, but in recovery, I have learned that I am not alone. My sponsor helps me understand how to apply the steps in my daily life so that I don't have to act out today, no matter what.

Admitting I was powerless over my addictive sexual behavior didn't come easily. At first, I couldn't see how that was going to help. That sounded like failure. I wanted to get power over this. I was raised to believe you could accomplish anything if you set your mind to it. But I had spent years trying to control my addiction without success, so I guess I worked most of the First Step during my years of acting out.

I had to admit I was powerless over my addiction and unable to control it on my own before I could work any of the other steps. I had to be completely willing to do anything necessary to recover, willing as only the dying can be. If this were just a "bad habit," then perhaps logic, counseling, psychotherapy, or behavior modification techniques would be able to change that behavior. My experience with addiction is that it doesn't respond to reason, medicine, or psychiatry. I needed a spiritual solution. But first, I had to exhaust any hope of reforming myself. It sounds paradoxical, but it was only when I admitted I was powerless that I was able to stop. It was only when I gave up trying to do it on my own that I was ready to consider asking for help from a Power greater than myself.

To complete my First Step, I needed to define exactly what it was I was powerless over—what specific behaviors constitute acting out for me. Defining sexual sobriety was the biggest single difference between working the Twelve Steps in Sex Addicts Anonymous and in my twelve-step program for alcoholism. In that program, I completely abstain from alcohol in order to stay sober. Very simple. Don't take the first drink. However, it wouldn't be healthy for me to completely abstain from sex for the rest of my life. In fact, that could constitute an equally unhealthy obsession. My sexuality is a beautiful part of my humanity, a God-given gift. It's only when my addiction looks to certain sexual behaviors to give me things they cannot give me that my sexuality becomes a problem.

So I needed to define what behaviors are addictive, what behaviors are healthy, and what behaviors are in-between, hence, the Three Circles (as described in one of our SAA pamphlets). I started with my inner circle, the behaviors that are addictive and destructive, the behaviors I can't control. Once I defined these, defining sobriety was simple again: I completely abstain from these inner-circle behaviors, a day at a time, and I stay sexually sober. My inner circle includes exhibitionism, voyeurism, pornography, strip clubs, and any sex without emotional honesty, mutual respect, and genuine intimacy.

At my home group (a local SAA group where I attend regularly and do service work), we all state what our inner-circle behaviors are and how long we have been sexually sober. It has been really important to me to have clear definitions (so that I know if I'm sober or not) and to celebrate time in continuous sobriety. I have been sexually sober since September 9, 1997, over four and a half years at this writing.

It took a lot of honest reflection, some sharing with others, and a little trial and error to sort out what belonged in the inner circle. This process itself was very valuable. I really appreciate that SAA members define for themselves what behaviors they are powerless over. If someone had just handed me a definition, it wouldn't have been as meaningful, it might not have worked or made sense for me, and I probably would have rebelled against it anyway.

There really are behaviors that some addicts can safely engage in from which other addicts find they must abstain. Some things in my outer circle (healthy sexual behavior) are in other people's inner or middle circles, and that's okay. I found definitions that work for me.

When it came to Step Two, I had a big problem with the "God" thing. I was not agnostic but antagonistic when it came to anything "spiritual." I defiantly insisted that everything could be explained and understood without resorting to unscientific beliefs. I had engaged in grand debates in high school about the existence of God and evolution vs. creation, and anytime someone mentioned God, religion, or anything that smacked of spirituality, my mind was closed. I didn't hear anything else that was said, as I was busy constructing arguments against it. When I read the Twelve Steps and saw God mentioned in half of them, I didn't think this program would work for me. I shared in meetings that I was having trouble with the God stuff, and other members shared that they had had the same problem but had found a way to make it work for them. A wise member with over ten years of sobriety approached me after one meeting and said, "Don't try to figure it all out. Just keep coming back."

By this time, I had been beaten into a state of reasonableness by my disease, and I had to accept the possibility that maybe I didn't have it all figured out. I had always considered human intelligence the highest power in the universe. The idea that there were some things I was incapable of comprehending was a big blow to my ego, but once I got over that, I was able to learn. People assured me that I could have my own conception of a Power greater than myself, that it didn't have to be the "God" that others had described to me in my youth. I had investigated numerous religions over the years and found that they each had something to offer, but I could never completely swallow any of them. I was very relieved to learn that I could develop my own definitions for spiritual terms.

One day, after about two months of coming to meetings daily, I was sitting in a meeting, and I started thinking about the phrase "God is love." I kept repeating it silently to myself. When I shared, I said, "If God is love, I guess I can handle that." I started to cry. This broke the ice for me. Here was something simple and non-threatening. I saw that love was a Power greater than myself, and that love was what I needed to fill the emptiness inside me that I was trying to fill with my addictive behavior. When I just opened up and let God's love in, I was filled. I knew everything was going to be okay.

Having accepted that I couldn't stop acting out on my own and that some Power greater than myself could help me, I had to decide, "Do I really want the help?" This may seem obvious, but I had to take this Third Step seriously. I had to decide if I wanted to go back out and try it "my way" one more time, or stick around and try what was working for people in SAA.

In order to turn my will and life over to God, I really had to get my ego out of the way. My self-centeredness had blocked the entry of a Higher Power into my life. My ego tells me that I have to control everything around me in order to get what I need and make everything okay. It means I have to be perfect.

One definition of ego that I've found useful is that "ego is the illusion that I am separate"—separate from others, separate from the rest of the universe, separate from God. This illusion leaves me feeling alone and afraid. In truth, I'm really part of a greater whole; I'm really one with everything. There really is no point at which I stop and God starts. My ego-centered life is based on fear and scarcity, but a God-centered life is based on love and abundance. I have come to believe that everything happens for some reason, even if I can't figure it out at the time. In turning my will and life over to the wisdom and care of this Higher Power, I am assuming that the universe knows what it's doing. I have faith that if I turn things over to God, everything will work out the way it's supposed to without my having to "make" things happen. This doesn't mean I don't work or make plans, I just let go of the outcome of things I can't control.

So, just how do I go about turning my life over to the care of God? I thought turning my life over to God would mean I would have to become a monk, give all my possessions to the poor, or sell flowers at the airport. That was the sort of all-or-nothing thinking that was typical of my active addiction. As it turned out, it didn't take anything so extreme. I learned that the Twelve Steps were designed to help me learn to live on a different basis, and that it was through working the Twelve Steps that I could turn my will and my life over to the care of a loving Higher Power. I noticed that Step Twelve says, "having had a spiritual awakening as the result of these steps." This means that I don't have to get spiritual all at once. I can take it a step at a time and gradually work my way toward spiritual health. The decision that I made in Step Three was a decision to work the rest of the Twelve Steps.

Someone asked me once at a meeting, "If there are three frogs on a log, and one makes a decision to jump off, how many are left on the log?" The answer is, "Three. One just made a decision, she didn't take action." I had to follow my decision with action if I wanted to stay sober. This meant taking a good, honest look at myself in Step Four.

I took inventory of my feelings, attitudes, and behavior. My Fourth Step was a simple, straightforward, written inventory, not a novel or an autobiography. It was important for me to write my inventory, because I can turn things over and over in my head and get nowhere. Writing it down made things concrete and finite, and it helped me get a perspective on the things in my life that weren't working. I think writing can be helpful on any of the steps, but this is one of the two steps (along with Step Eight) that require writing.

I took inventory in four major areas: resentments, fears, sex conduct, and harms done to others. I worked through each item systematically to find the personal shortcomings within myself that had brought about, perpetuated, or aggravated each situation.

Sharing my inventory with my sponsor in Step Five was a powerful and liberating experience. There were things I had done that I was never going to tell anybody, and I thought that if I told somebody all this stuff he might beat the hell out of me. That didn't happen. Sharing these things with someone else was an incredible release. It helped me let go of the shame and cleared the way for God to work within me. I didn't have to do it all by myself anymore.

I've heard Steps Six and Seven referred to as "the forgotten steps," but I've also heard them called "the heart of the program." It is through these steps that I really begin to change. Instead of simply trying to regulate my behavior, I ask God to help me change. I had to become completely willing to let God take those things away that didn't work in my life, things that had been the source of all my troubles. Sometimes I still want to cling to a defect of character because I'm getting some sort of "payoff" from it, but I have found that living by spiritual principles means letting go of my old way of doing things, old "survival skills" that no longer work. Once I acquire the humility to let God help me, all I have to do is ask. I do the footwork, then get out of the way and let God do the heavy lifting.

I don't believe I would ever have stayed sober this long if I hadn't made amends for the harms I'd done to others. I had to take responsibility for my past actions to be able to live with myself. I already had a list of harms done to others from my Fourth Step, which I re-wrote as my Eight Step list, so most of this step was about becoming willing to approach people I had hurt. My sponsor helped me with this by saying, "Just forget any idea that you're going to come out of this 'looking good,' then go ahead and do it." I had to be willing to go to any length for my recovery, and let go of any expectations about how people would respond to my amends.

I also worked with my sponsor to make sure that I didn't cause any more injury in trying to make amends. When my stepdaughters didn't want to hear my amends, I asked my sponsor if I should write a letter or something. He said, "Don't push it. You've expressed that you're willing to. Let it go at that. When the time is right, it will happen."

I didn't go in expecting forgiveness or acceptance, but that is almost always what I received. Most people were just happy to see that my life was getting better, and because I had worked all the steps leading up to Nine, they could see that I had changed. My ex-wife did throw my amends back in my face, because she didn't believe I was sincere. I can't say that I blame her. I had lied to her for years. Perhaps someday she will see that I have recovered, but the important thing is that I have admitted where I was wrong and done what I can to set things right. I can look the world in the eye today, and I'm doing everything I can to make sure that I never hurt anyone else that way again.

To stay spiritually healthy, keep growing, and avoid further harm to others, I continue to take personal inventory and follow through with the actions suggested in Step Ten. I'm glad that I never "graduate" from this program. I just keep asking for help in removing those character defects that stand in the way of my usefulness to God and to the people around me. One shortcoming that I continue to work on daily is my tendency to be judgmental of others. It's not my job to judge any other human being, and it never helps me to do so. It's always about thinking that I'm better than someone else. When I'm in judgment of someone else, I have no peace, so I try to stick to taking my own inventory instead of everyone else's.

I also maintain my spiritual health through daily prayer and meditation. I don't have a rigid practice, but I try to remember to meditate every morning and pray before I go to bed at night, as well as throughout the day when needed. The morning meditation helps me get centered for the day, and I find I am much less likely to become irritable or frustrated when I remember to spend a few minutes with myself and become aware of God's presence within me and around me. Skipping my morning meditation is like skipping breakfast; I usually notice about halfway through the morning that I'm easily upset or thrown off balance. When this happens, I stop, take a deep breath, and think, "Oh yeah, that's right, it's not about me." In this way, I can start my day over any time I want to.

In my evening prayer, I give thanks for all the blessings in my life and ask for help to remove my shortcomings. I've learned not to ask for specific things, for that would be expecting God to do my will. I try to ask only for God's will in my life as it says in Step Eleven, and express my willingness to accept whatever God has in mind for me.

Sometimes life is full of uncertainty, anxiety, and fear. When facing major changes or stress, my solution is to turn it over to God. Unfortunately, it seems I usually have to get really desperate before I ask for help. Prayer becomes a last resort, when it could be my first resort. When I finally give up trying to do it all by myself, I say, "God, I'm scared, I'm confused, I don't know what's going to happen, I don't know what I'm supposed to do, but I'm willing to accept whatever your will is for me." Once I do this, everything works out fine, often in ways I never even imagined. Things line up that I never could have forced or manipulated into happening. When my plans don't work out, it's because God has something much better in mind.

Perhaps the most important thing I do to stay sexually sober is to carry the message of recovery through the Twelve Steps of SAA to other sex addicts who are still suffering from this disease. When nothing else will keep me sober, working with another sex addict will remove my desire to act out. Whether it's walking someone through the steps, getting information about our meetings to the general public, sharing my experience at a meeting, or just putting away the chairs afterward, service work has been a huge part of my recovery. I got involved with service in my first thirty days in recovery, and I haven't been without a service position since. The primary purpose of every SAA group is to carry the message, so anything that helps a group function is helping to carry the message. By using my experience to help someone else, I can turn the tragedy of my addiction into my greatest asset. A person who has recovered from addiction through the Twelve Steps can get through to another addict when no one else can. This means that I feel a responsibility to use my experience to help others, to pass on what was so freely given to me. "Service is gratitude in action," and the gift of my recovery is so great that the only fitting demonstration I can think of for my gratitude is to give it away.

I want to close by sharing how much I enjoy life today. In my addiction, I was alone, afraid, and without hope. I really didn't want to be here for life. I just wanted to "check out." Since coming into recovery, I've completed my education, and I'm doing the work I always dreamed of doing, a career that sex addiction would have destroyed. I've married a wonderful woman, and I have a healthy, honest relationship with her. I can enjoy true intimacy with another person. My sex life is better than it ever was in my addiction, because (for me, anyway) real intimacy is what great sex is all about. Last month I witnessed the birth of our first child, and I know that I can be a good father to this child because of my recovery in SAA. I show up for life today, and I'm really glad to be alive. I love this program! It works.